IMAGES
of America

UPPER MILFORD TOWNSHIP

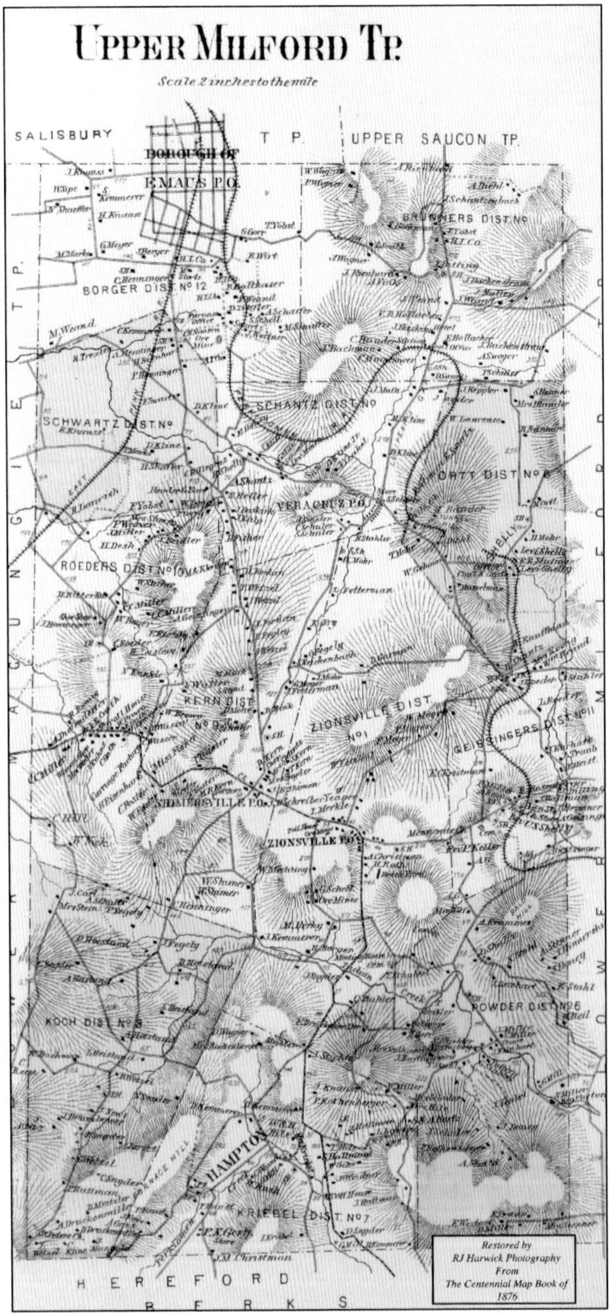

This 1876 map of Upper Milford Township is packed with information. It divides the township into the school districts of that time, including some areas no longer part of Upper Milford. Locations are given for churches, factories, waterways, roads, ore mines, tollhouses, and more. The names of residents are included on the map. (Courtesy of Esther Martin.)

On the Cover: The tobacco factory of the early 1900s in Powder Valley is pictured with owner Thomas Stahl and his workers. See page 50 for more details about the group. (Courtesy of Richard Zacharda.)

IMAGES
of America

UPPER MILFORD TOWNSHIP

Upper Milford Historical Society

ARCADIA
PUBLISHING

ISBN 978-0-7385-9258-9

Published by Arcadia Publishing
Charleston, South Carolina

Printed in the United States of America

Library of Congress Control Number: 2011945637

For all general information, please contact Arcadia Publishing:
Telephone 843-853-2070
Fax 843-853-0044
E-mail sales@arcadiapublishing.com
For customer service and orders:
Toll-Free 1-888-313-2665

Visit us on the Internet at www.arcadiapublishing.com

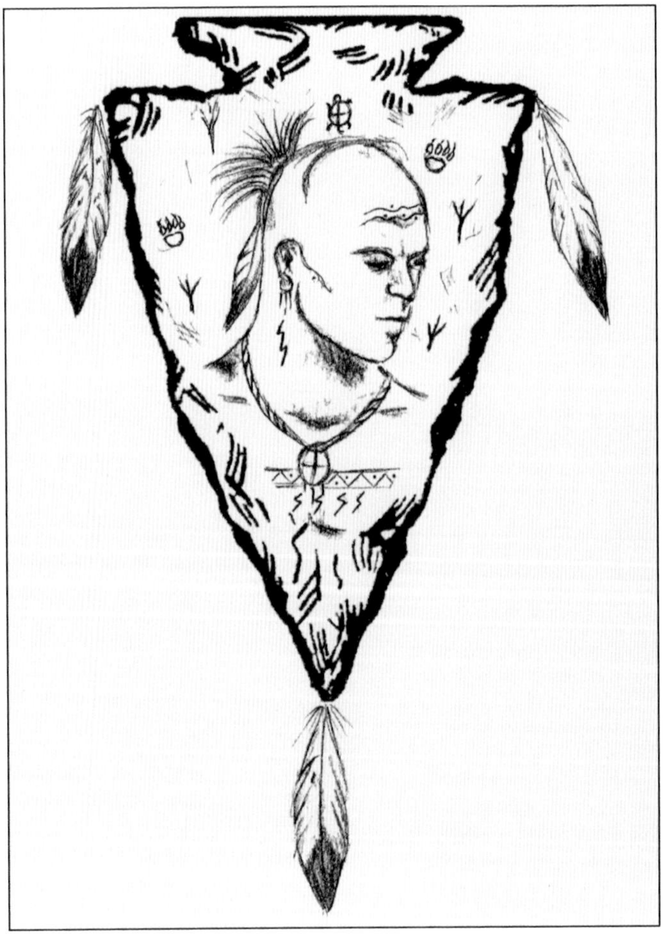

The native inhabitants of the Upper Milford area were the Lenni Lenape branch of the Delaware Indian Nation. The preserved Jasper Park Quarries in Vera Cruz are one of few remnants left of Lenape mining, which provided raw material for tools traded throughout the eastern part of the country. A statue representing Lenape chief Lapowinsa stands at the entrance to the park. The site was placed in the National Register of Historic Places in 1983. Lenape descendant Glenn Wolf; wife, Karen; and son Joshua created this design representing the arrowheads, the jasper, and their Lenape heritage.

Contents

ACKNOWLEDGMENTS

This book is the result of the untiring efforts of many, many people. The Book Committee of the Upper Milford Historical Society spent countless hours gathering the pictures and historical information presented within these pages. Committee members, each one invaluable, were Henry Beitler, Joseph Benner, John Fegley, Pauline Fritz, Barbara Harris, Barbara Heist, Beulah Miller, Neil Moser, Roselyn Parry, and Sidney Unser.

We are indebted to the township residents, current and former, and many friends whose names appear in the courtesy lines under each photograph for sharing their treasured pictures and histories. Courtesy lines with UMHS denote materials from Upper Milford Historical Society's files. Information for many pictures was taken from the following: Alfred Mathews and Austin Hungerford's 1884 *History of the Counties of Lehigh and Carbon in the Commonwealth of Pennsylvania*, Charles Rhoads Roberts's 1943 *History of the Lehigh Valley*, the 1951 *Vera Cruz Community Association Centennial Celebration Booklet*, *The Hearthstones of the Shelter House*, and Beulah Batman Miller and Barbara Miller Heist's 1976 *The History of Powder Valley*. Another important source was the copious notes and writings of Old Zionsville native Richard E. Stauffer, pictured on page 98, whose materials were donated to the society after his death. All information has been gleaned and recorded with the utmost care for accuracy.

The committee greatly appreciates the cooperation and assistance provided by township personnel in printing working copies of materials used in this book. Finally, these images could not have been restored and reproduced without the expert assistance of Sidney Unser's Spring Hill Picture Framing and Photography.

Filled with a deep respect for the dignity of the rural people remembered herein, the historical society offers these pictures and text to friends and families of the township and their future generations. Let this history stir memories and bring new insight into the lives of Upper Milford's past residents and the villages they created.

Introduction

Upper and Lower Milford Townships were originally part of Bucks County in a larger territory called Milford Township. As surveyed by John Chapman in 1738, Upper and Lower Milford were pulled out of the larger Milford Township to become one as Upper Milford Township, the first township organized in Lehigh (Lecha) County. Eventually, on December 6, 1852, Upper Milford and Lower Milford were made separate townships. Because of these early Milford connections, Hosensack, Corning, and Dillingersville, now in Lower Milford, have been included in this Upper Milford history.

Nearly all of the early settlers were Germans (Pennsylvania Dutch), such as the Schwenkfelders, the Mennonites, the Moravians, the Lutherans, and the Reformed religious denominations who moved into the Hosensack Valley and beyond. They found the fertile farmlands, sheltered valleys, rich timberlands, abundant springs and streams, and rolling hills to their liking as reminders of their homeland.

Besides homes, churches were a high priority in building their settlements stemming from their strong religious beliefs. Thus, churches became the heart of their villages. The Upper Milford Mennonite Church began as early as 1735; the Old Zionsville Church, now United Church of Christ (UCC), started as early as 1740; Zionsville Lutheran Church was established in 1758; Vera Cruz Baptist Church (now Evangelical Congregational) began in 1758; St. Peter's Union Church existed as early as 1773; Salem United Methodist Church started as early as 1829; Bible Fellowship (Mennonite Brethren In Christ) was established in 1857; Salem Bible Church (Salem Evangelical Lutheran) began in 1873.

These Pennsylvania Germans brought their language, family traditions, and traits of patience, courage, thrift, and hard work as they established the settlements briefly outlined here:

- 1732 – Michael Moser took up 100 acres that became Dillingersville
- 1734 – Durk Jansen (Derrick Johnson) took up 352 acres that became Shimerville (Scheimersville, Shimersville)
- 1734 – Christian Crall (Kraul), 25 acres north, and Philip Herzog took up 102 acres south, first called Zionsville, now Old Zionsville
- 1734 – Henry Keiber took up 150 acres that became Hosensack
- 1738 – John Baumgartner took up 100 acres that became Vera Cruz
- 1760 – Melchoir Schubert had a home in Powder Valley, the Schubert/Graber Cabin
- 1829 – Henry Kemmerer established Powder Mill on Indian Creek
- 1872 – Sigmund formed around the F.N. Gery store
- 1876 – (New) Zionsville formed around Abraham Geissinger's hotel and store at the Perkiomen Railroad
- 1876 – Shelly's Station or Dillinger's Station or Dillinger formed around Levi N. Shelly's feed storehouse
- c. 1877 – Corning formed around Elias Trump's store

The early German settlers came with a fair share of learning and quickly established schools to educate their children, largely in their churches. Many of these private church schools were discontinued or later assimilated into the public school system after the 1834 Common School Act. Some of the school subdistricts were Berger's (Kemmerer's), Borger's, Brunner's (Bildhaus), Geissinger's, Kern's (Upper Milford High School), Koch's, Kriebel's (Yoder's), Miller's (Mill), Ortt's, Powder Valley (Schubert), Roeder's, Schantz's Mill (Vera Cruz), Schwartz's, Sigmund (Hampton), and Zionsville (now Old Zionsville).

The township developed prosperous, though small, industries, such as brick making; mills of every kind, especially grist and sawmills; iron-ore mining from large rich ore deposits throughout the area; tobacco factories; a creamery; Hampton Furnace; and Stahl's Pottery in Powder Valley whose fame has increased through the years. Businesses flourished with the building of the Perkiomen Railroad, an extension of the Reading Railroad, the King's High Road (Kings Highway), and the Great Philadelphia Road. But, these avenues also facilitated commerce and communication to larger surrounding cities and promoted the demise of most of the indigenous industries and businesses in the villages.

Early residents remained heavily dependent on agriculture as a way of life. These Pennsylvania German farmers operated very productive farms, employing farming methods that yielded most of their own daily food staples and provided a living. But, in many cases, increasing economic necessity forced a continuous decrease in working farms and farmers. Today, many barns remain in the township, but few are used for farming purposes. Many have been changed into living quarters. The Upper Milford Historical Society has archives with photographs of well over 100 of these structures and is constantly working to add information about each one.

In more recent times, Upper Milford Township has seen homes and housing developments spill into once-open fields, sloping hillsides, and expansive valleys. However, the township has not experienced the extensive growth that creates large towns. One can still scan the landscape, breathe in the rural atmosphere, and capture the essence of life in the country.

One

Faith and Worship

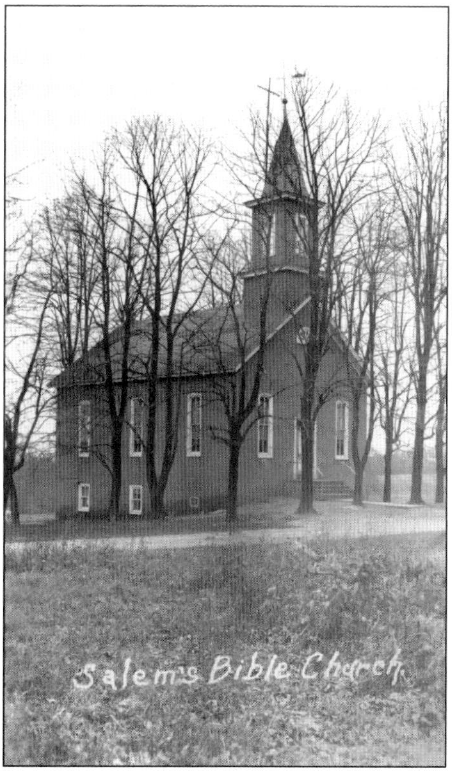

Salem's Bible Church is on the road of the same name at the very southwestern edge of the township where Lehigh County and Berks County meet. The old church pictured was built in 1873. When the congregation outgrew it, a second church was added in 1978. This building is now used for the middle and high school youth ministry, part of the Christian school run by the church. (Courtesy of C. Edward Mosheim.)

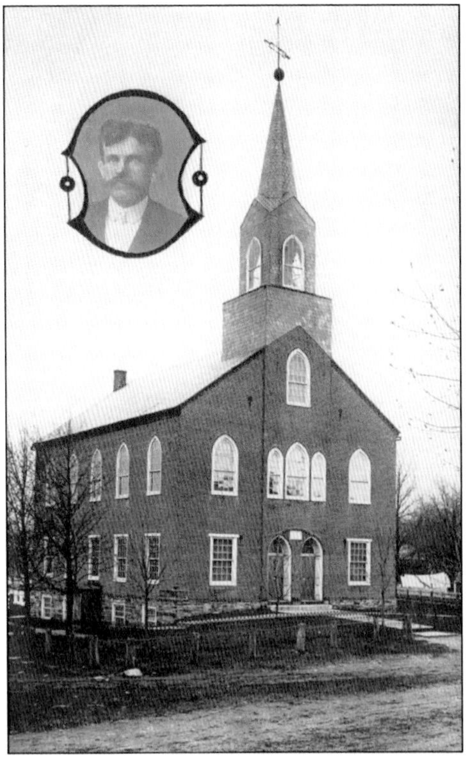

The third church of the UCC congregation in Old Zionsville was built in 1858. Rev. James Blatt is pictured in the insert. This brick building was torn down in 1908 to make way for the current granite church pictured below. Notice the strikingly different architectural styles of the two churches. (UMHS.)

Located at the intersection of Fountain Road and Kings Highway, this church was built in 1909 on the very same spot as the brick church shown at left. The granite for the new church came from Gehman's Quarry on Church View Road about 1.5 miles from the village center. The children of Rev. Eli Keller donated the cost for one of the beautiful front windows, and the Ortt sisters paid for the other one. (Courtesy of Jean Iobst.)

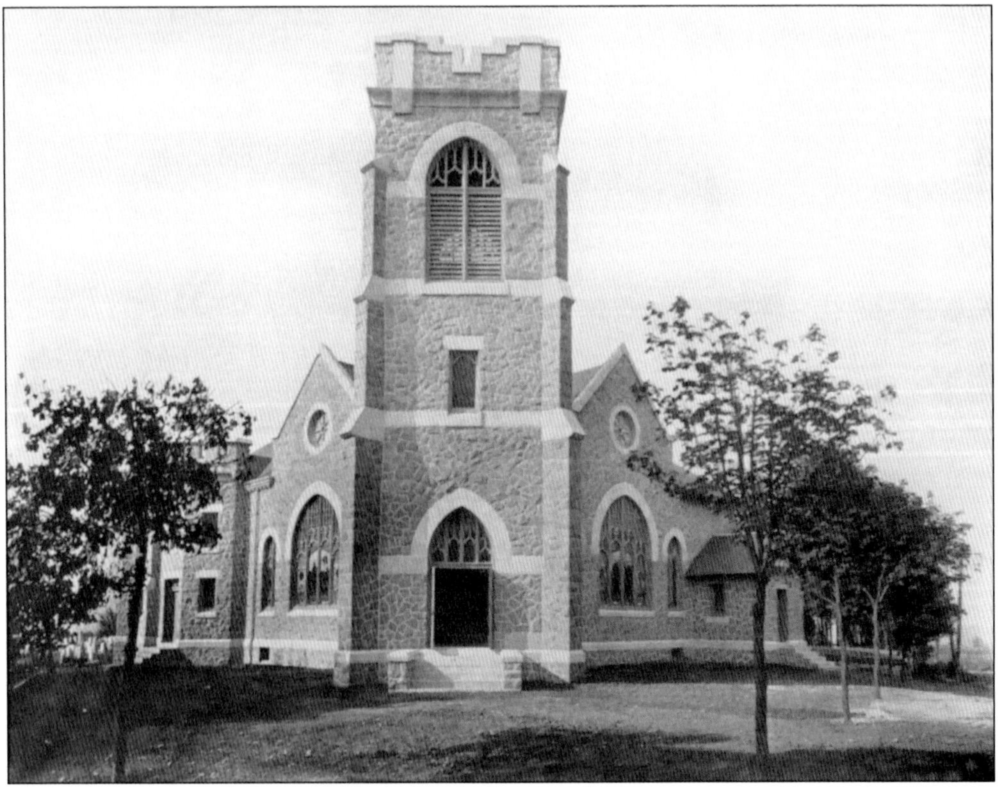

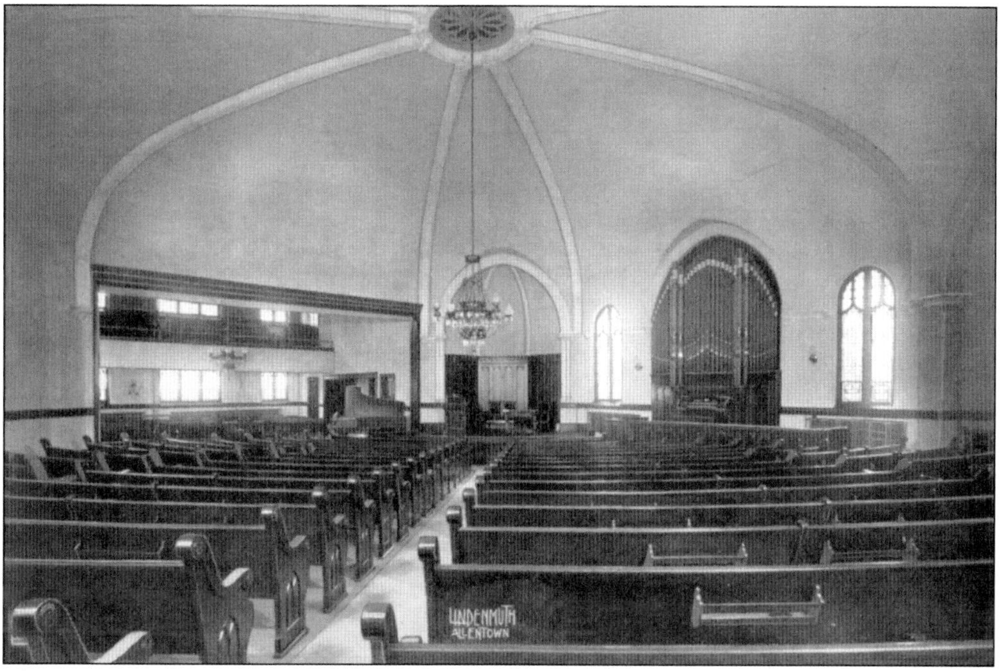

The interior of the granite 1909 Old Zionsville Reformed Church has two rooms. The smaller section on the far left can be closed off from the main church with an adjustable curtain. The organ is from Bake and Culley in Philadelphia. The lights were gaslit until after 1921, when electricity came into use. Originally, heating was done by a vapor vacuum system, later by pipeless heaters, and, since 1974, by a gas furnace. (Courtesy of C. Edward Mosheim.)

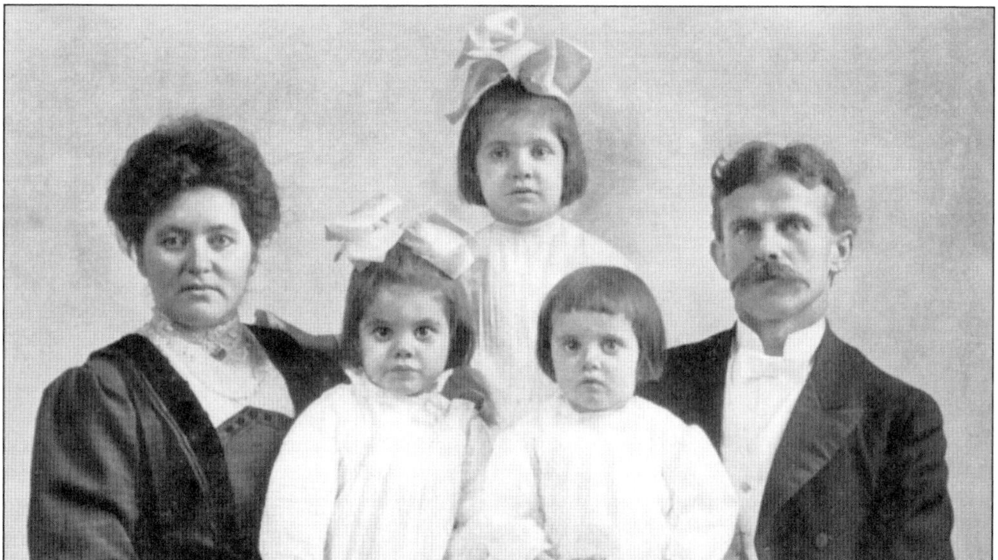

Rev. James Blatt was pastor of the Old Zionsville UCC Church from 1907 to 1948. Shown here with wife, Lizzie, and daughters Marguerite, Mabel, and Mary, Reverend Blatt also taught at Upper Milford High School. He was the pastor when the granite church was built. Blatt served his congregation and community for 41 years. (UMHS.)

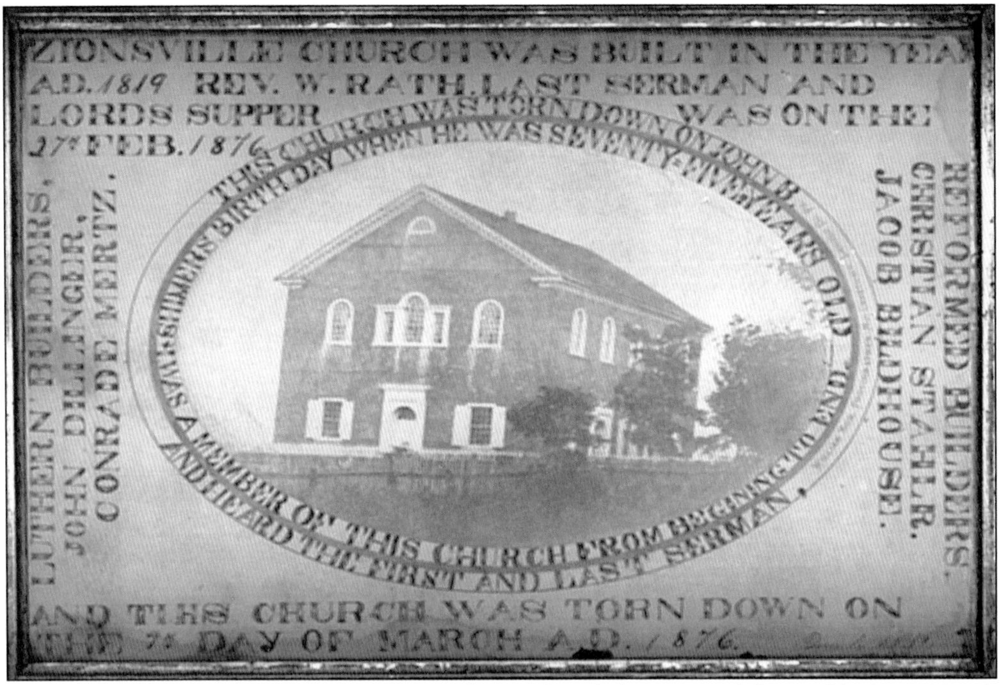

The Zion's Lutheran Church in Old Zionsville was founded on ground donated by Peter Hittel. The original building was a log structure in use from 1758 to 1819. The second church, pictured above, was used from 1819 to 1876. The inscription framing this picture proclaims the history of the building. John H. Shimer heard the first and last sermons in this church and was a member from beginning to end. The church was torn down on his birthday, March 7, 1876. Below is the third and present Zion's Lutheran Church with its 175-foot steeple, which commands the crest of a small rise and is often photographed in its picturesque setting. (Both, courtesy of Zion's Lutheran Church.)

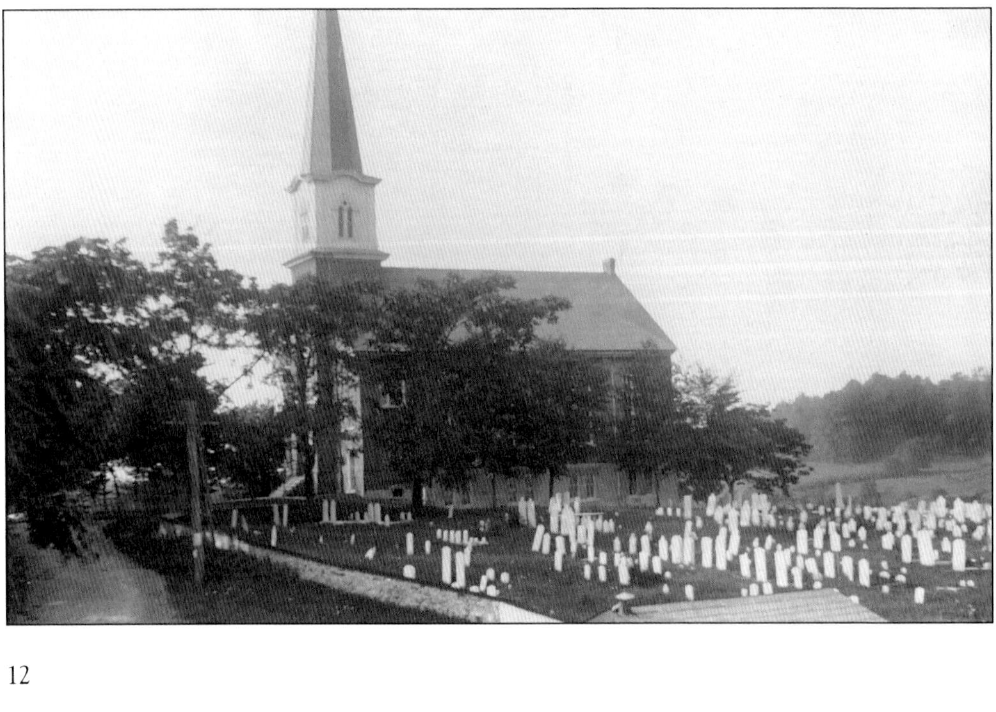

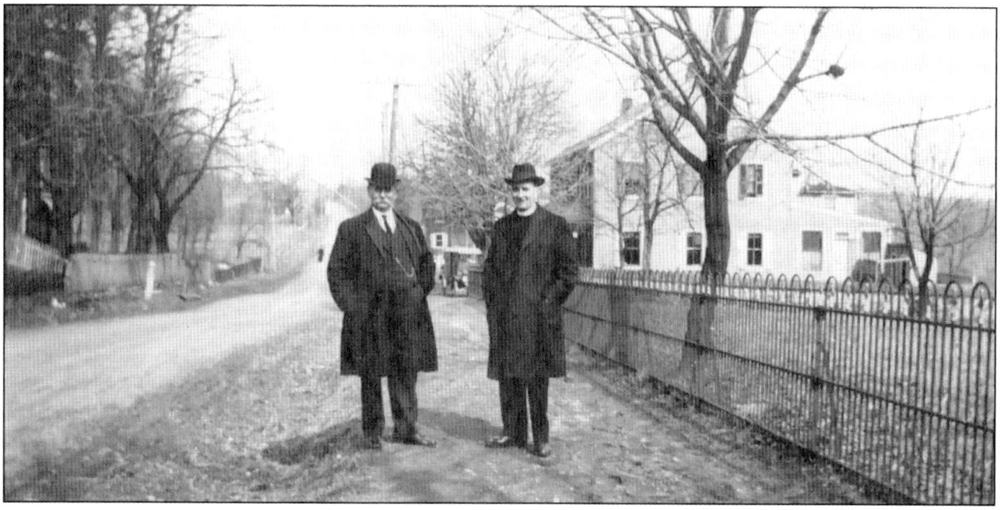

Rev. David C. Kaufman, left, is photographed with an unidentified man standing on Kings Highway North in front of the Zion's Lutheran Church lot in Old Zionsville. Kaufman served his congregation from 1907 to 1955. The church fence remains, but the Old Zionsville Hotel seen in the background burned and was torn down. Notice that Kings Highway is still a dirt road. (Courtesy of Barbara Harris.)

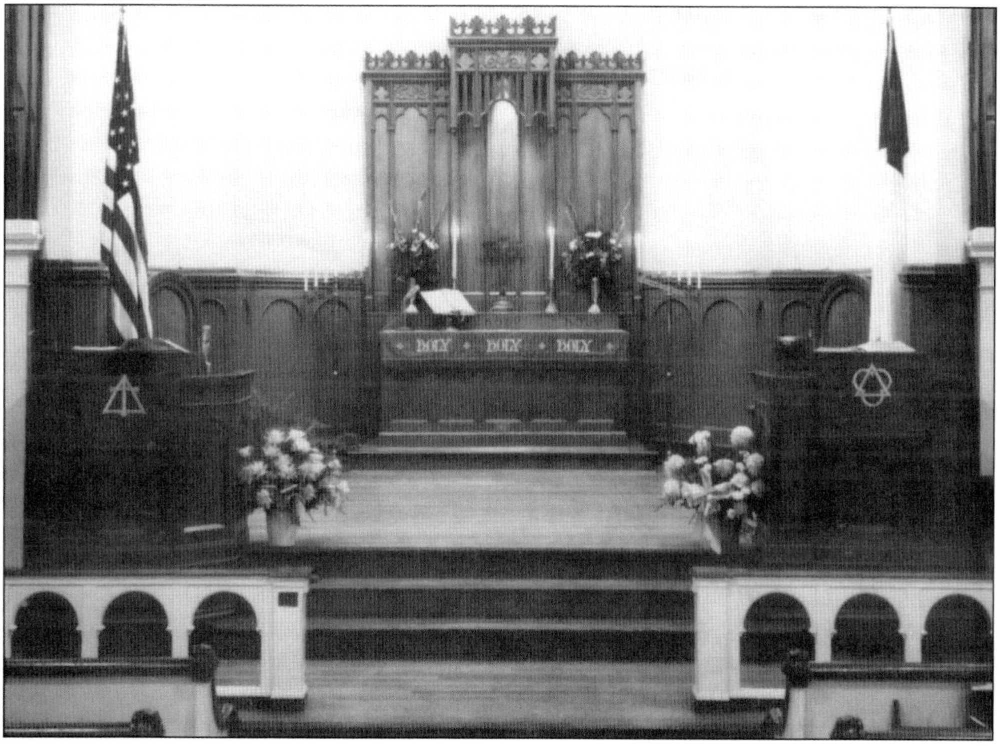

The interior of Zion's Lutheran Church underwent renovations of about $31,000 in 1974, as this photograph reflects. Included in the work were a new nave ceiling, painting inside and outside, and repairs to and enlargement of the 1915 Durner organ. Some of the earlier pastors serving the church have been the Revs. I.B. Ritter, David Kaufman, Luther Linn, and Sherwood Dieter. (Courtesy of Zion's Lutheran Church.)

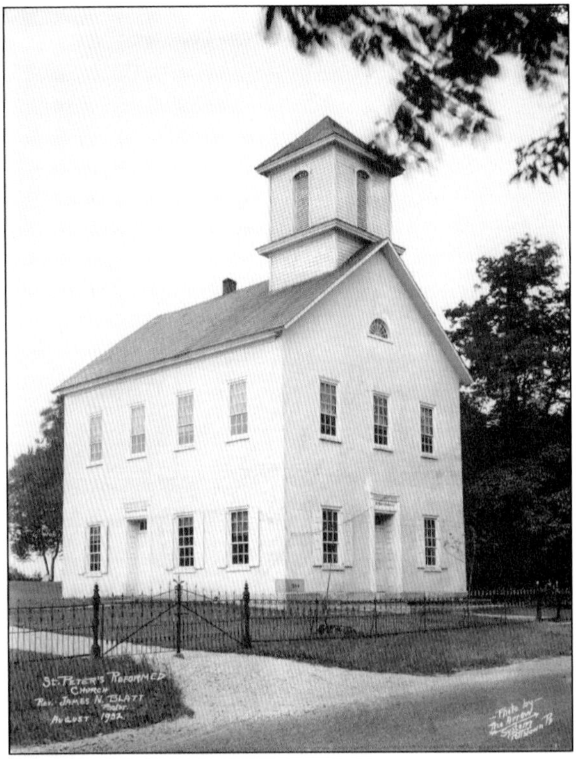

The 1932 St. Peter's Union Church is three miles west of Shimerville on St. Peter's Road. The original acreage was purchased from George Adam Bortz in 1773. The earliest known services were held in a small stone building called "Da Barrick Schule" a few hundred feet northwest of the present building. A new building was dedicated on Christmas Day 1844 that retains its original character to this day. (Courtesy of St. Peter's Union Church.)

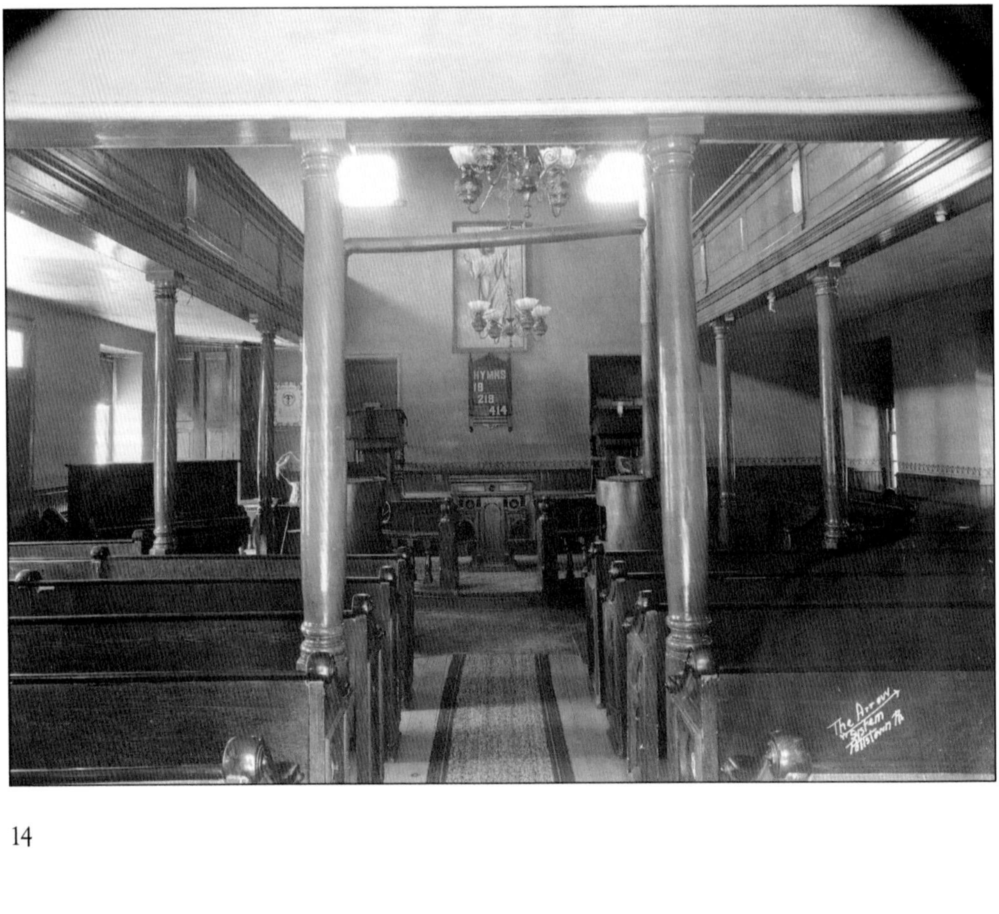

The interior of St. Peter's Union Church projects an ambience of warmth with its wood construction and soft lighting. Mennonites, Moravians, and Schwenkfelders all held services here and had the right to bury their dead in the cemetery. It is said that Native Americans are also buried on this church property. (Courtesy of St. Peter's Church.)

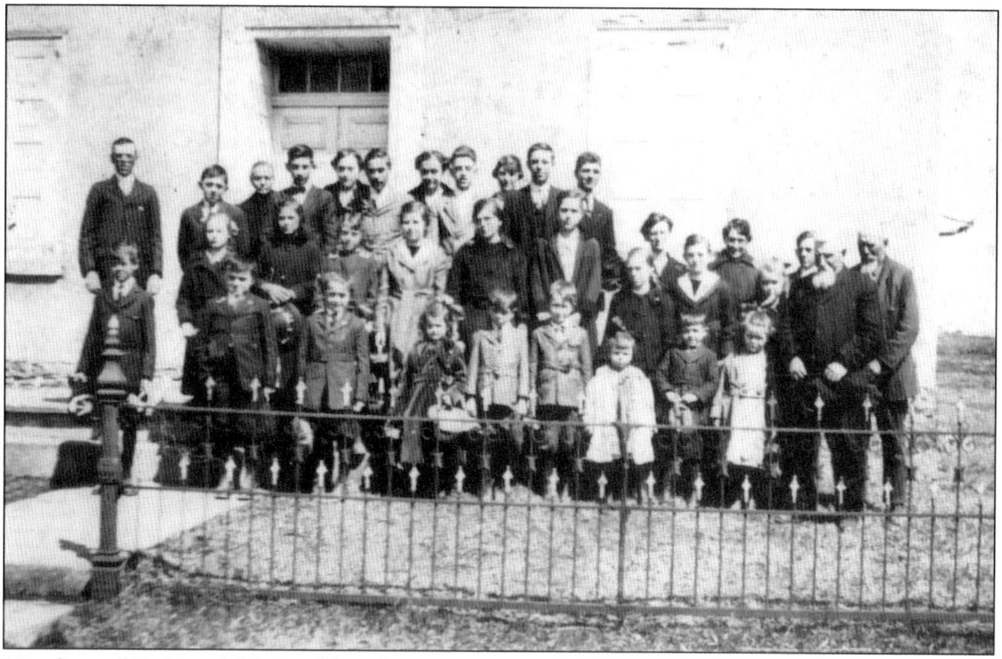

Members of St. Peter's Union Church gathered in the early 1920s for a group photograph, shown above. Four members of the Wetzel family are identified. In the first row are Wilson Wetzel (sixth from left) and Minerva Wetzel (seventh from left). In the second row is Maria Wetzel (fourth from left). In the third row is Ambrose Wetzel (fourth from left). Notice the decorative fence and the closed shutters. The 1941 program for homecoming, shown right, advertises a good supper for 50¢. The event was held in the grove next to the church, which still hosts many special church functions. Rev. D.C. Kaufman was also pastor at the Old Zionsville Lutheran Church, and Rev. James Blatt was pastor at Old Zionsville Reformed Church. (Both, courtesy of St. Peter's Union Church.)

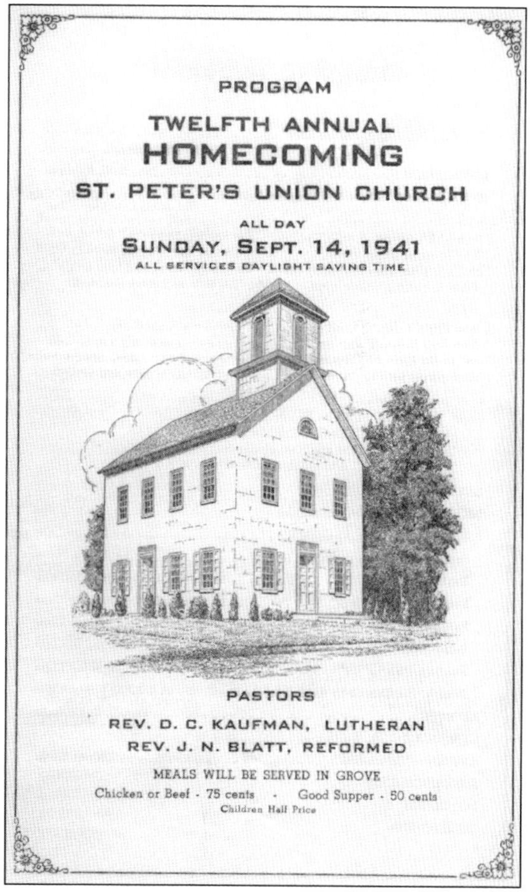

PROGRAM

TWELFTH ANNUAL

HOMECOMING

ST. PETER'S UNION CHURCH

ALL DAY

SUNDAY, SEPT. 14, 1941

ALL SERVICES DAYLIGHT SAVING TIME

PASTORS

REV. D. C. KAUFMAN, LUTHERAN

REV. J. N. BLATT, REFORMED

MEALS WILL BE SERVED IN GROVE

Chicken or Beef - 75 cents - Good Supper - 50 cents

Children Half Price

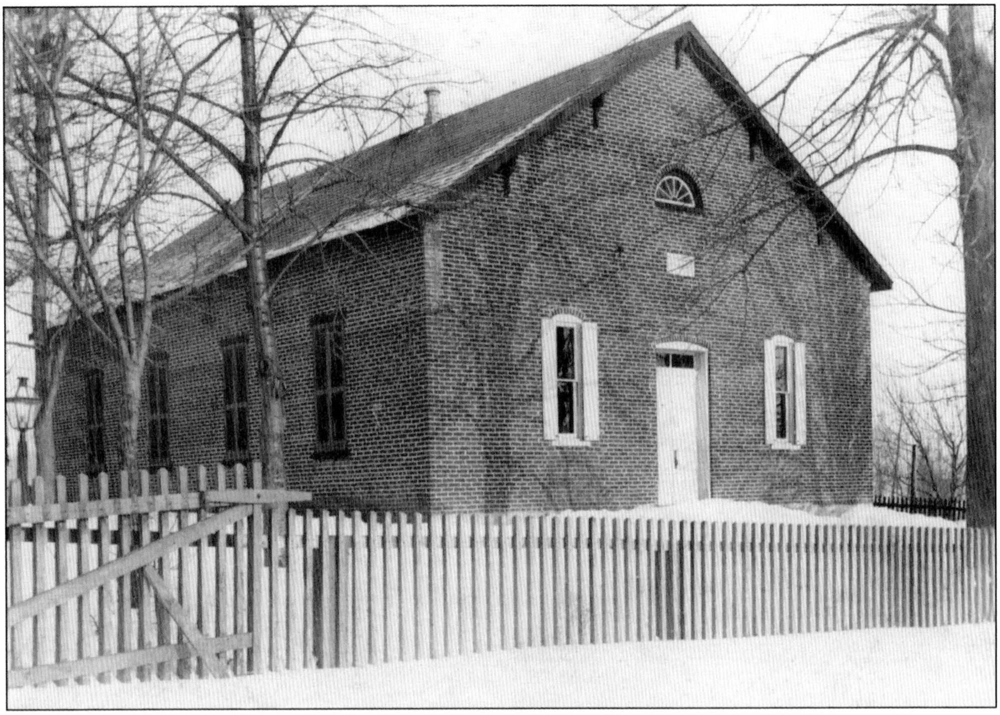

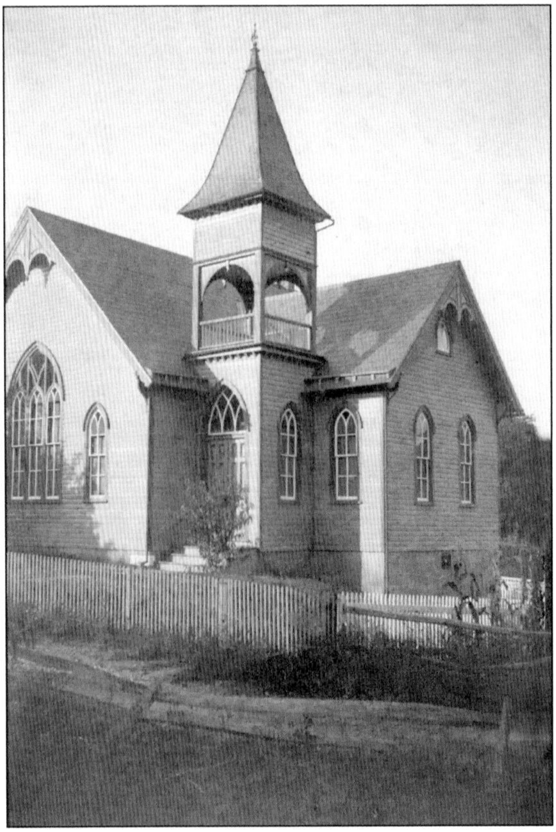

The Mennonite Brethren in Christ Church, now known as Bible Fellowship Church, was started in 1857 by Rev. William S. Gehman and a group of dissatisfied Mennonites. Their first church was built on Vera Cruz Road in Zionsville in 1859 and known as "Nummer Drei" (Number Three) to distinguish them from former Mennonite affiliations. A large portion of the church property was donated by Abraham Kauffman. (UMHS.)

The Grace (Hosensack) Evangelical Congregational Church on Buhman Road in Powder Valley was built in 1897 at a cost of approximately $3,300. Later, a bell was added to the steeple. The original windows were replaced with stained-glass windows in 1952, but much of the distinctive interior architecture and wood trim are original. A parsonage was added in 1970 next to the church. (Courtesy of Barbara Heist.)

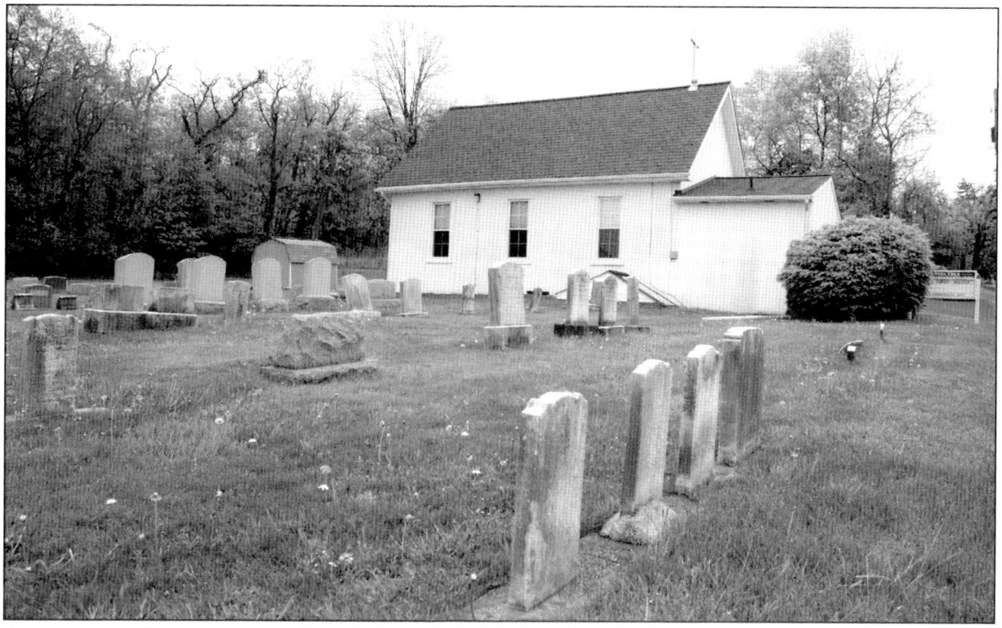

A one-story frame Baptist church was erected in 1853 just south of Vera Cruz on a tract of land that had originally been issued to Bernhard Derr. William Desh and William Mohr were ordained as the ministers and served many years until the church was discontinued by attrition of membership. In 1900, a small congregation of United Evangelical members purchased the property and remodeled the church, and has conducted regular services there ever since. Among the pastors for "the Little Church on the Hill" have been the Revs. J.K. Freed, Ralph Hillegass, Paul Kern, Paul Lykens, and M.E. Detterline. (Courtesy of Sidney Unser.)

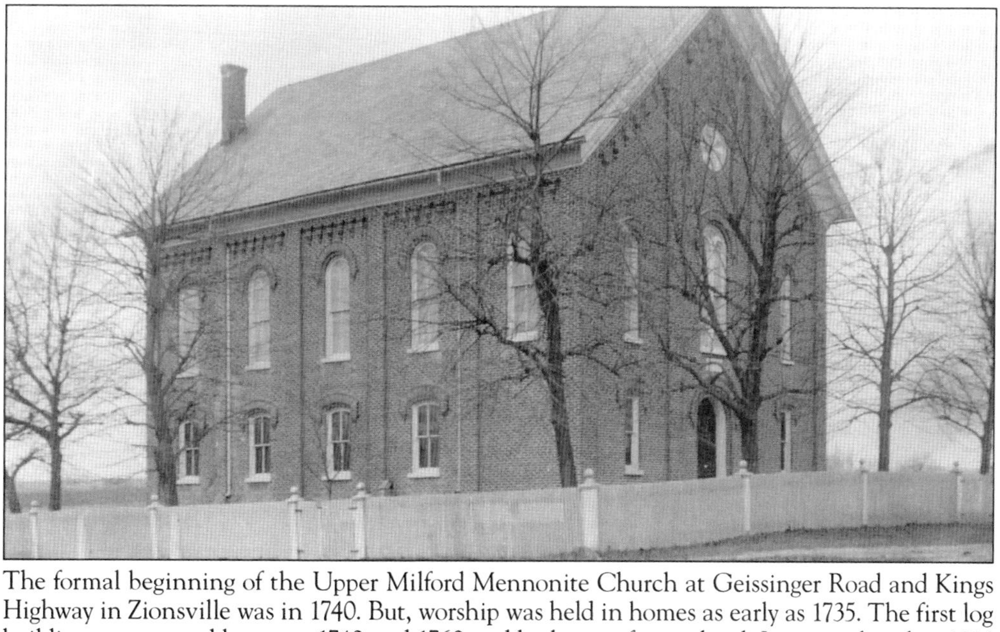

The formal beginning of the Upper Milford Mennonite Church at Geissinger Road and Kings Highway in Zionsville was in 1740. But, worship was held in homes as early as 1735. The first log building was erected between 1740 and 1760 and had space for a school. It was replaced in 1816 by a stone building and by the brick church pictured in 1876. Members provided all of the labor to build their church. (UMHS.)

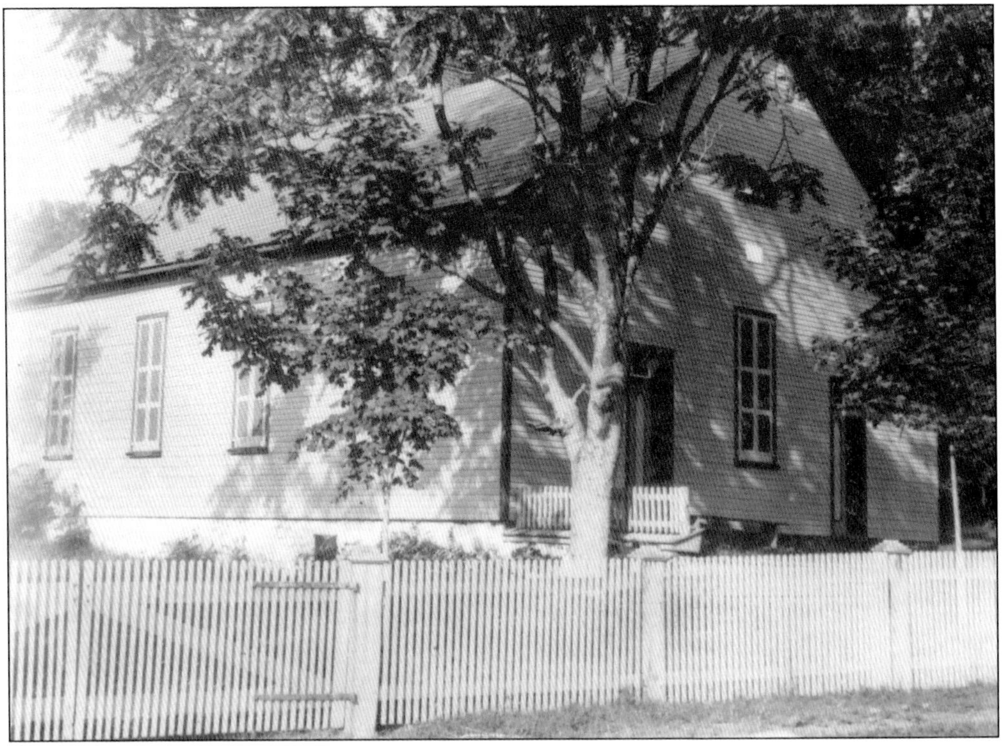

The building pictured here is the Salem United Methodist Church in Powder Valley, as it looked around 1891. It was erected in 1858 and called the "Evangelisch Versomlungs Haus" (Evangelical Meeting House). Notice the separate entry doors for men and for women. The white fence was removed in 1916 as were most of the trees in front. The oldest legible tombstone in the cemetery behind the church is for someone who was born in 1721 and died in 1793. (Courtesy of Beulah Miller.)

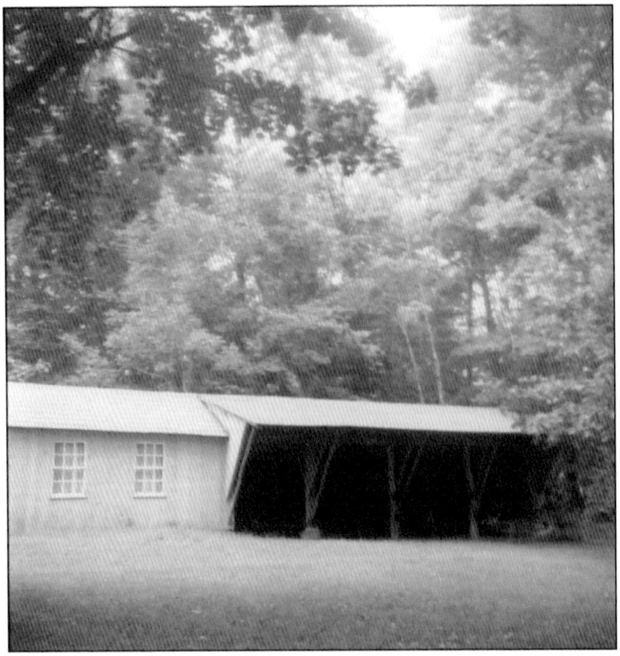

The original horse sheds located to the side of the Salem United Methodist Church are still in place. Horses were driven into the sheds with the buggy or wagon attached to keep them out of the weather. The horses were fed while their owners attended the sometimes-lengthy church services. These sheds predate the present church building. (Courtesy of Beulah Miller.)

Two

Schools and Scholars

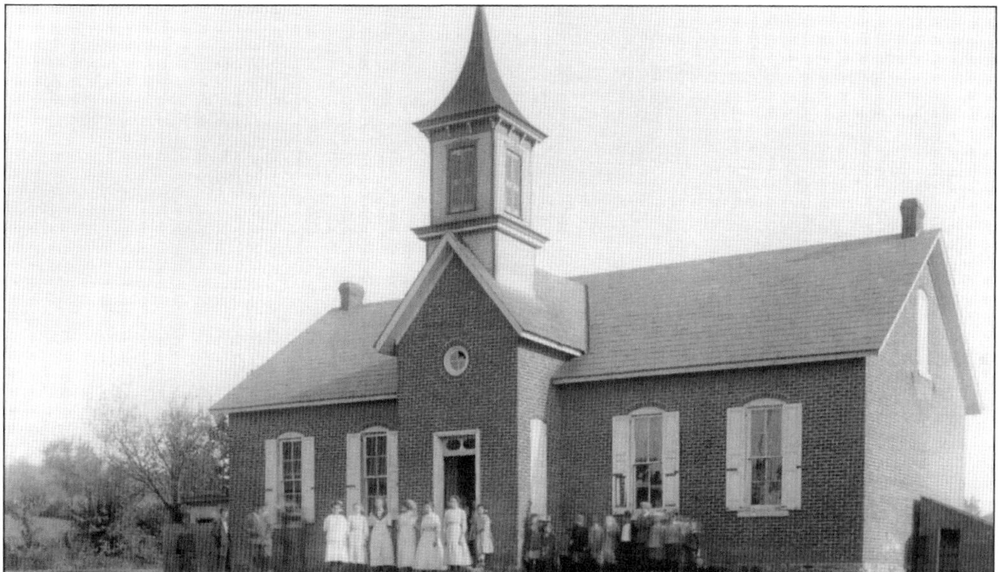

Truly, the home at the "Y" in the Shimerville Road was once a school with a bell tower. Built in 1865, the Kern School had two rooms and was used for grades one through eight until 1907, when there were enough pupils to form a high school. Then, one room was used for Upper Milford High School and the other for lower grades. The Kern family carp pond was across Main Road West from this building, hence the school's name. After the building was sold and renovated into a home, the bell from the tower found its way to a pole at the Swain School on the outskirts of Allentown. (UMHS.)

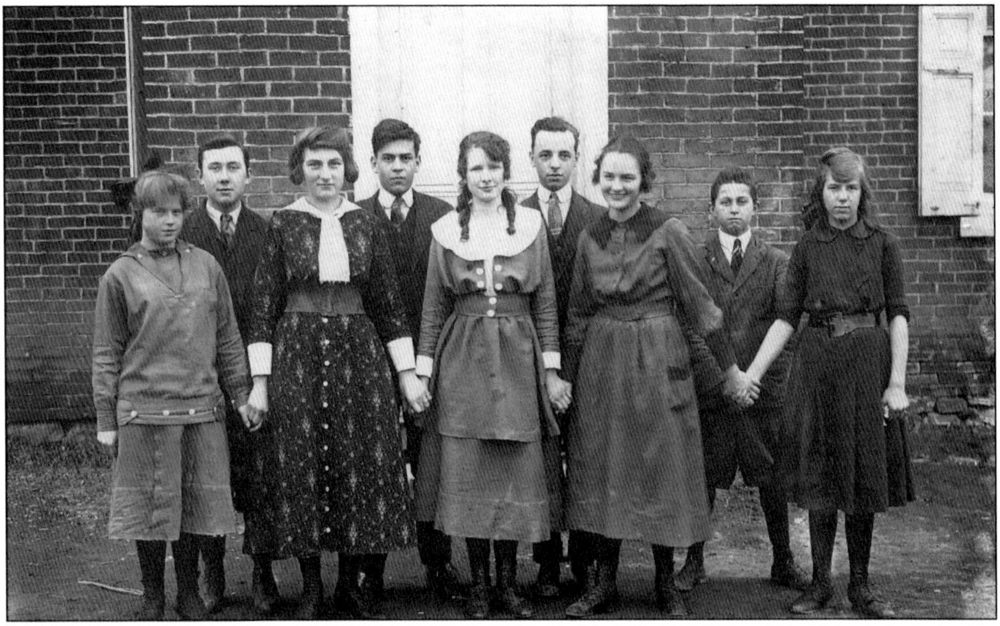

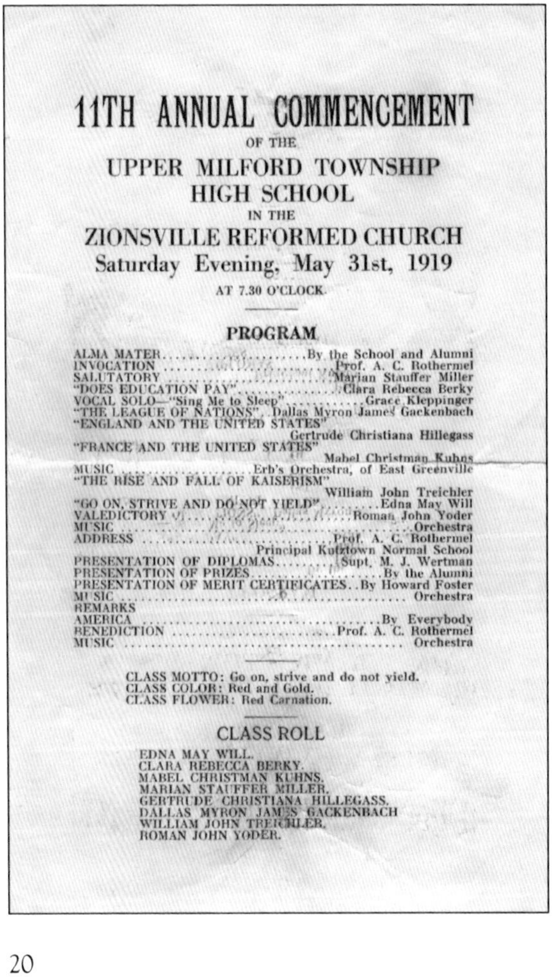

11TH ANNUAL COMMENCEMENT
OF THE
UPPER MILFORD TOWNSHIP
HIGH SCHOOL
IN THE
ZIONSVILLE REFORMED CHURCH
Saturday Evening, May 31st, 1919
AT 7.30 O'CLOCK

PROGRAM

ALMA MATER .... By the School and Alumni
INVOCATION .... Prof. A. C. Rothermel
SALUTATORY .... Marian Stauffer Miller
"DOES EDUCATION PAY" .... Clara Rebecca Berky
VOCAL SOLO—"Sing Me to Sleep" .... Grace Kleppinger
"THE LEAGUE OF NATIONS" . Dallas Myron James Gackenbach
"ENGLAND AND THE UNITED STATES"
Gertrude Christiana Hillegass
"FRANCE AND THE UNITED STATES"
Mabel Christman Kuhns
MUSIC .... Erb's Orchestra, of East Greenville
"THE RISE AND FALL OF KAISERISM"
William John Treichler
"GO ON, STRIVE AND DO NOT YIELD" .... Edna May Will
VALEDICTORY .... Roman John Yoder
MUSIC .... Orchestra
ADDRESS .... Prof. A. C. Rothermel
Principal Kutztown Normal School
PRESENTATION OF DIPLOMAS .... Supt. M. J. Wertman
PRESENTATION OF PRIZES .... By the Alumni
PRESENTATION OF MERIT CERTIFICATES . . By Howard Foster
MUSIC .... Orchestra
REMARKS
AMERICA .... By Everybody
BENEDICTION .... Prof. A. C. Rothermel
MUSIC .... Orchestra

CLASS MOTTO: Go on, strive and do not yield.
CLASS COLOR: Red and Gold.
CLASS FLOWER: Red Carnation.

CLASS ROLL

EDNA MAY WILL.
CLARA REBECCA BERKY.
MABEL CHRISTMAN KUHNS.
MARIAN STAUFFER MILLER.
GERTRUDE CHRISTIANA HILLEGASS.
DALLAS MYRON JAMES GACKENBACH
WILLIAM JOHN TREICHLER.
ROMAN JOHN YODER.

The class roll listed eight graduates from Upper Milford High School in 1919, pictured above. The girls in the first row are Edna Will (second from left), Marian Miller (far right), Clara Berky, Mabel Kuhns, and Gertrude Hillegass. The boys in the second row are, from left to right, valedictorian Roman Yoder, Elton Miller, Dallas Gackenbach, and William Treichler. Elton Miller chose not to graduate due to issues with the teacher. However, in a true success story, Miller later became an important member of the school board. (Courtesy of Ruth Yoder-Taylor.)

Part of the May 31, 1919, commencement program held in the Old Zionsville Reformed Church is shown. That was the 11th graduating class from Upper Milford High School. The last class graduated in 1925. (Courtesy of Ruth Yoder-Taylor.)

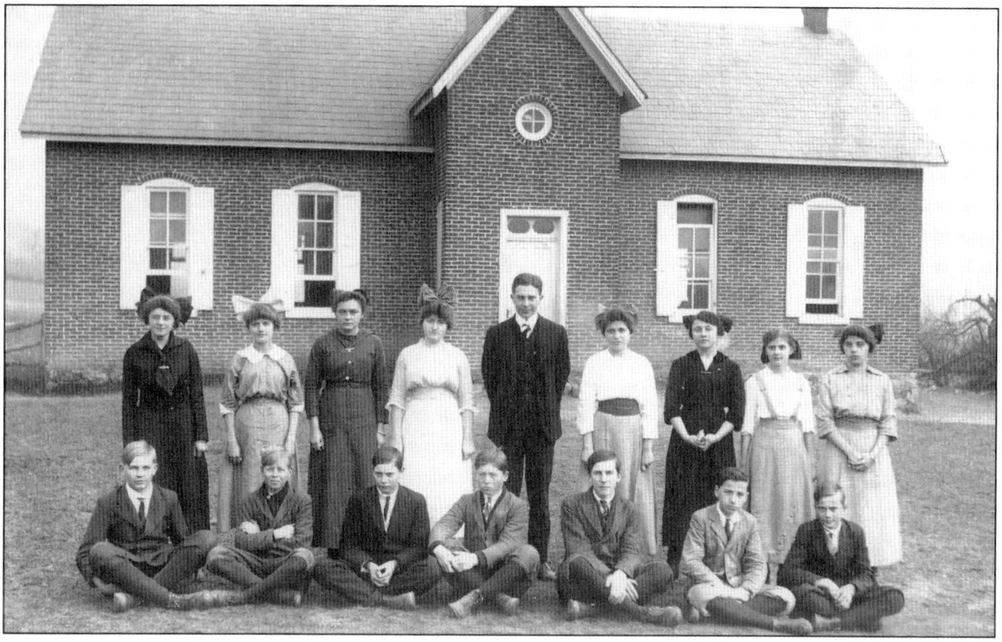

Another picture of Upper Milford High School from 1915 shows some of the prominent graduates, such as the teacher Henry Snyder, who, along with fellow graduate Horace Schantz, became a Pennsylvania state senator. Future township teachers Tillie Kuhns and Ella Miller Schreiber are second from right and far right of the second row, respectively. The school had a fine reputation and was widely respected for its excellent teachers. Future teacher Franklin Faust is the first student on the left in the first row. Monthly, on a Friday evening, literary society programs were conducted to overflow audiences with music, recitations, and debates. In the photograph below, teacher Rev. James Blatt, also a graduate of the school, is posing with his upper grade students. Blatt taught at the school from 1918 to 1924. Future teacher Roman Yoder is in the back row, second from right. (Both, courtesy of Barbara Harris.)

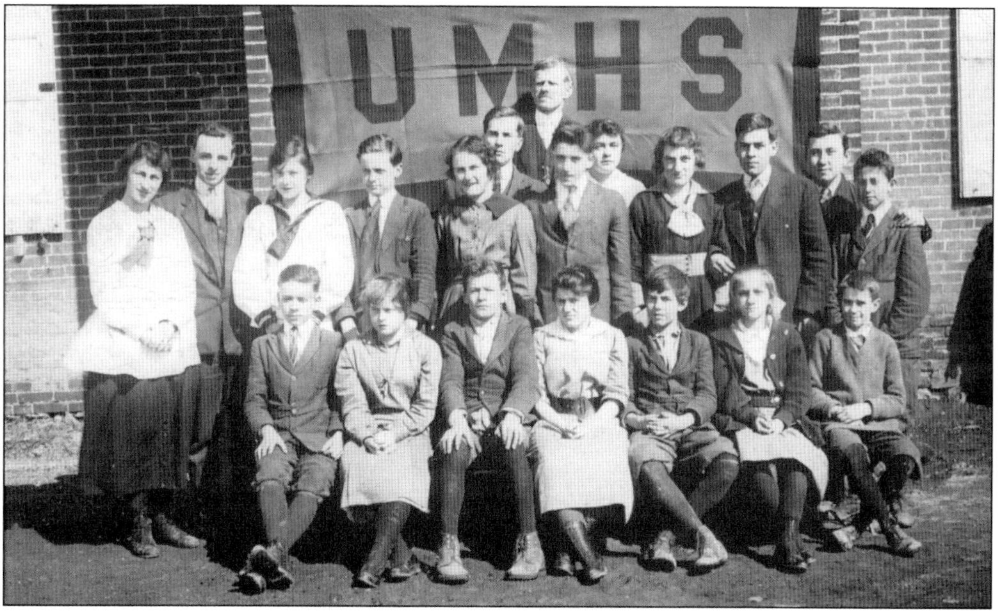

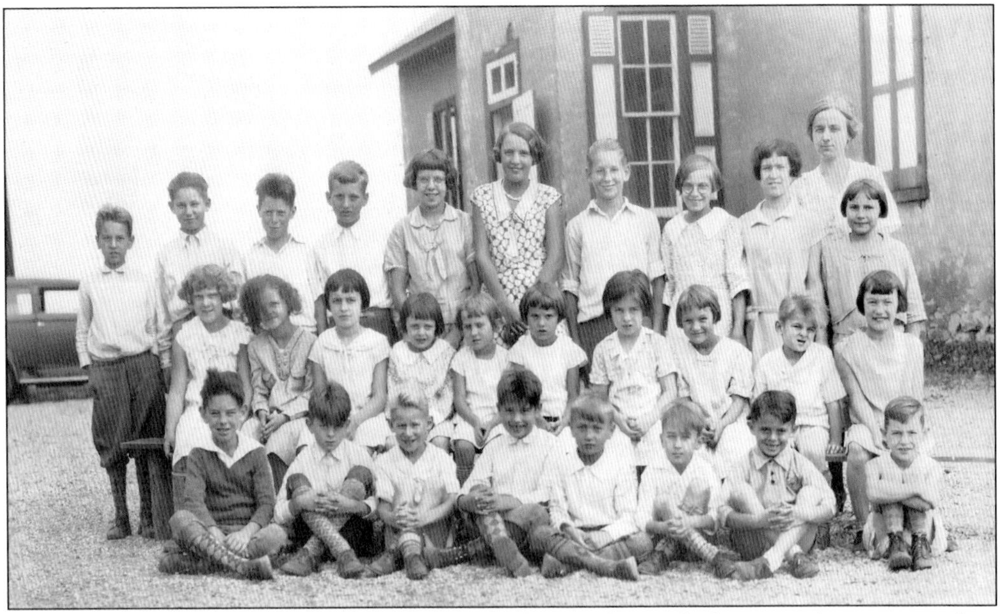

Teacher Lulu Miller was in the earlier years of her long and storied 45-year teaching career when this photograph was taken in 1930. Miller taught the elementary grades in the Old Zionsville School and the Kings Highway School. Look for her in many family group pictures throughout this book. When the Old Zionsville School closed, Miller moved to the newly built Kings Highway School, shown below, where she closed out her long career in 1958. In the photograph below, Sidney Unser is the first child on the left in the first row. (Both, courtesy of Barbara Harris.)

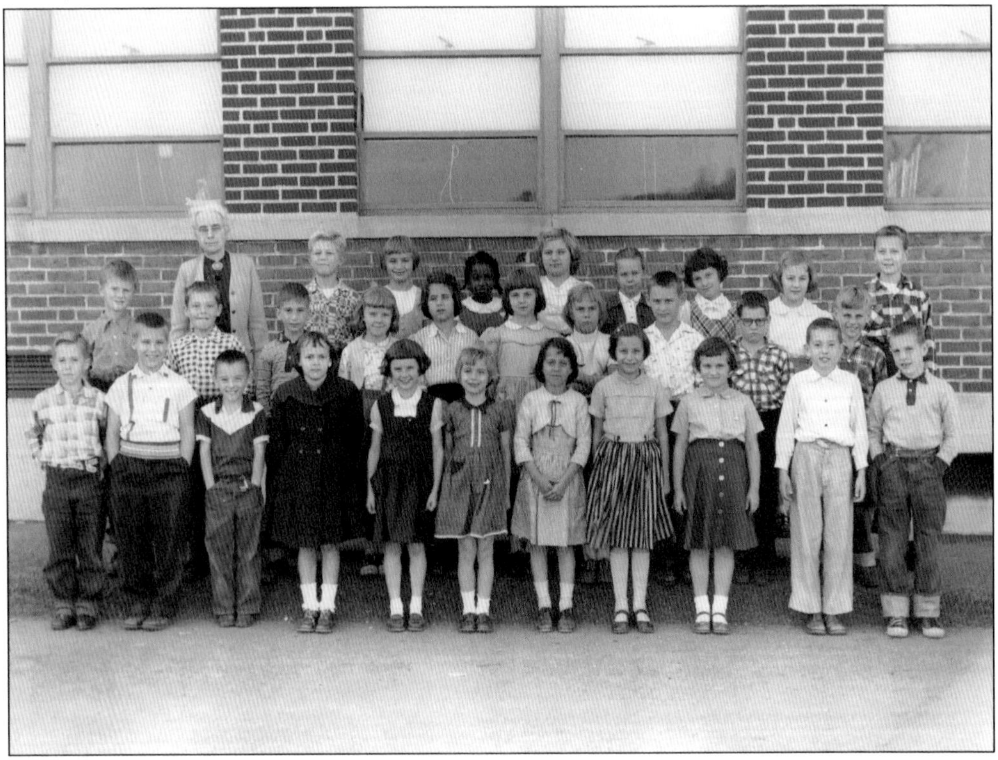

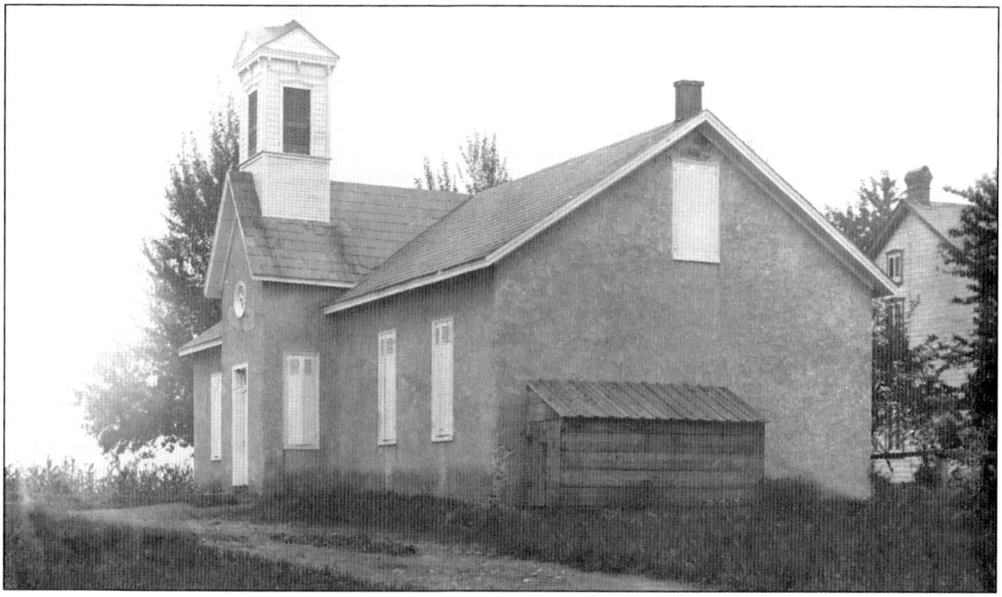

The Old Zionsville School was built as a one-room structure in 1874 on a half acre bought from Charles Wieand. An addition was constructed in 1892, making it two rooms. Prior to this building, an 1841 church sponsored Old Zionsville School and stood a short distance to the north. It was accepted as a public school by the township in 1844. This new 1874 school had a steeple with a bell claimed from the 1841 building. The school is now the home of the Brown family on the lane going into Lenape Park. (UMHS.)

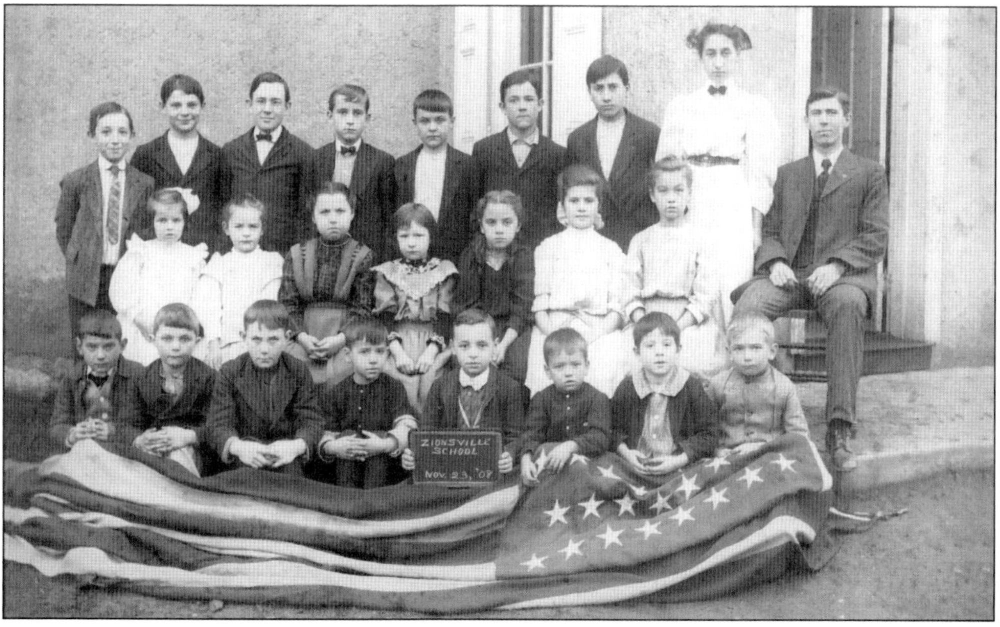

In 1908, the students at the Old Zionsville School were very serious when this photograph was taken. Teacher Ella Reese Schantz is the woman standing in the third row. The male teacher is unidentified. Dallas Gackenbach, a future teacher, is holding the school sign. In the second row, Mazie Miller is third from the left, and Ella Miller Schreiber is fifth. Notice the unusual draping of the flag to enhance the picture. (Courtesy of Barbara Harris.)

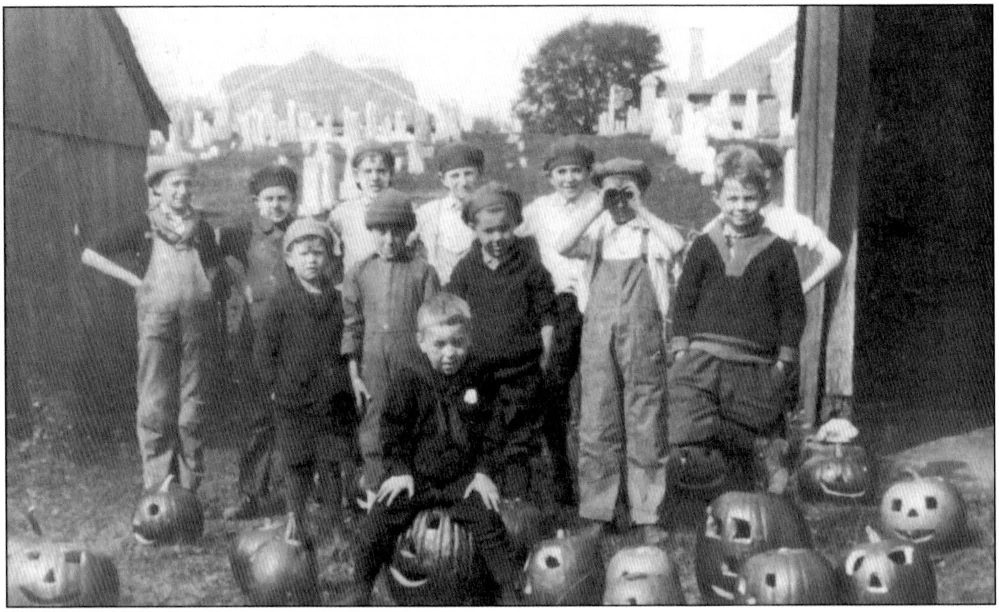

These schoolboys are shown at the Old Zionsville School with their Jack-o-lantern creations. Claude Schultz is perched on a pumpkin, and one of the Stauffer brothers is shown using his hand "binoculars" to zero in on the photographer. The cemetery of the Reformed Church was an inspired background for "Trick or Treat!" (Courtesy of William and Carolyn Lagler.)

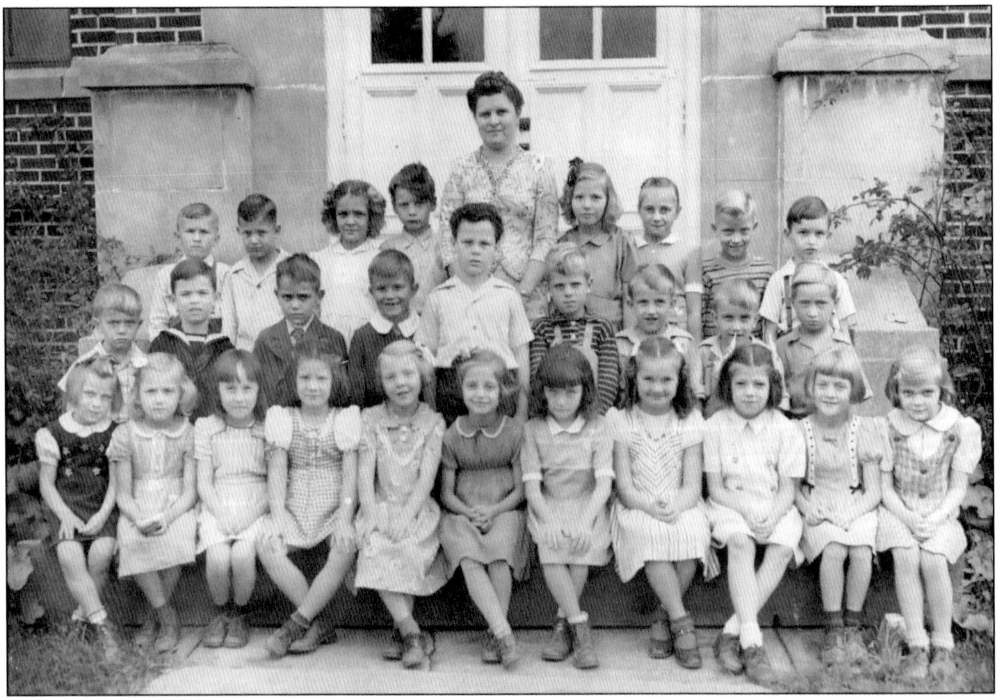

Jolann Klan Ozvatics was the teacher of these elementary grade students at the Vera Cruz School in 1946. Mary (Schantz) Snyder is the smiling girl in the dark dress in the middle of the first row. Teacher Ozvatics graduated from Kutztown State Teachers College and taught at the school for 30 years. (Courtesy of Mary Snyder.)

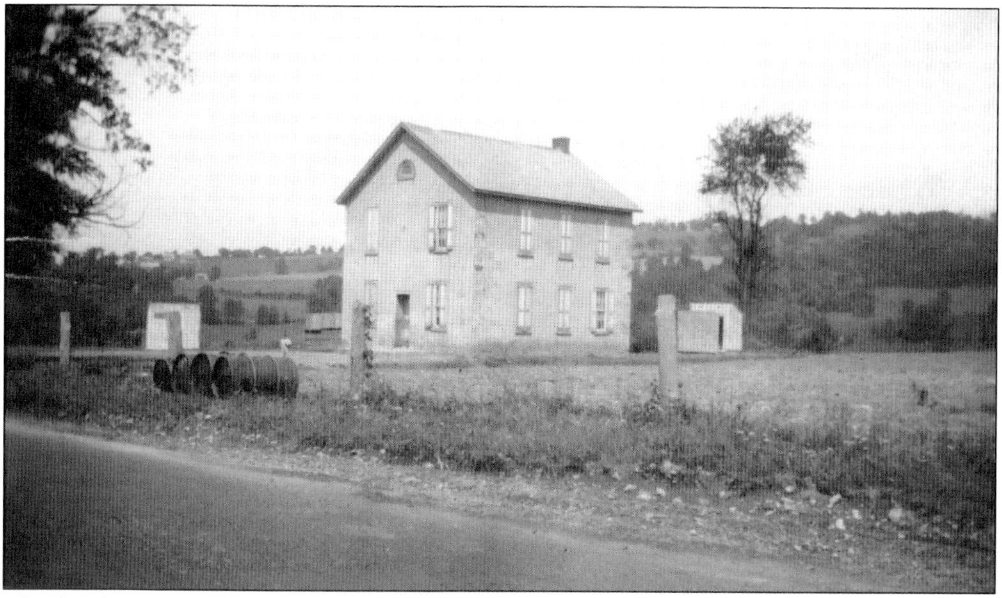

The first known school in Vera Cruz was Schantz Mill, built in 1850. It was sold to Henry M. Shelly in 1881 when the building above was built for a new school on land purchased from Samuel Schuler. This Vera Cruz School was in use until 1927. In 1928, teacher Charles D. Treichler bought the school and made it into his home. Treichler was an avid collector and historian of the Vera Cruz area with a special interest in arrowheads and jasper. He also served the township as tax collector for many years. (Courtesy of Joseph Benner.)

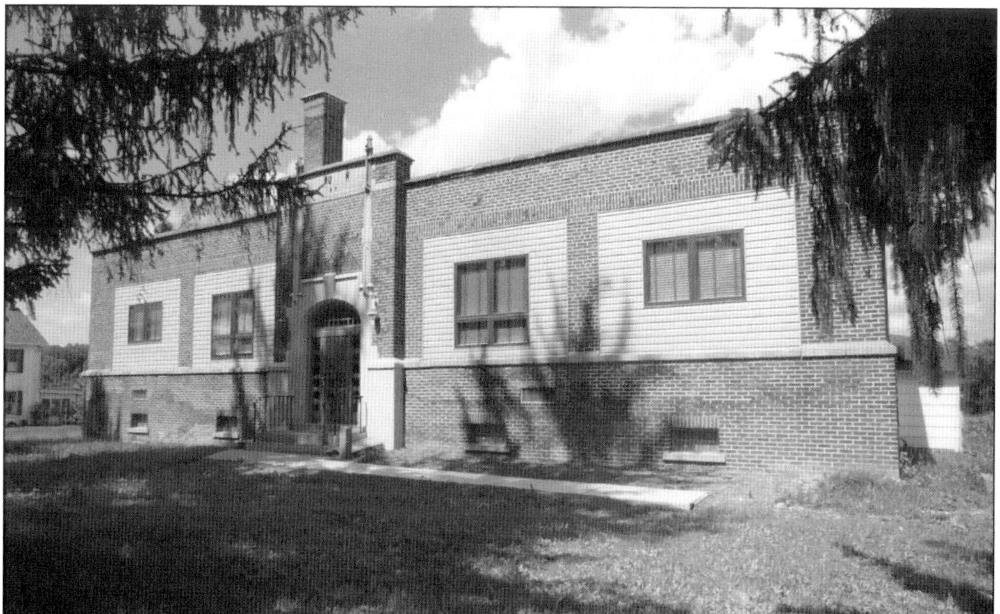

A new Vera Cruz School was built in 1927, just 50 feet south of the old school on Vera Cruz Road. Besides Charles Treichler, who became principal, the first teachers in the four-room building were Wesley Kehl, Helen Mohr, and Gertrude Keller, who had transferred from the old building. After this school closed, it was turned into Harry Rinker Enterprises. (Courtesy of Sidney Unser.)

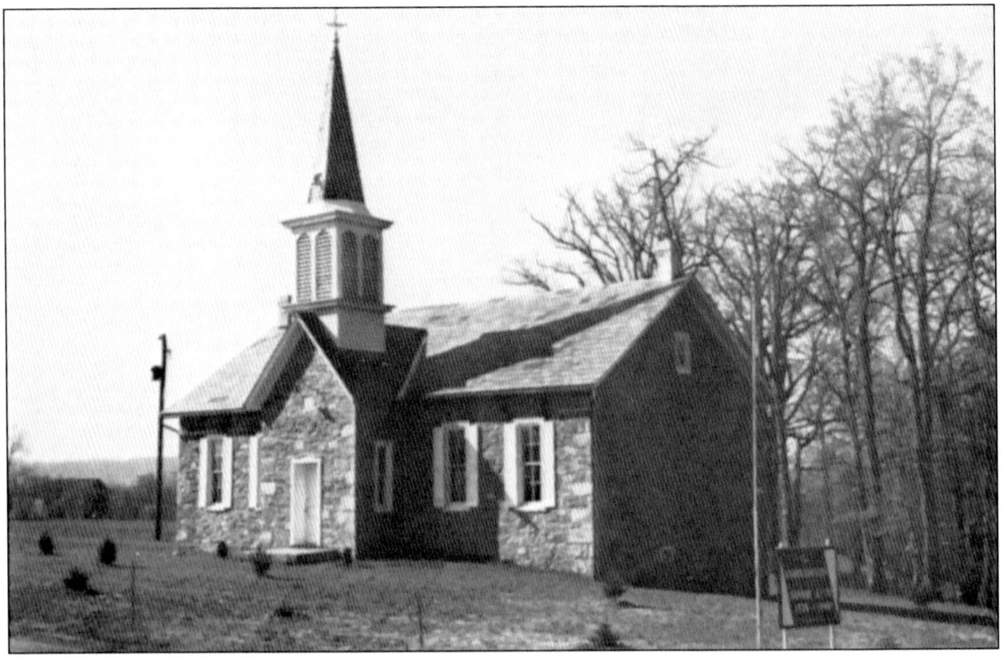

The fourth and present building of the Dillingersville School is shown in 1885. The first building in 1735 was of logs, the second one in 1799 was half school and half dwelling, and the third building was erected in 1848. The school is a registered historic site and is preserved by the Dillingersville Union School and Church Association, which holds a yearly gathering at the school. (Courtesy of Joseph Benner.)

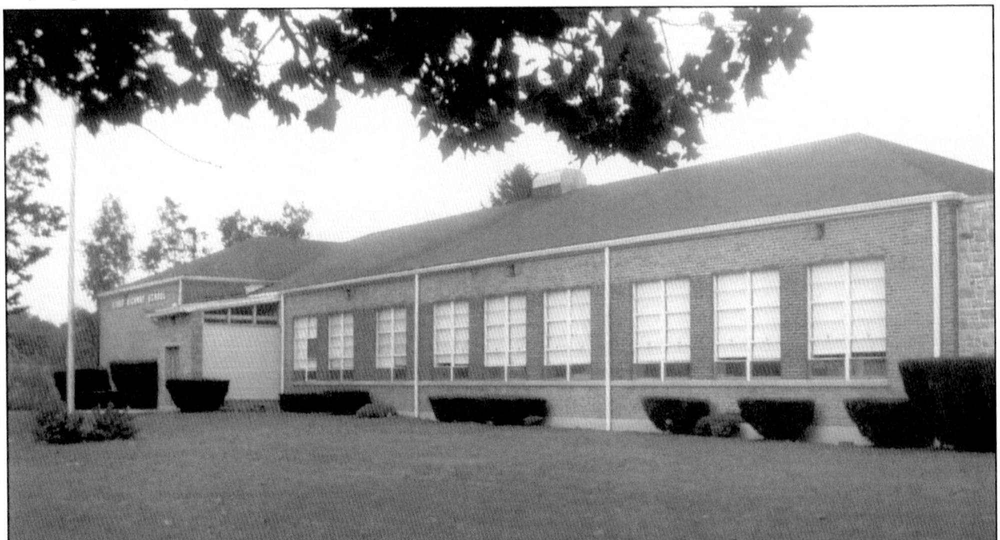

The Kings Highway School on Chestnut Street in Old Zionsville was built by the Upper Milford School Authority and opened in 1951. It was transferred for $1 to the newly merged East Penn School District in 1979. In 2005, East Penn closed the building as a school. Upper Milford Township bought the building back from the district for $875,000 in 2007. It has since been remodeled into the current Upper Milford Township Municipal Center and is home to the Upper Milford Historical Society. (UMHS.)

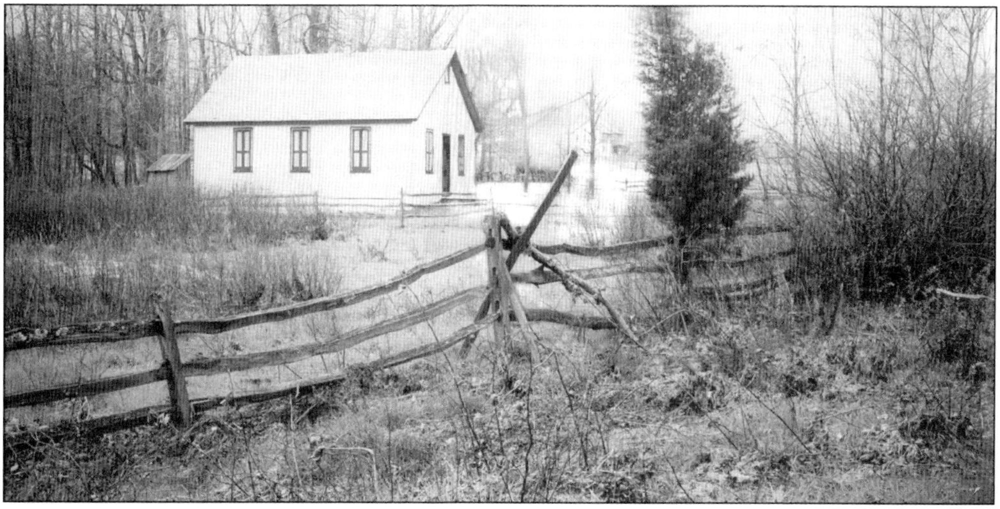

The Sigmund School Subdistrict bought a quarter acre from William Rausch in 1880 in the area of the Hampton Furnace for a school. Pictured here in the 1909–1910 term, the stone building cost about $1,000. A few of the teachers were C.P. Heller, A.E. Heimbach, and O.F. Gery. The school has been converted into an attractive home, as are most of the previous township school buildings that have managed to endure over time. (UMHS.)

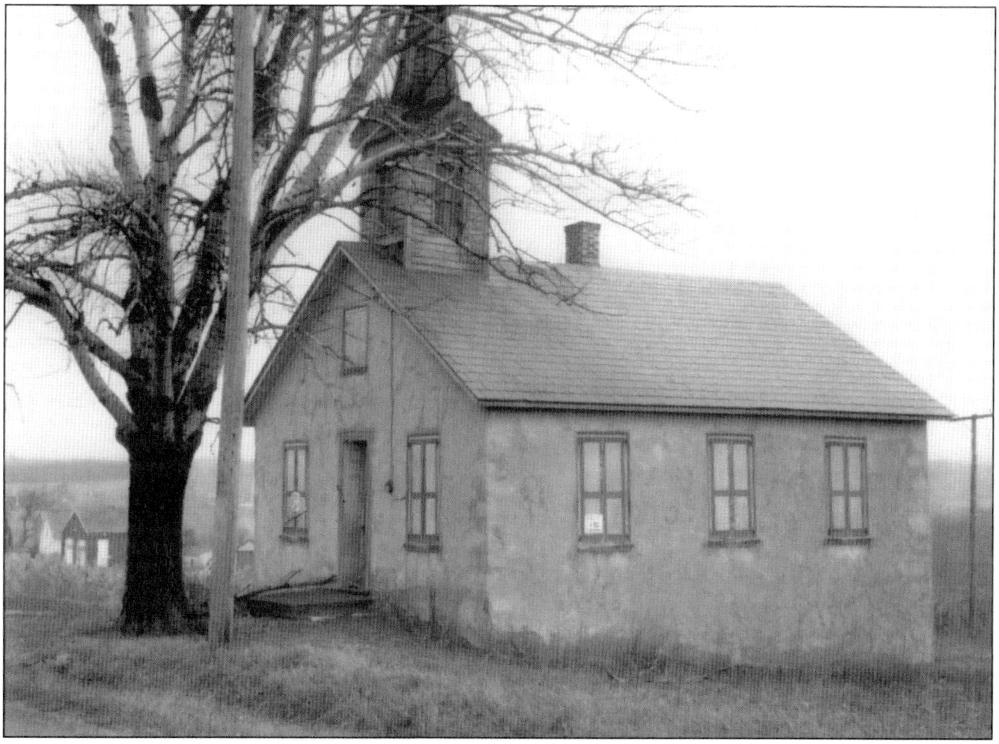

The Geissinger School was erected in 1874 on Kings Highway in Zionsville on a quarter acre of land purchased from Abraham Geissinger. The school actually predated the village of Zionsville, which was established two years later in 1876. The first teacher was John N. Bitting, employed for five months at $40 per month. The building has been plastered over and is now the proud residence of the Steiner family. (UMHS.)

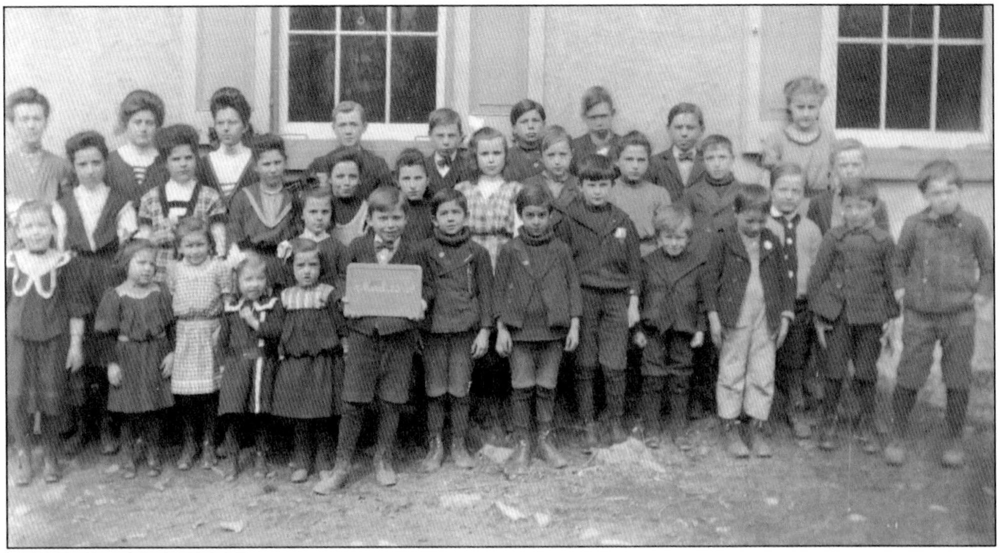

A March 1909 class picture of the entire student body at the Powder Valley School shows the younger and older brothers and sisters grouped together, as was the rule in early schools. There was an advantage to this arrangement. Young children heard the lessons of their older siblings and, in some cases, absorbed enough of the teachings to be skipped a grade. Powder Valley families included in Schubert School had surnames such as Bartholomew, Batman, Carl, Miller, Schultz, and Stahl. Newton and Elton Miller are in the first row on the right side of the sign holder. (Courtesy of Barbara Heist.)

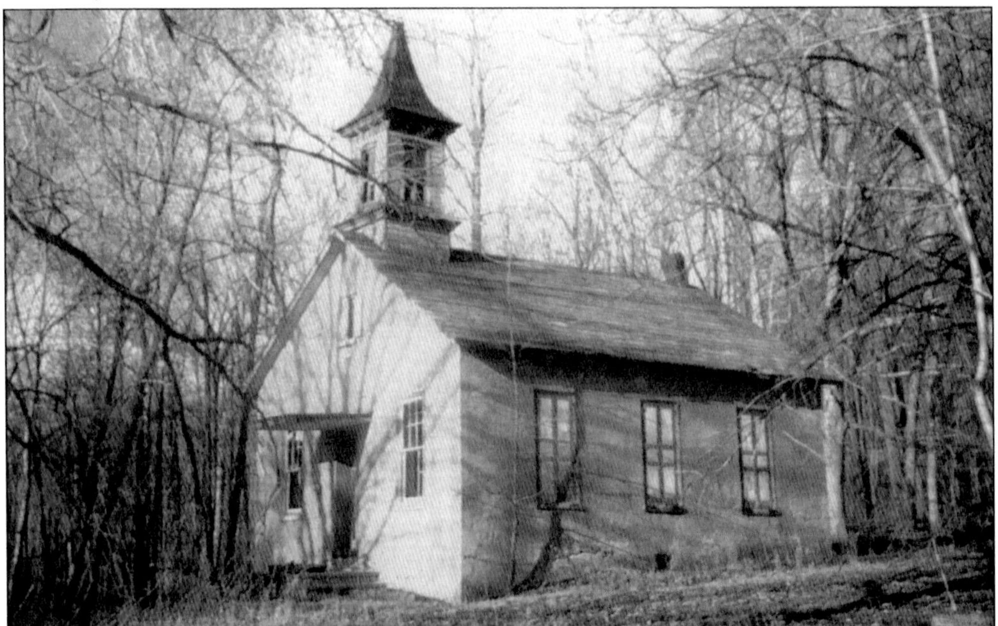

The Schubert School on Sell Road in Powder Valley was built in 1888. It replaced the first school known as Powder School, built by contractor William Weidner in 1855. That first school building has been remodeled into an attractive home on Powder Valley Road. This new building was Schubert School until 1951. It, too, has been renovated into an attractive home. (Courtesy of Beulah Miller.)

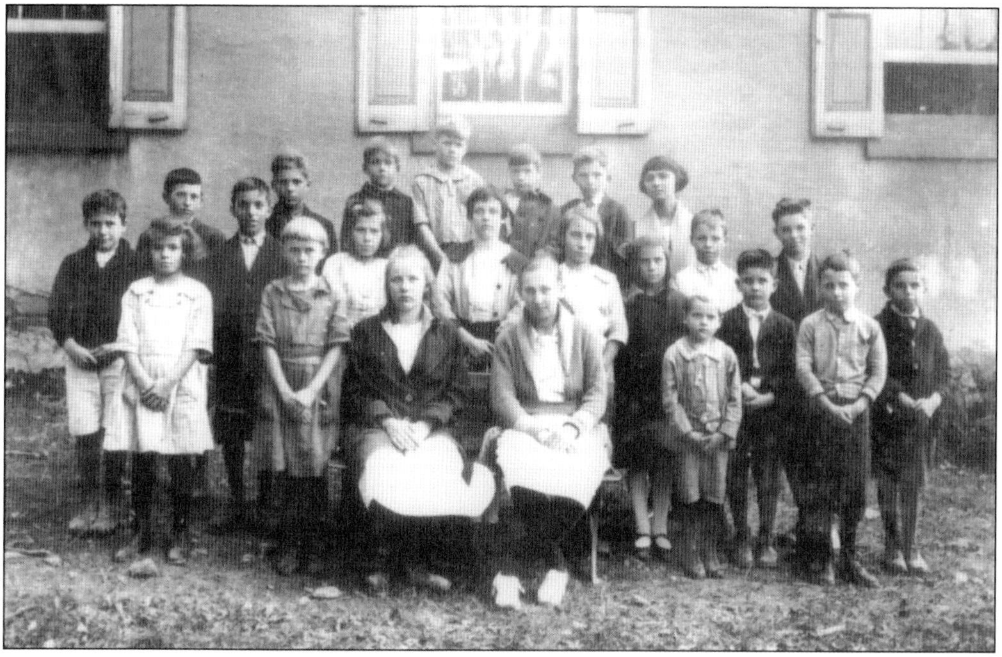

It is not easy to find the young-looking teacher Esther Moyer in this 1923 group picture of the students at the Schubert School in Powder Valley. She is on the right end of the last row. Otto Miller is the tall blonde lad in the middle of the last row. Powder Valley surnames represented in this class are Cassler, Geary, Hillegass, Kleinsmith, Mohr, and Pillar. (Courtesy of Beulah Miller.)

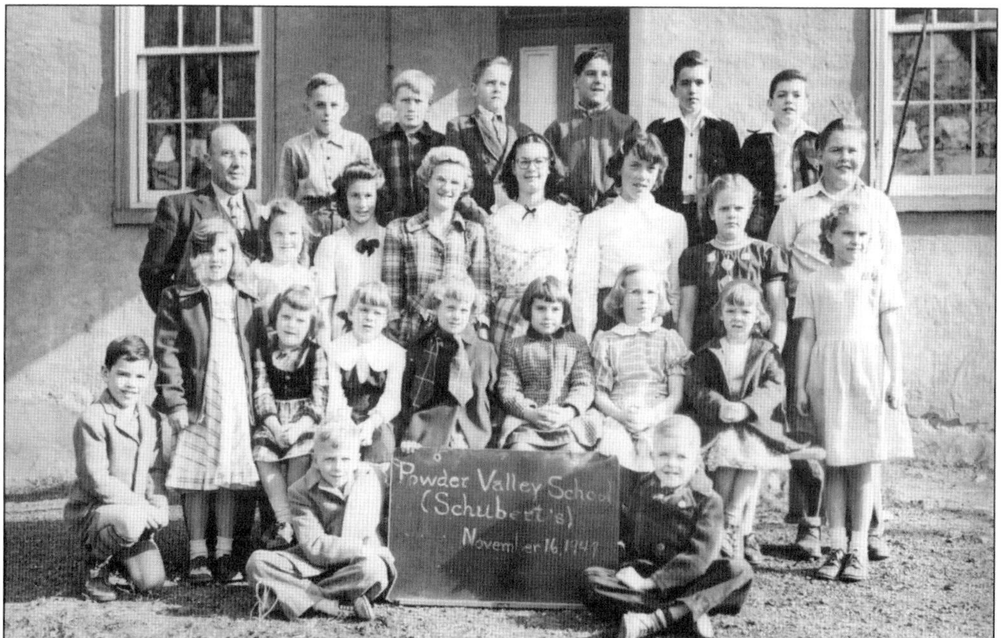

Students at the Schubert School are pictured in 1949. The teacher on the far left is Roman Yoder, a well-respected educator in the township for over 40 years, who is pictured as a youth in many photographs throughout this book. Barbara Miller Heist stands directly behind the school sign, and Pauline Miller Fritz is two students to the left of Barbara. (Courtesy of Barbara Heist.)

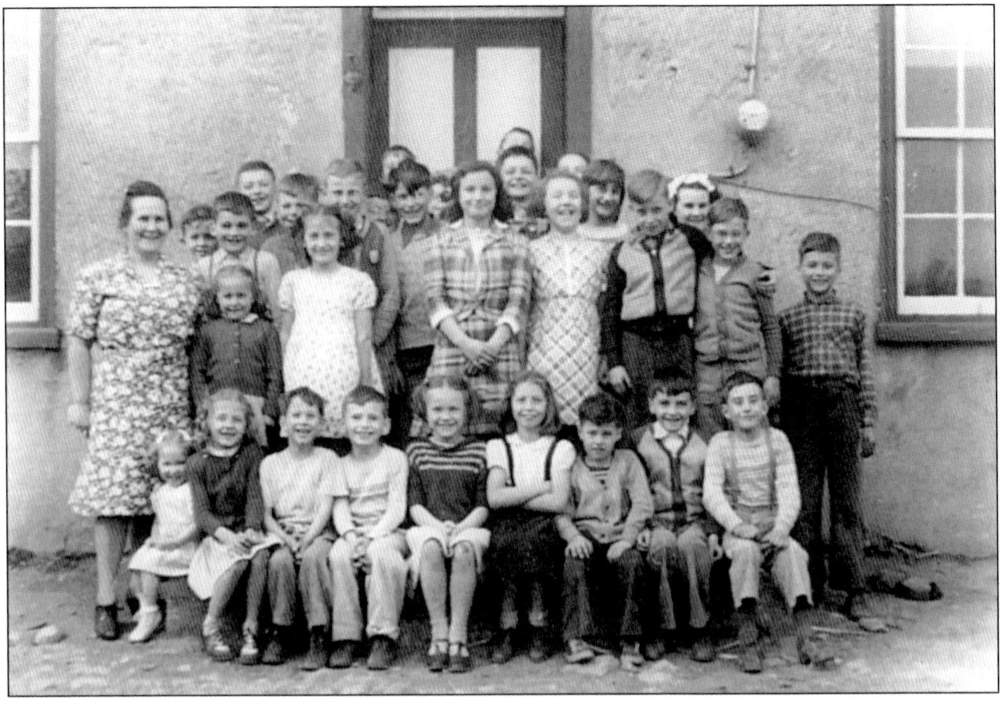

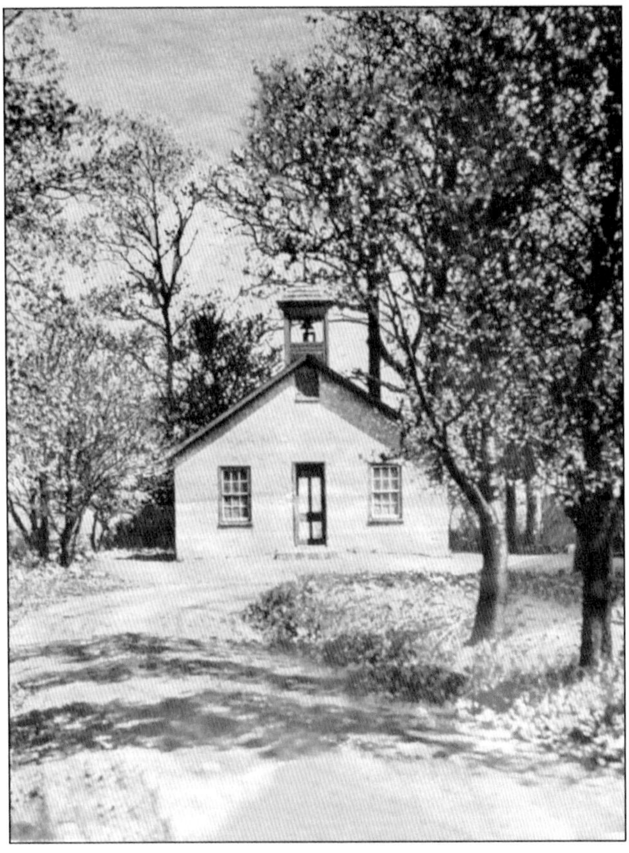

Northwest from Shimerville on Mill Road near the intersection with Rose Drive was the Miller School, at left. It was also called Miller's Mill because of the nearby mill of that name. For a time, it was also called the Roeder School. It was built in 1844 by George Neumoyerhile while the Milfords were still one township a year after the common school act was adopted by the township. The first teacher was Albert Bogen. The teacher in the 1940s photograph above is Annie Hosfeld. Surnames in this school district included Dietrich, Gardner, Merkel, Reichlederfer, Rohrbach, Schnellman, Wetherhold, and Zadravecz. (Both, UMHS.)

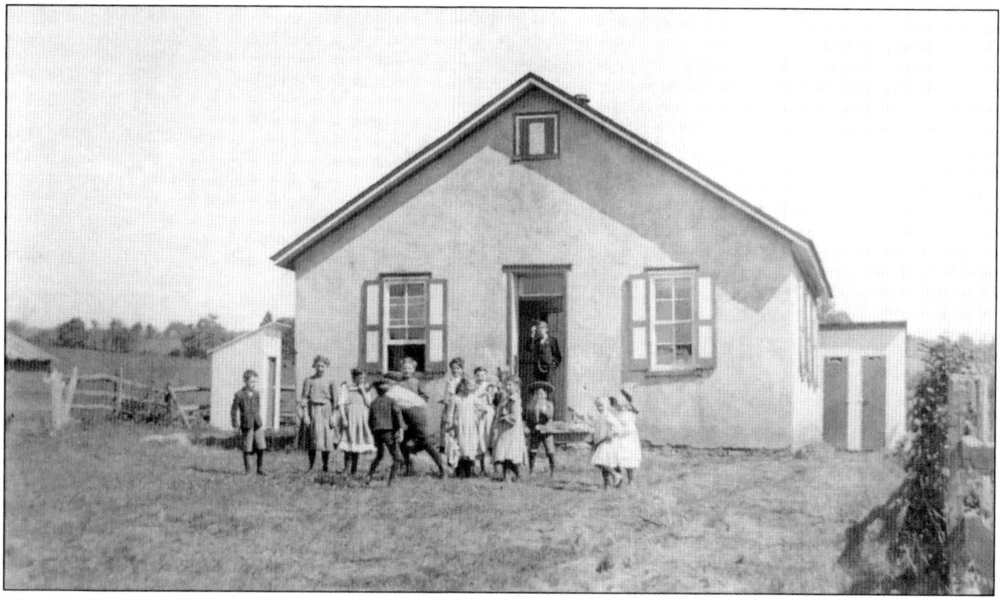

The Yoder School, shown around 1917, was located on Tollgate Road in Zionsville. Prior to 1882, this Subdistrict No. 7 was known as Kriebel's School. Built in 1882 on the premises of Christian Mensch, the school had 75 pupils at one time, but by 1931, enrollment had dropped to 35 students. In the photograph above, students are outside for recess, perhaps playing favorite games of the time such as baseball, leapfrog, or "bolly over." (Courtesy of Ruth Yoder-Taylor.)

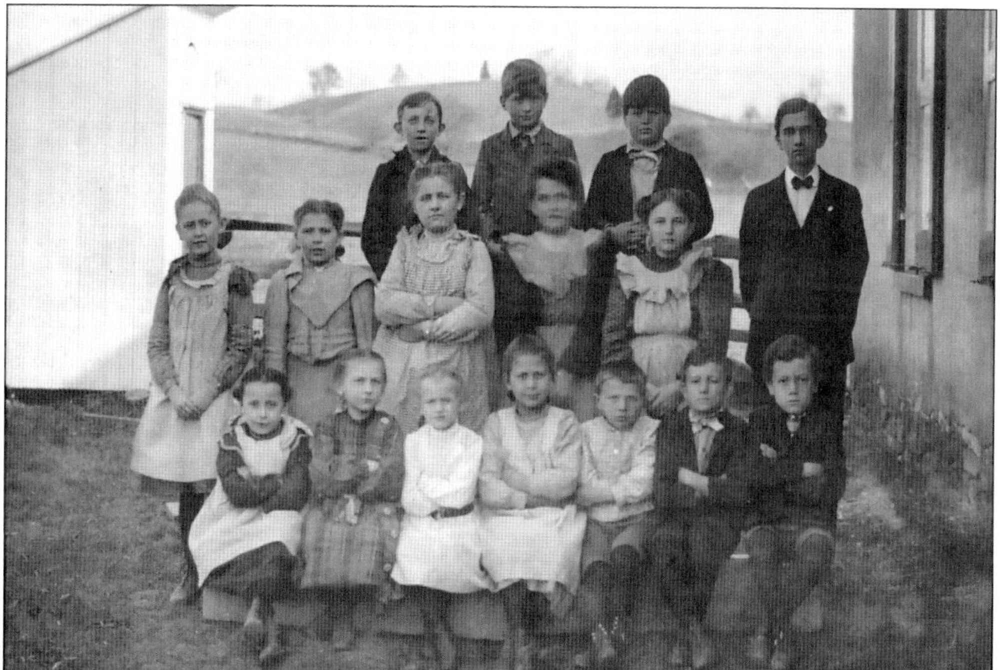

A young Harry S. Miller, later the hardware storekeeper in Old Zionsville, is the teacher pictured here with his students at Yoder School around 1915–1916. Roman Yoder was the last teacher at this school, the same school he had attended as a child, when it closed in 1939. See page 93 for the story of Miller as a World War I soldier. (Courtesy of Ruth Yoder-Taylor.)

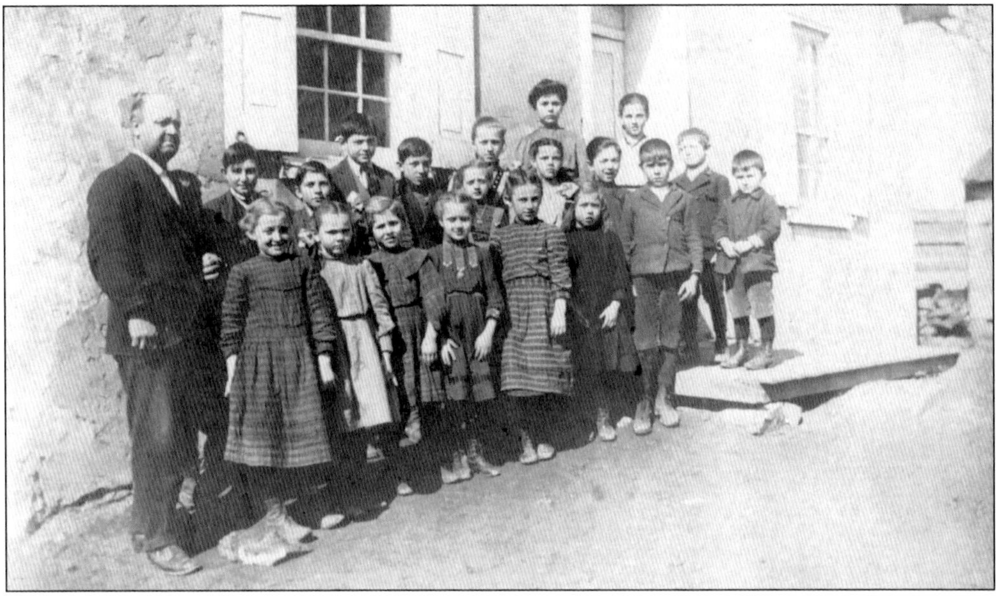

The Ortt School, Subdistrict No. 4, was first established in 1820 for the Dillinger Station area with a log building on the premises of John Ortt (Johannes Ord), an early settler of Upper Milford. In 1845, a new school was built less than a mile west on the premises of Jacob Schantz. William Weidner was the contractor for this building just as he was for the 1855 Schubert School. In 1872, a third school was built southeast from Vera Cruz, which was used until it was torn down to make way for the Pennsylvania Turnpike. The teacher in the school photograph above is unidentified, but Hulda Shelly is the teacher in the picture below. Surnames in this school were Christman, Derr, Fehnel, Heist, Kemmerer, Paules, Sadrovitz, and Shelly. (Both, courtesy of Joseph Seem.)

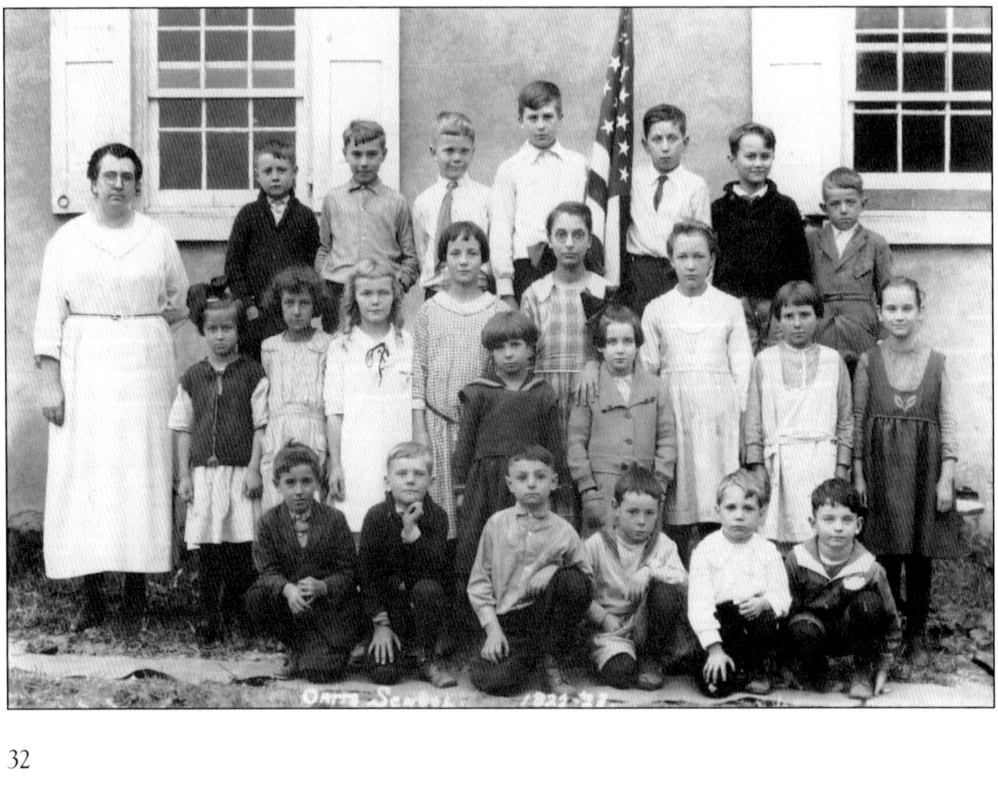

Three

Businesses and Merchants

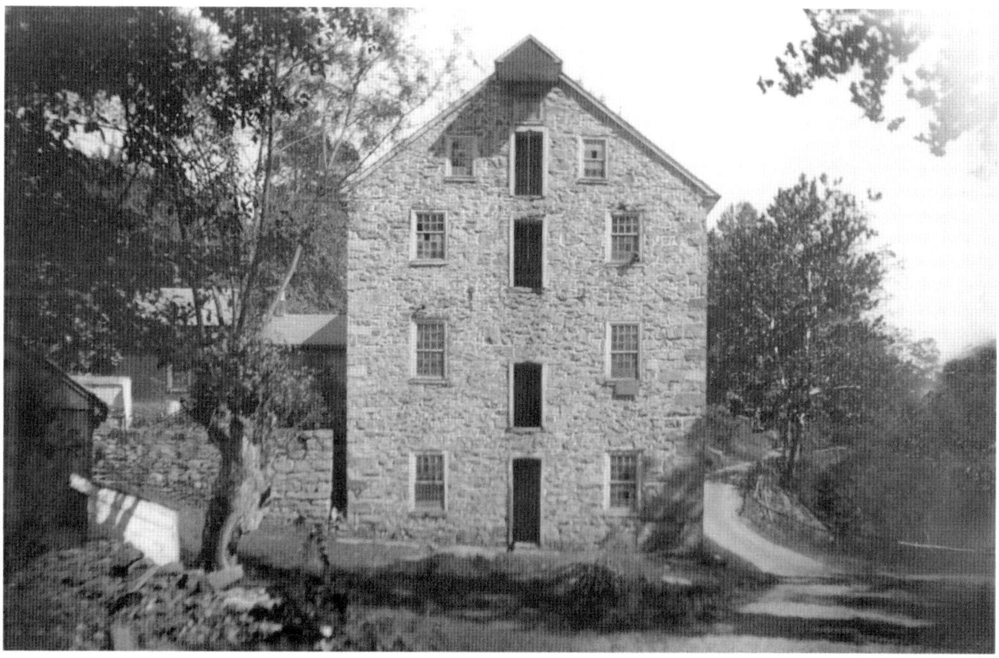

In 1812, Abraham Yeakel bought the four-story stone mill and house on Buhman Road in Powder Valley. The Yeakel Mill was an oil mill and gristmill and considered the finest in the whole area. In 1918, it was converted into a sawmill, which also sold shoe soles, novelty wooden boats, and butter paddles. The mill burned down in 1957. (Courtesy of Schwenkfelder Library and Heritage Center.)

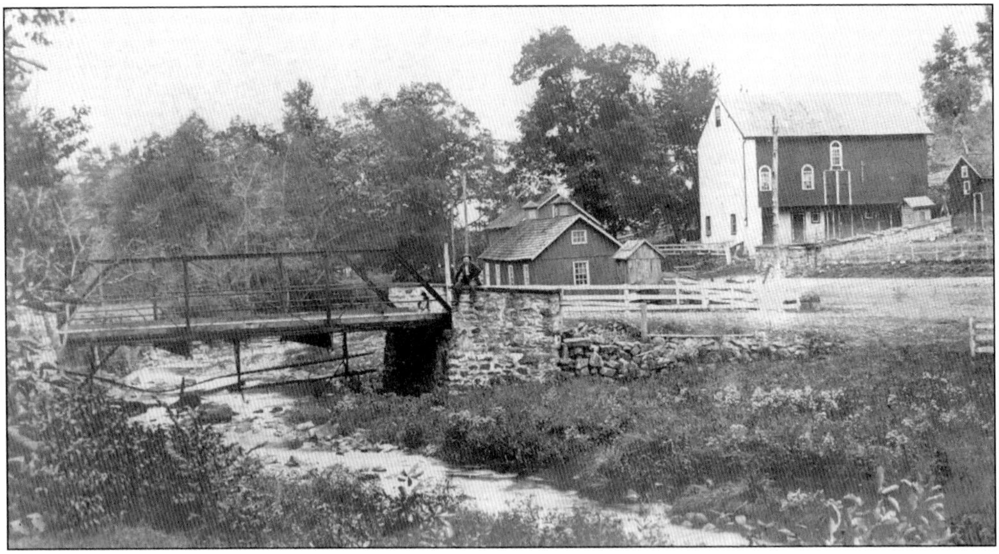

This is the Hiriam Yeakel Mill on Sigmund Road, not to be confused with the Abraham Yeakel Mill in Powder Valley. Hiriam was Abraham's son. Yeakel bought this grist and sawmill from C.W. Wieand in 1865, hence it is also sometimes referred to as Wieand's Mill. At this mill, logs were cut for lumber and wooden rakes were made. The mill stopped grinding in 1938 but still stands. Area mills changed owners frequently over the years, thus often leading to confusion in accurately identifying and locating them. (Courtesy of Ruth Yoder-Taylor.)

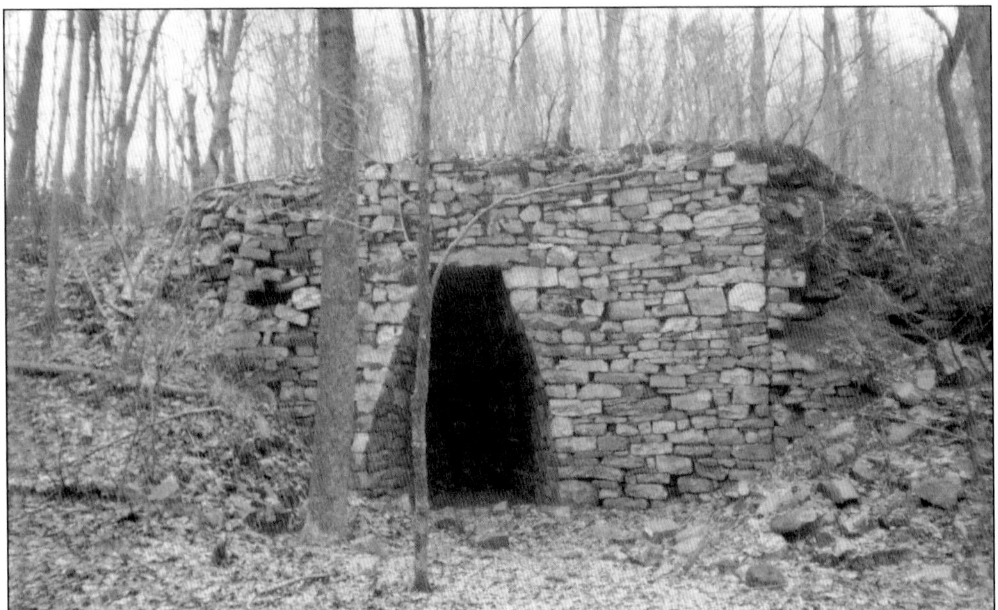

During the 19th century, limestone was burned in limekilns, like the one pictured, and sold for whitewashing buildings and for liming farm fields. Remains of at least four such limekilns can be seen on Sigmund Road near Victory Valley in the township, the same location as the Hampton Furnace. Purchased by Frederick Sigmund in 1850, Hampton Furnace was one of the most prosperous iron plants in the state. The iron was used to make cannonballs for the Civil War. The furnace blew up in 1874. (Courtesy of Barbara Rohrbach.)

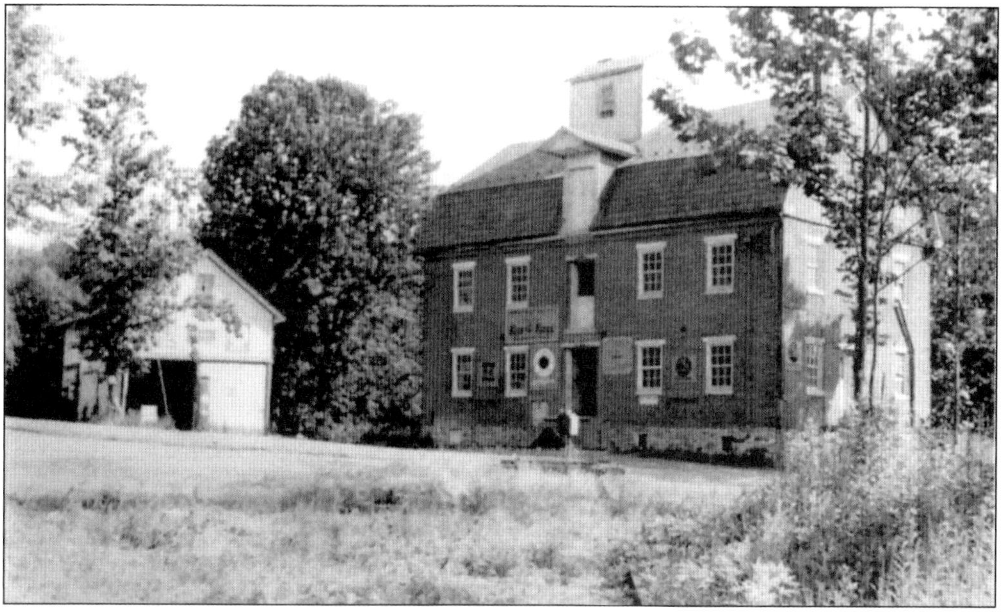

The mill at Powder Valley, above, is located at the very southern end of Powder Valley beside the railroad tracks, now in Lower Milford Township. It was an oil mill run by Samuel Roeder during the 1860s, but later owners converted it into a gristmill. John C. Hancock bought it in 1885 and conducted an ice business using the waters flowing from the dam pictured below. In this hazardous business, local workers cut ice from the lake and shipped it via the Hosensack Railroad to Philadelphia. Oswin Stahl purchased the mill in 1912, and within three weeks, fire destroyed it. But Stahl rebuilt the mill, not with the original flat roof, but this time with a mansard roof, as seen above. Shortly after Elmer Stahl bought the mill in 1935, the dam broke in the great flood that swept the entire area. Wilbur Schultz had the mill from 1949 until 1967, when the Heinz family bought it and remodeled into a private residence, which it remains today. (Courtesy of Schwenkfelder Library and Heritage Center.)

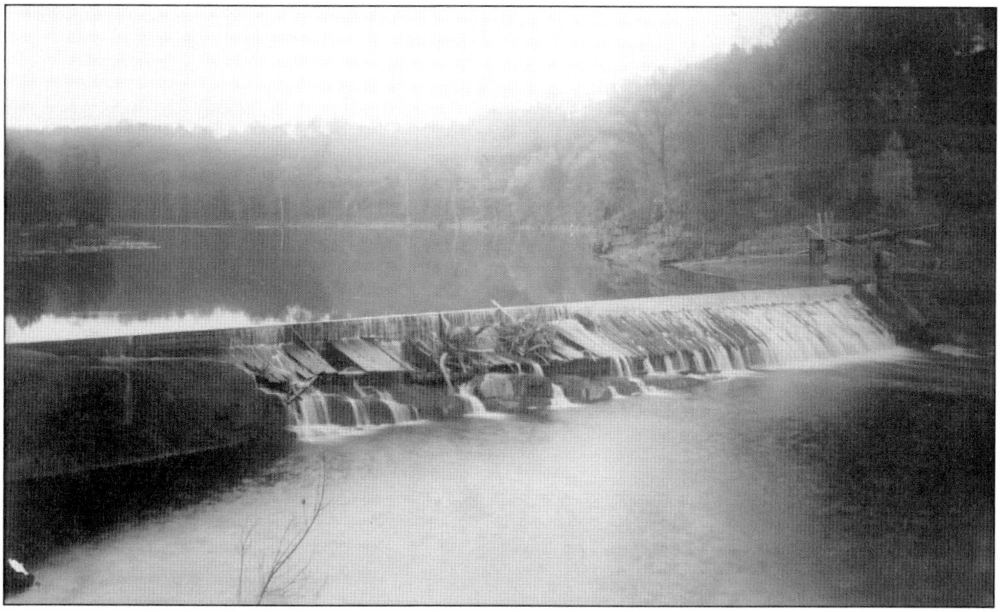

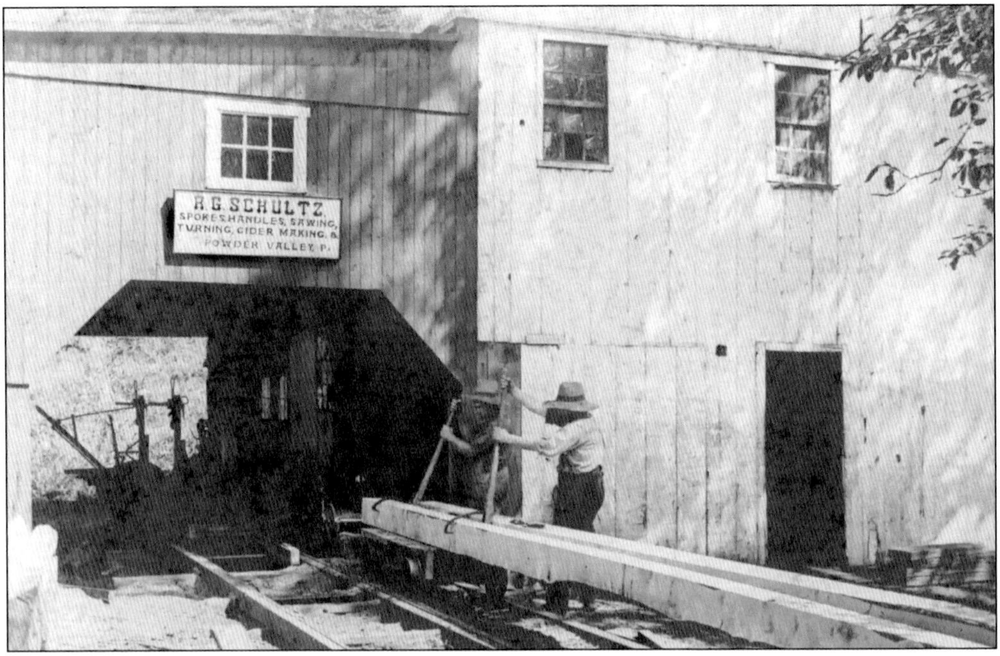

The Rob Schultz sawmill on Powder Valley Road was just below the Yeakel Mill. Schultz's versatile services, as advertised on his sign, were making cider, making spokes and handles, and doing sawing and turning jobs for customers. The mill is also reported to have produced hundreds of barrels of vinegar. (Courtesy of Ruth Yoder-Taylor.)

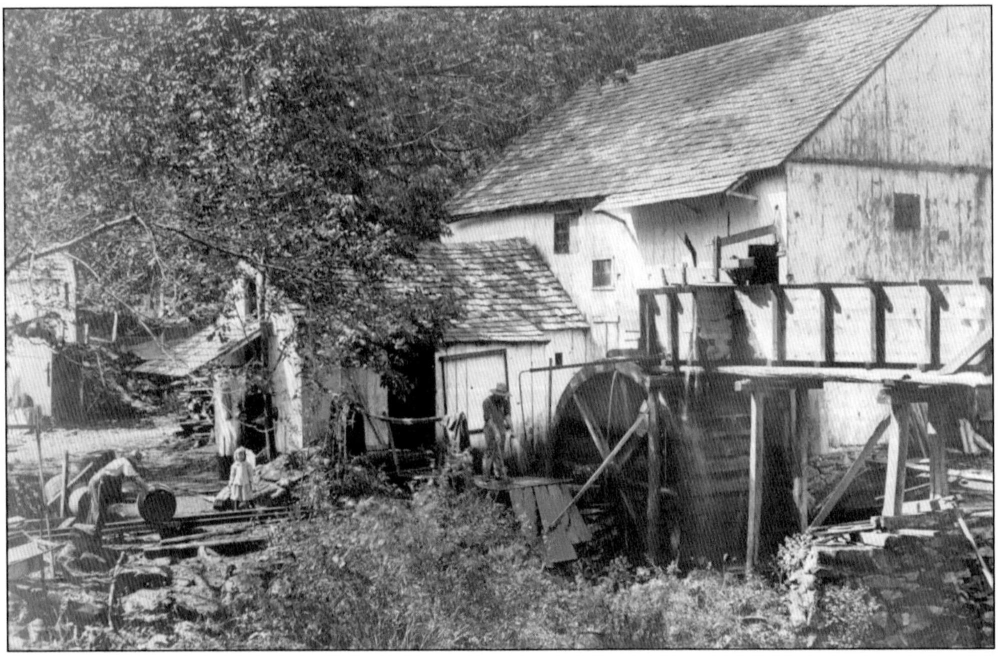

Rob Schultz is shown at his cider press and sawmill on Powder Valley Road. The waterwheel and flume that ran the mill are clearly seen. Hanging on the posts are cloths that were used to filter the cider. Schultz and his daughter Mabel are pictured. The mill washed away in the July 9, 1935, flood that devastated the Powder Valley area. (Courtesy of Beulah Miller.)

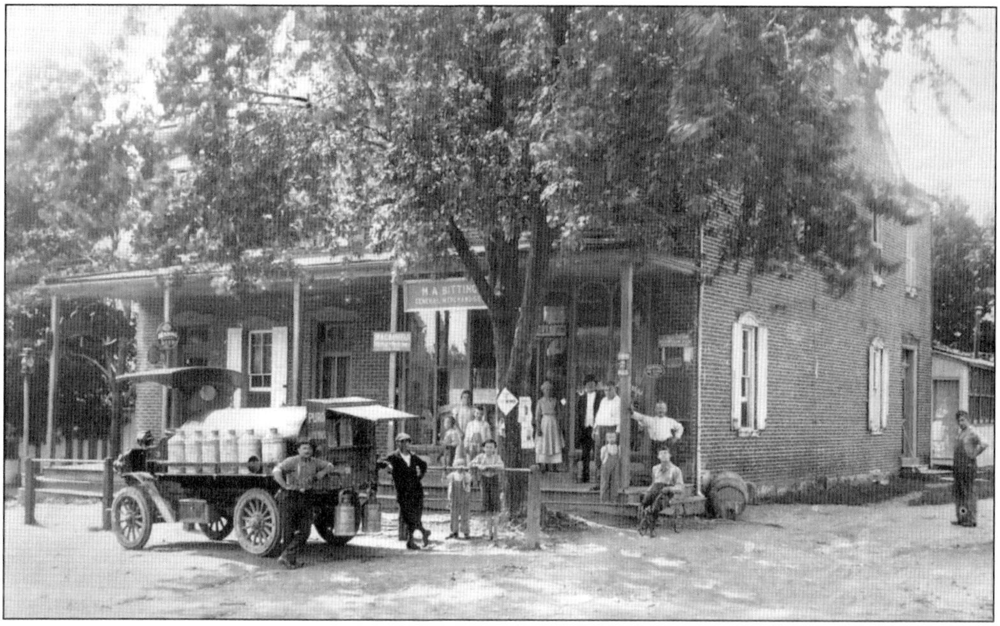

The Zionsville Store was originally also a hotel run by William M. Gehman from 1876 to 1883. It was the direct result of the coming of the railroad and flourished as the hub of the Zionsville countryside. E.P. Yeakel bought it in 1921 as a store only and moved his stock from the store his family had operated in Hosensack since 1913. At various times, Lee Roeder, George Summers, and Norman Schantz had the store. From 1962, Henry and Janet Kradjel were the proprietors of the store until its final closing in about 1987. (UMHS.)

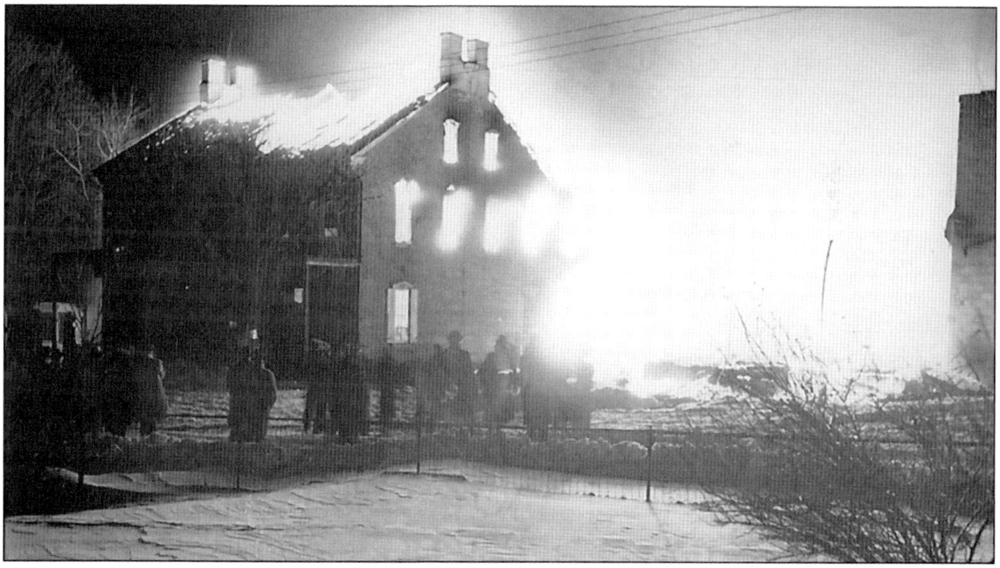

E.P. Yeakel and his wife, Eva, were roused from their home around 1:30 a.m. on March 2, 1941, by two passing milk deliverymen who saw that Zionsville's Yeakel's Economy Store, as it was known at that time, was on fire! The blaze had apparently started in the boiler room of the Clover Sportswear Factory beside the store. The spectacular nighttime fire threatened the whole village for a time. Undaunted, Yeakel built a new store on the same site, which opened to customers on November 20, 1941. (UMHS.)

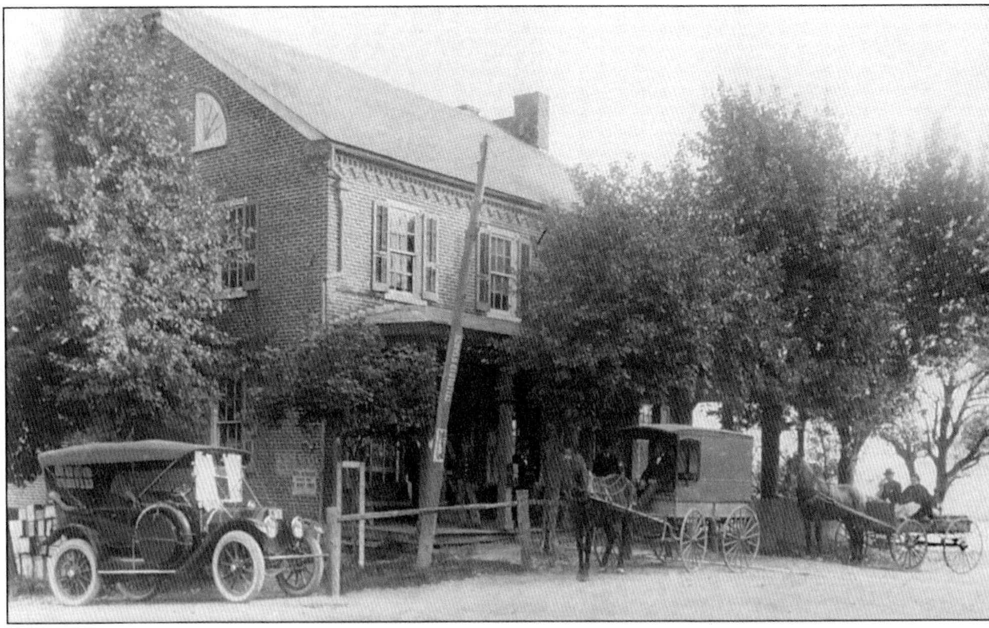

The Shimerville Store was started in 1839 by Joshua and Reuben Stahler. Later, Llewellyn Shimer ran the business for about 40 years. The above photograph is from about 1915 when Henry S. Kern was the store owner and transportation was largely by horse and buggy. But the automobile was also coming on the scene, as the photograph indicates. The store's interior is seen in the picture below. George Stauffer is wearing a sweater, ? Bittenbender is the woman in the apron, and owner Henry Kern is holding one of the items for sale. Theodore Knauss was the last proprietor of this general store business. In recent years, a variety of shops have conducted business at this busy intersection. (Both, courtesy of Merle Leh.)

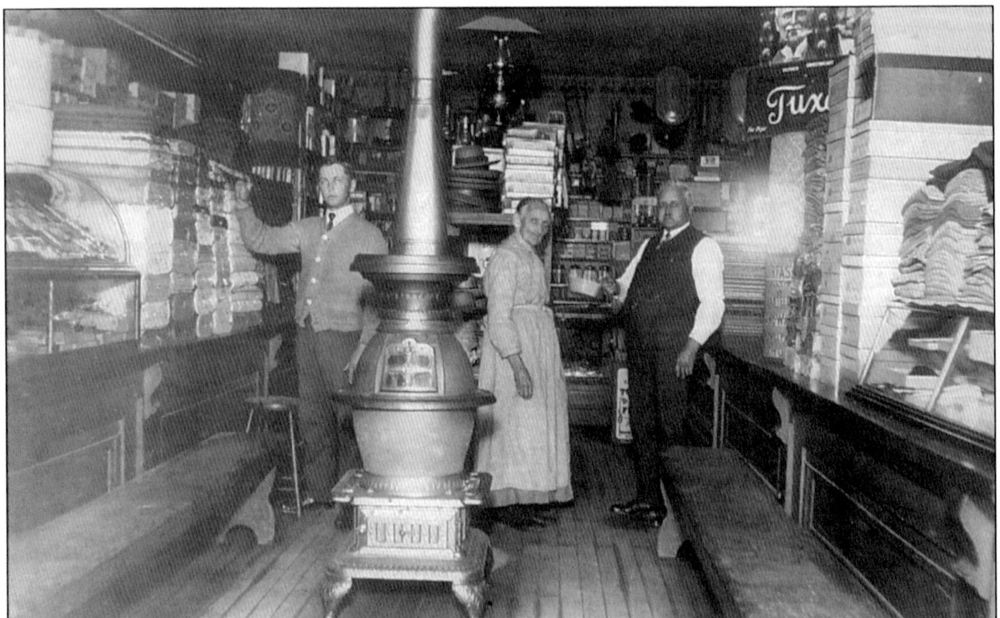

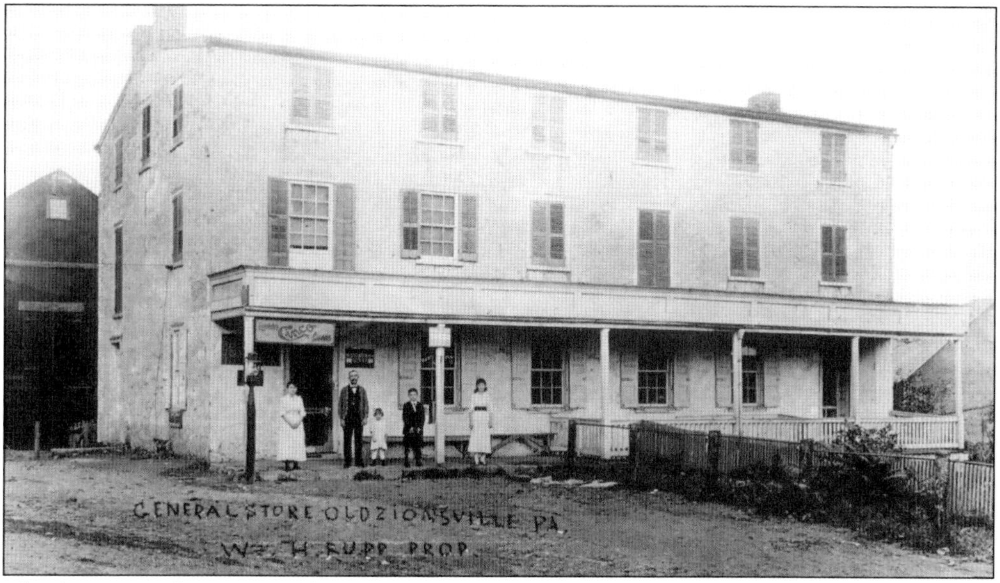

The first general store in Old Zionsville was established by Philip Hittel in 1810. Charles W. Wieand, a prominent figure in the development of the village, had the store by 1848 and rebuilt it as a large stone store. Subsequent proprietors were Albert Sterner, Milton Strausser, William H. Rupp (pictured), and J. Dallas Carl, the last owner. The Rupp family pictured was wife Lydia, son Herman, little daughter Mary, and tall daughter Viola, who married J. Dallas Carl. The store closed in 1962 and was torn down in 1972 to make way for the Reformed Church parking lot. (UMHS.)

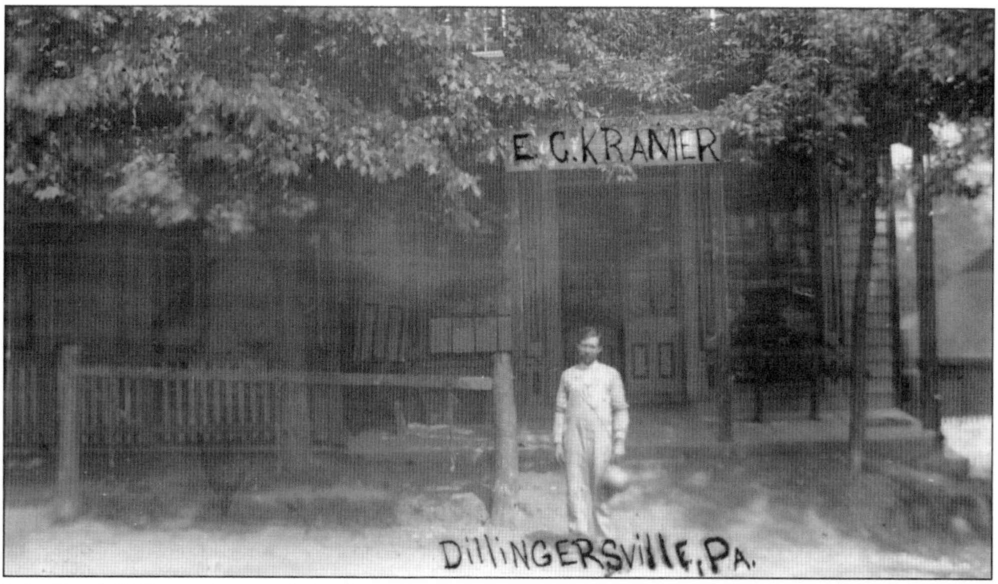

John Jacob Dillinger Jr. established a store about 1800 in Dillingersville, then part of Upper Milford Township. Dillingersville had first been settled in 1735 by Michael Moser, but the Dillinger family evolved into prominent landowners and business people. The Dillinger son had the store for about nine years, and another Dillinger, Henry, had it from 1829 to 1846. After that, there were many other storekeepers, including Daniel Stahler and E.G. Kramer (pictured), during the 1920s and 1930s. (Courtesy of C. Edward Mosheim.)

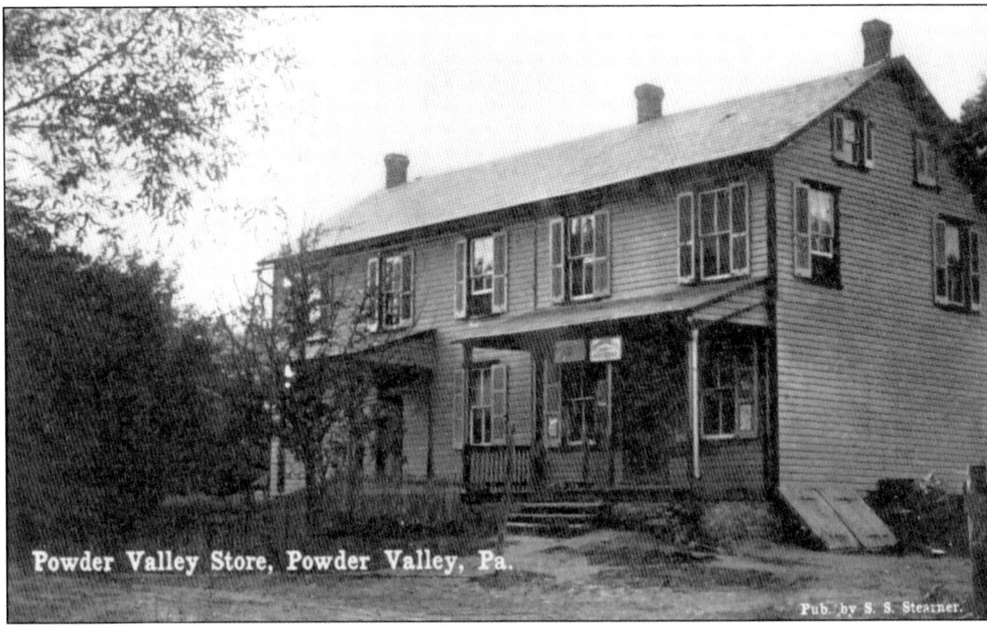

The Powder Valley Store/Post Office on Powder Valley Road was owned by Amandus Miller in 1900. It was the heart of the community and the gathering spot for special occasions, such as the patriotic Fourth of July celebration every year. In the 1920s, it was turned into Indian Lake House Hotel, a popular tourist destination. In the 1930s, Amandus Miller and his sons bought the place again and converted it into a home. Today, it is the attractive residence of the Bartholomew family. (Courtesy of Beulah Miller.)

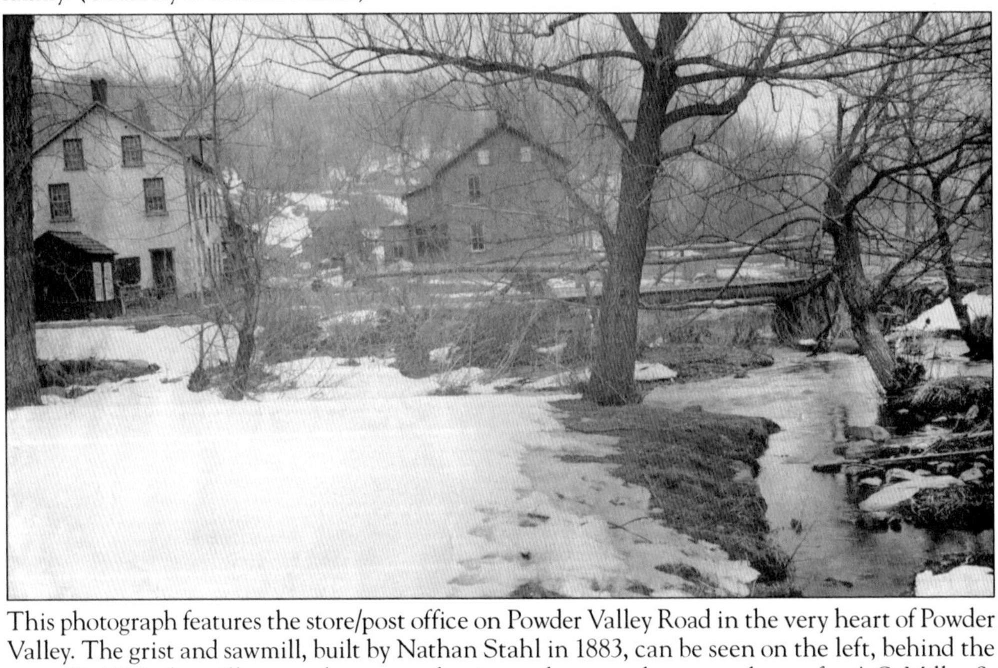

This photograph features the store/post office on Powder Valley Road in the very heart of Powder Valley. The grist and sawmill, built by Nathan Stahl in 1883, can be seen on the left, behind the store. By 1930, the mill was no longer productive and was used as a storehouse for A.S. Miller & Sons, feed and grain dealer. This mill has been razed. (Courtesy of Schwenkfelder Library and Heritage Center.)

In 1840, Seth Miller began crafting, repairing, and selling tinware house-to-house in the township and adjoining townships. He crafted many useful tin items needed for the kitchen and farm. Although he never had the store itself, his successful venture turned into the M.J. Miller and Son Hardware Store Business in Old Zionsville conducted through five generations of Millers: Peter, Levinus, Milton, and Harry. The Millers earned a reputation of integrity and fair dealings with customers. (Courtesy of Barbara Harris.)

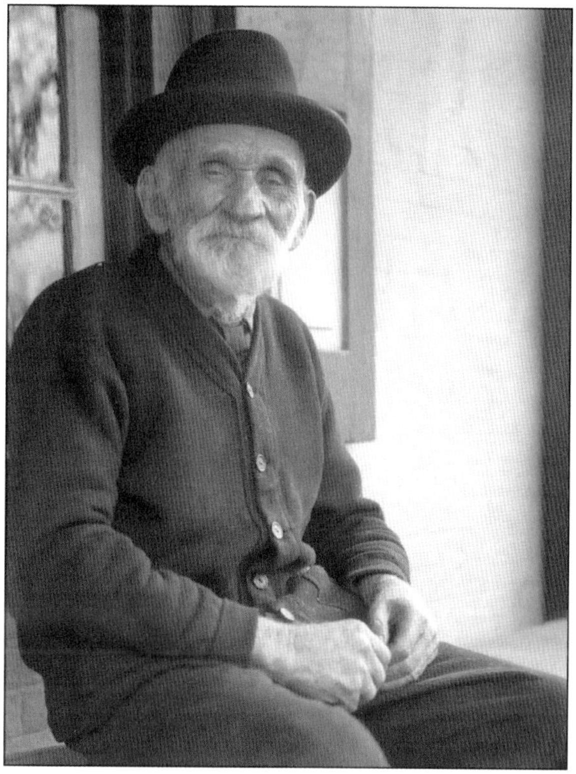

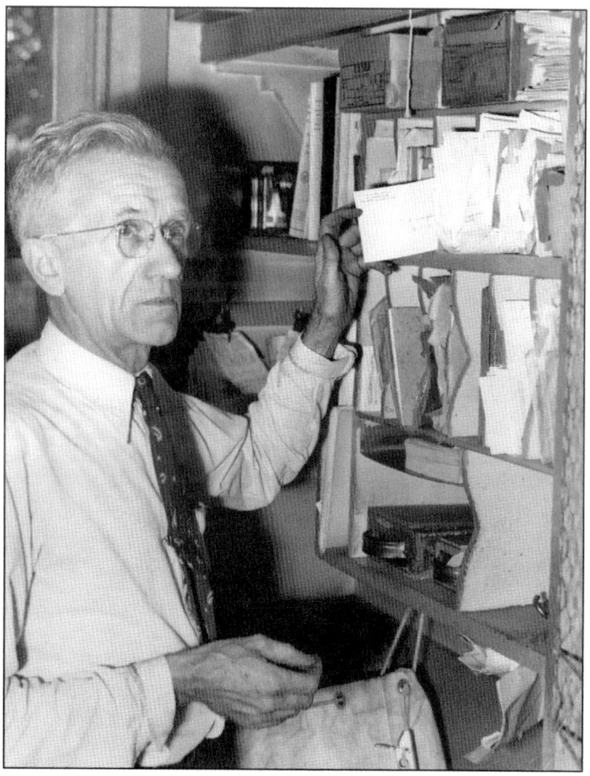

From 1921 to 1949, Harry Miller was a partner with his father, Milton Miller, in the M.J. Miller and Son Hardware Store on Kings Highway in Old Zionsville. He continued the Miller tradition of entrepreneurship as sole owner of the hardware business after the death of his father. Miller is shown working in the section of the store that held the post office. The 131 years of Miller ownership ended in 1971 when Miller closed the store and the post office was relocated to Church View Road. (Courtesy of Barbara Harris.)

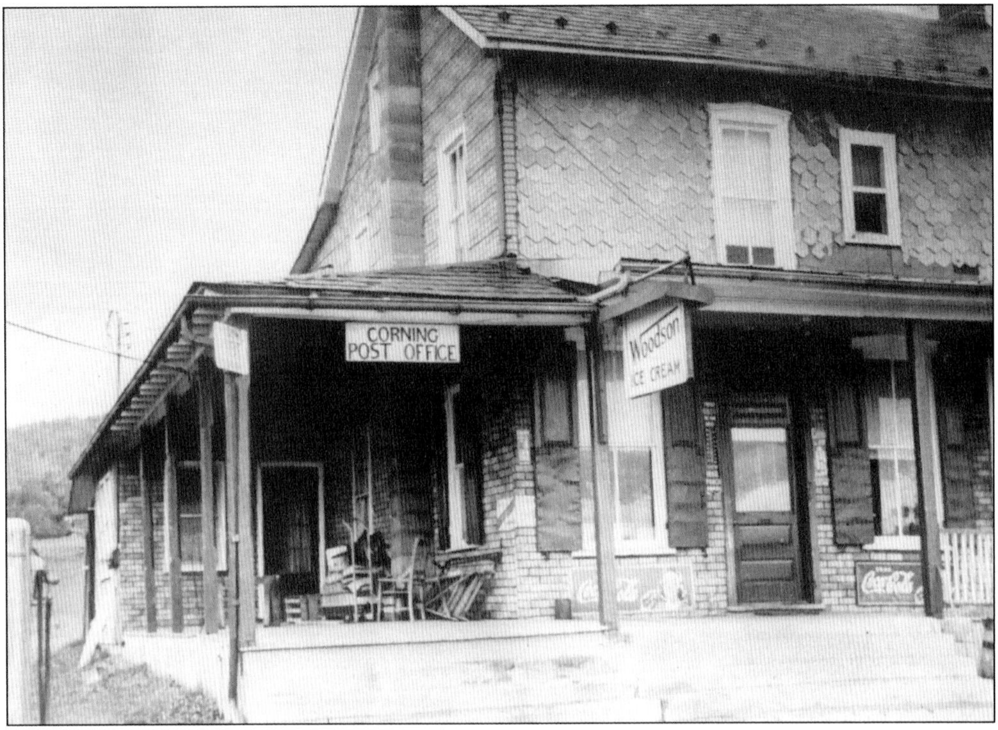

The Corning Store was also the post office, a railroad stop, and the hub of Corning. Daniel and Carrie "Mammy" Dries were the proprietors in the 1940s. In the early 1950s, Jean and Oscar Miller ran the store. Local youngsters stopped in regularly for their favorite candies. A popular product sold in the store was Woodson Ice Cream from the dairy in Red Hill, which is no longer in business. The building has been remodeled into a row of small homes. (UMHS.)

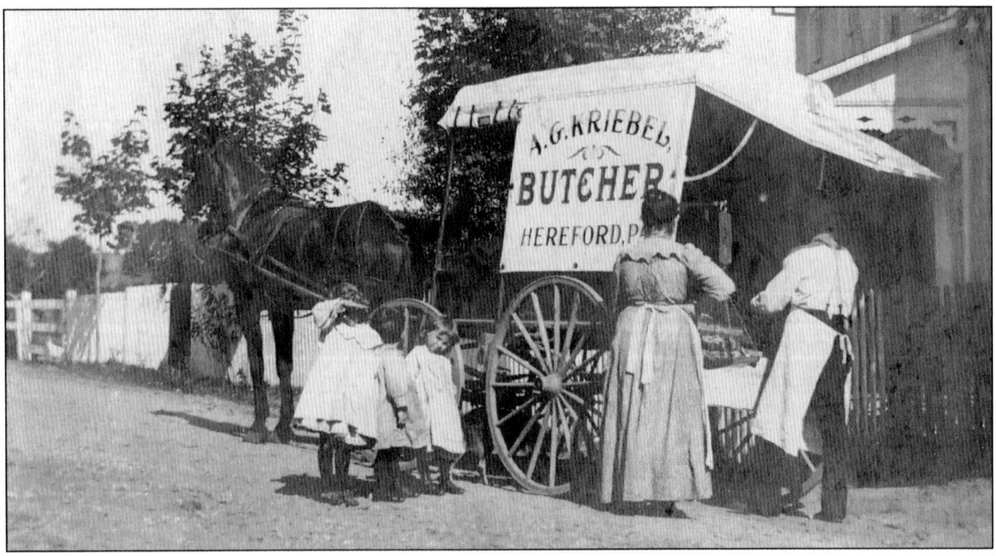

Andrew G. Kriebel had a butcher shop in Hereford, then Treichlesville, but he also served customers at their homes as he traveled a route in the nearby countryside with horse and wagon. Here, Kriebel has stopped at the Yoder farm in Zionsville along the old Route 100 Treichlersville Turnpike to deliver fresh meats. (Courtesy of Ruth Yoder-Taylor.)

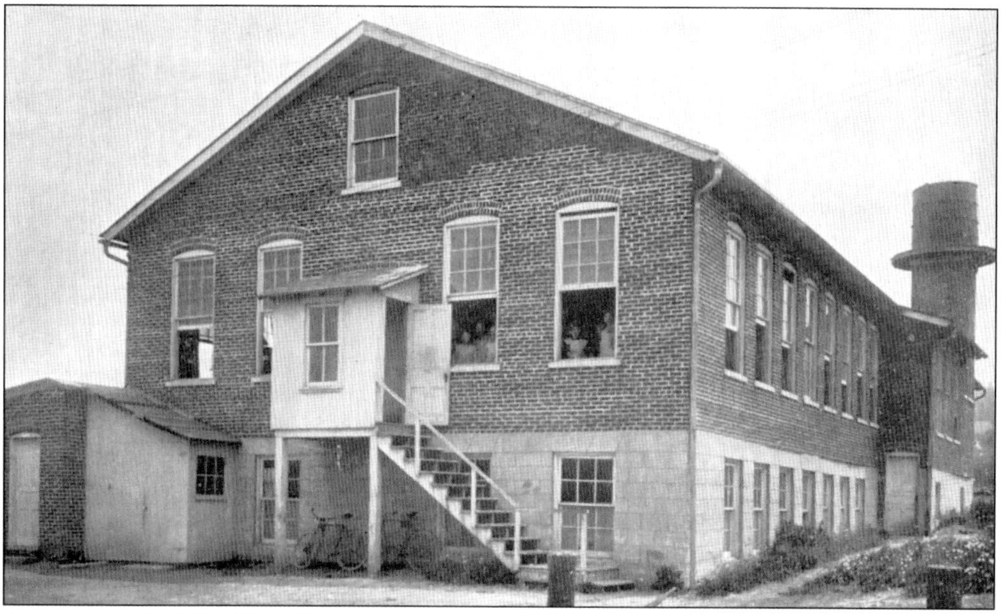

At one time, the Vera Cruz Silk Mill on Main Road East employed 40 people weaving broad silk. The photograph shows the mill in 1913. It was built in 1909 by a corporation that included A.R. Schuler and Dr. A.H Trumbauer. After William E. Yeakel bought the mill in 1945, the second floor became the silk mill and the first floor served as the center for Yeakel's Roofing. (UMHS.)

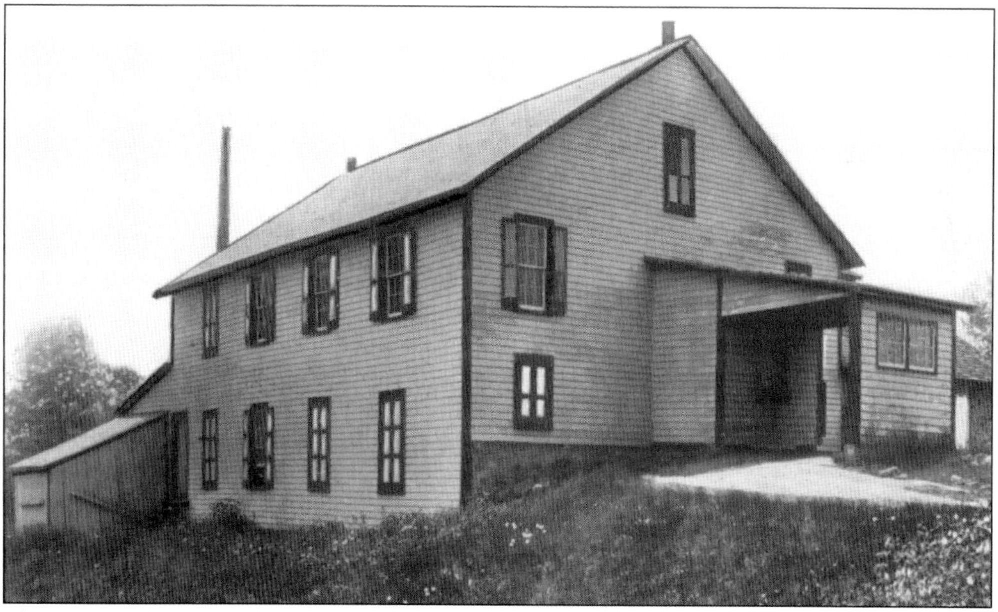

The creamery on Vera Cruz Road South was started in 1880 by David Schuler and was operated by Schuler family members until 1913. In 1883, the creamery produced over 36,000 pounds of butter and over 75,000 pounds of cheese. The second floor of the building was called Creamery Lodge Hall, the meeting place of the Mystic Chain Lodge, the Golden Eagle Lodge, and the Vera Cruz Band. It has been completely remodeled into a home. (UMHS.)

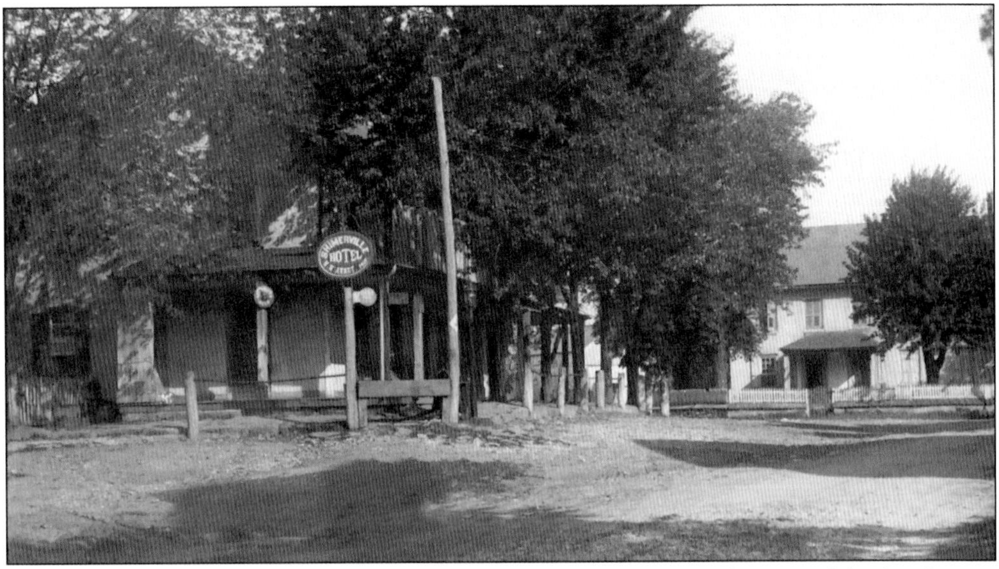

In the foreground is the Shimerville Hotel, and across St. Peter's Road is one of the first houses in the area. In 1792, all of this property belonged to John Shimer, after whom the village was named. The hotel has been an integral part of Shimerville history from 1734, when original land owner Durk Jansen claimed the acreage. Various Shimer family members followed as owners along with numerous merchants who have operated other businesses in the hotel building. Julius Christofaro had the hotel about 1960 when the popular Shimerville Drive-in Movie Theater was located beside it. Today, Hendrixson's Furniture occupies the building. (Courtesy of Ernest and Kathy Stoudt.)

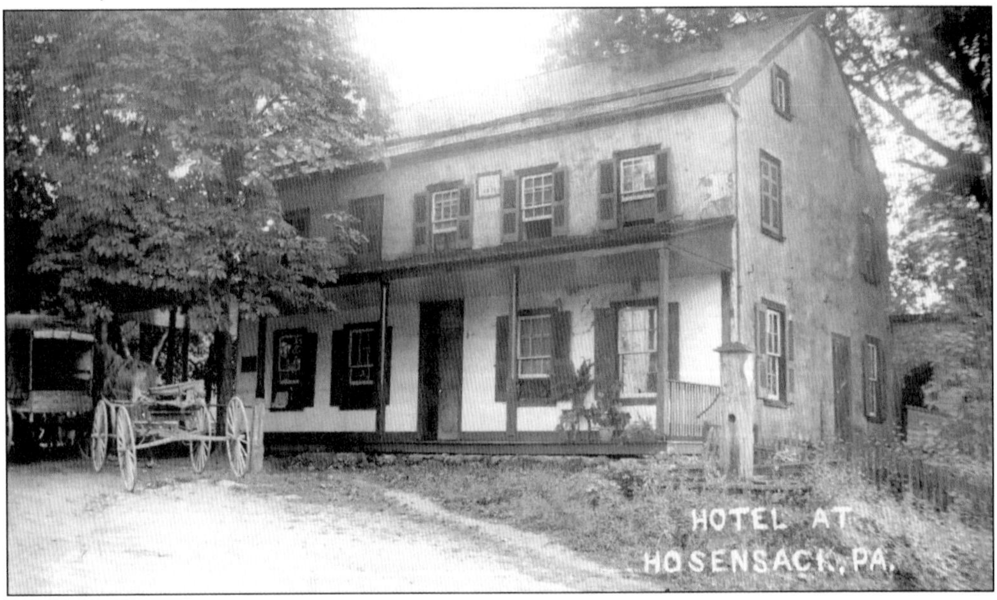

The first tavern in Hosensack was licensed to George Klein in 1757. It was part of the small area on old King's High Road called "Hosenhaason" in archival records. Klein had obtained a deed to a house there in 1757. The first house had been built by Henry Keiber (or Geber) on the 150 acres he took up in 1734. Hosensack was part of Upper Milford before the Milfords were separated in 1852. (Courtesy of C. Edward Mosheim.)

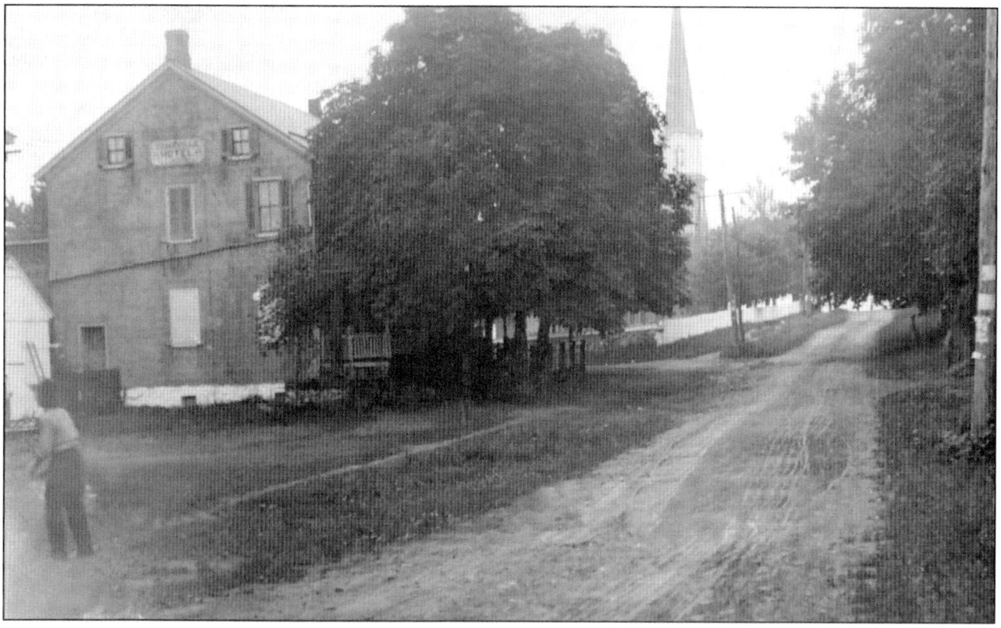

The stone hotel in Old Zionsville was built by Philip Hittel, a prominent area businessman, about 1830. Many landlords have conducted the business over the years, including Nathan A. Carl (1861–1879) and Carl's son-in-law James Gackenbach (1879–1910). William Themlin and his young family operated the hotel on March 30, 1942, when it burned down. The family was away at the time of the fire, and there were no casualties. (UMHS.)

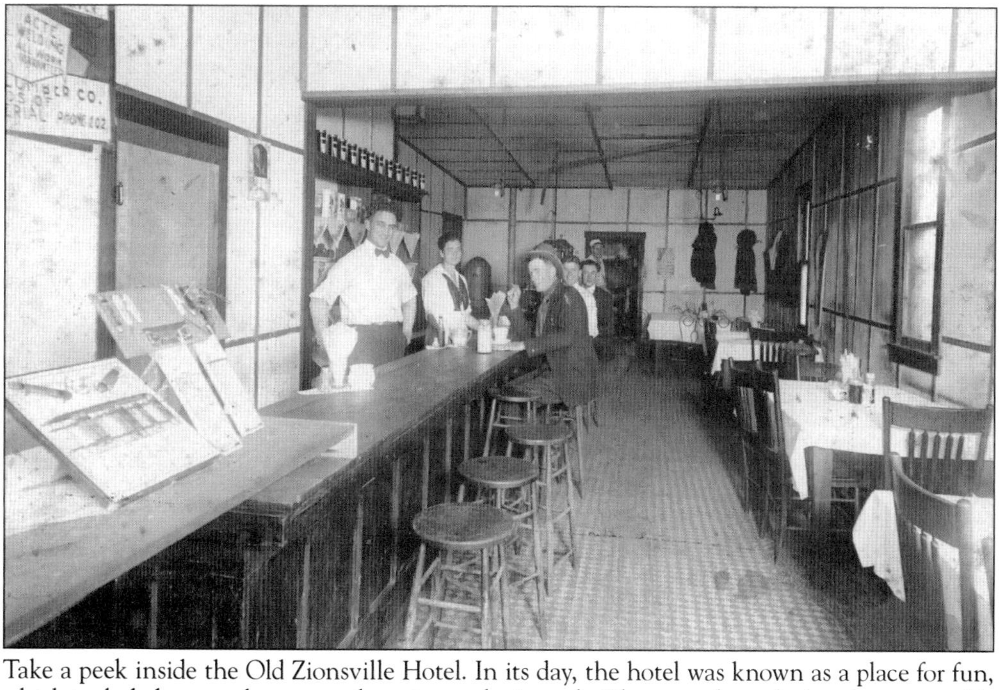

Take a peek inside the Old Zionsville Hotel. In its day, the hotel was known as a place for fun, which included square dances, card parties, and minstrels. The spot where the hotel once stood is now the parking lot at the former township/post office building on Church View Road. (Courtesy of Irene Frederick.)

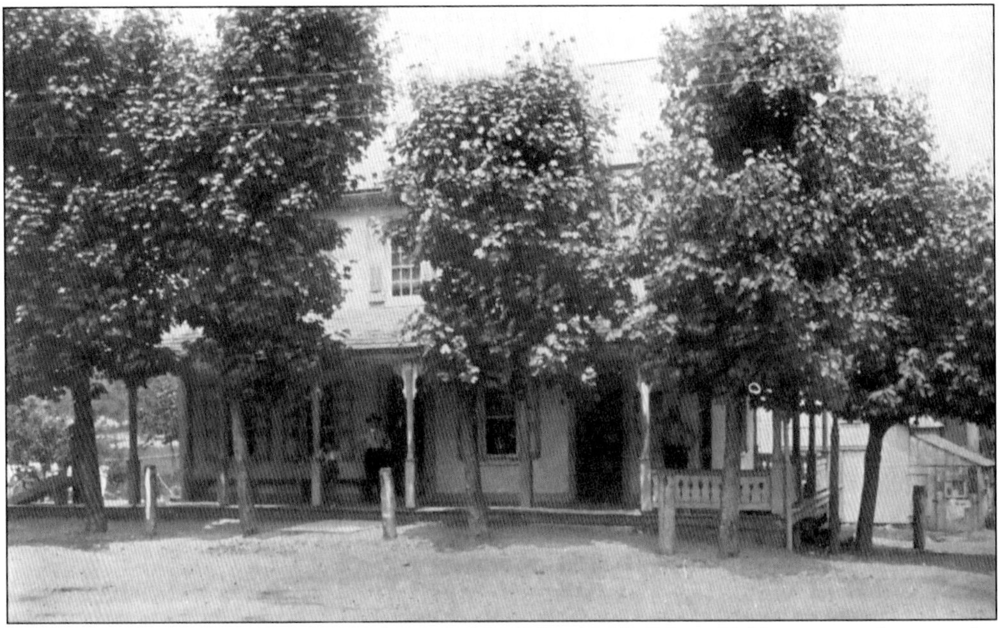

The hotel in Vera Cruz was started in 1786 by John Fischer, son of Christian, who was the second-known land owner in Vera Cruz. It is the oldest hotel in Lehigh County. Numerous owners had the place until it became Harvey Kinert's Hotel, pictured above. From 1911 to 1913, Uriah Schuler operated the hotel, as seen below during the winter. The right side porch was enclosed to enlarge the interior. Carl Schuster made extensive renovations to the hotel in the 1950s. (Both, UMHS.)

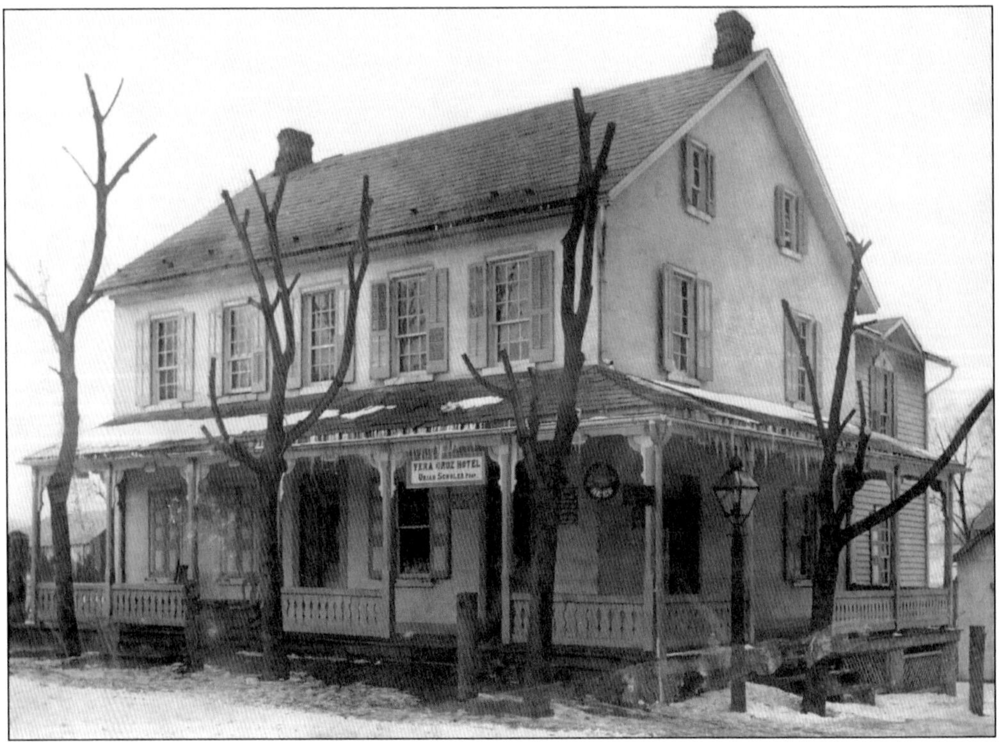

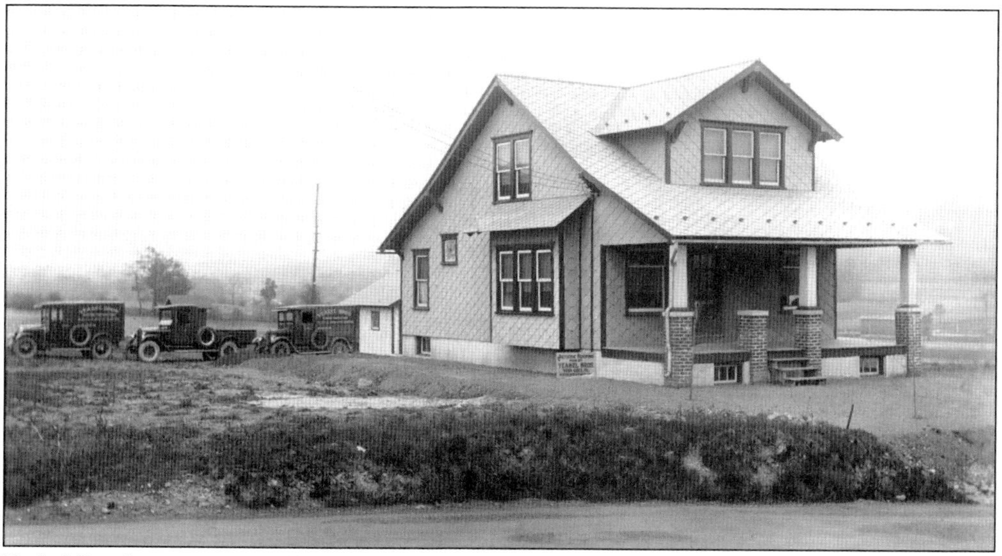

Yeakel Roofing was originally started by Charles F. Yeakel in a shop behind his home just past the railroad tracks in Vera Cruz. Then, his sons William M.E. Yeakel and, for a short time, Chester F. Yeakel moved the business to the home, shown above, on Main Road East in Vera Cruz. The fleet of Yeakel trucks is seen parked behind the house ready for work. Today, the Vera Cruz School and the Veterans Memorial fill the empty lot shown next to the house. (Courtesy of Yeakel Roofing.)

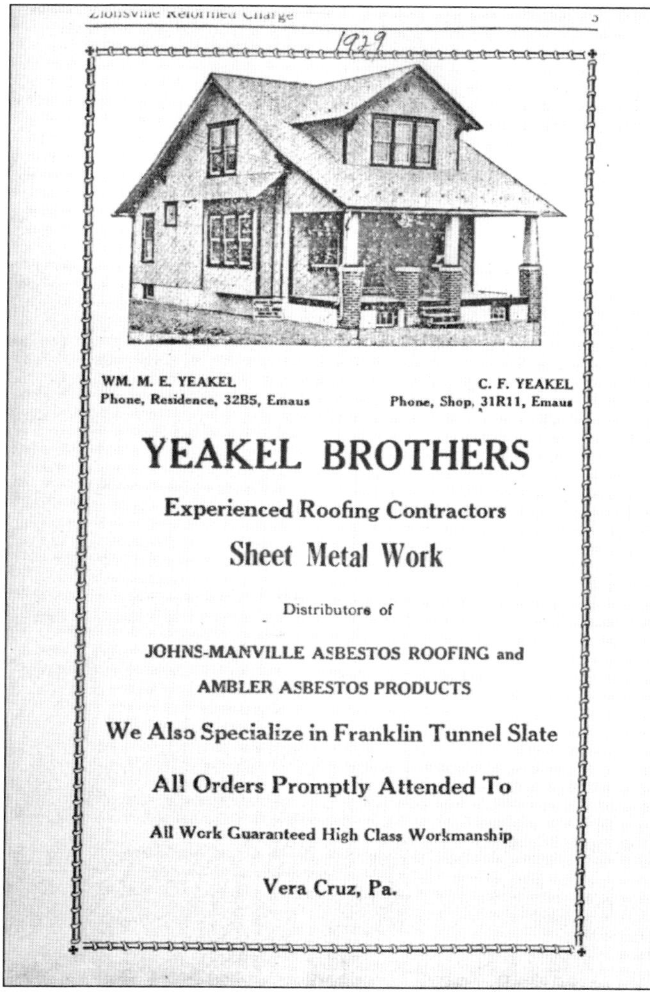

An early Yeakel advertisement specifies its roofing services. Notice the mention of asbestos products and the type of phone number used in earlier times. The business relocated to the Vera Cruz Silk Mill building in 1945. In the early 1950s, Yeakel Roofing moved again to its current location at the corner of Ridge and Williams Streets in Emmaus. (Courtesy of Yeakel Roofing.)

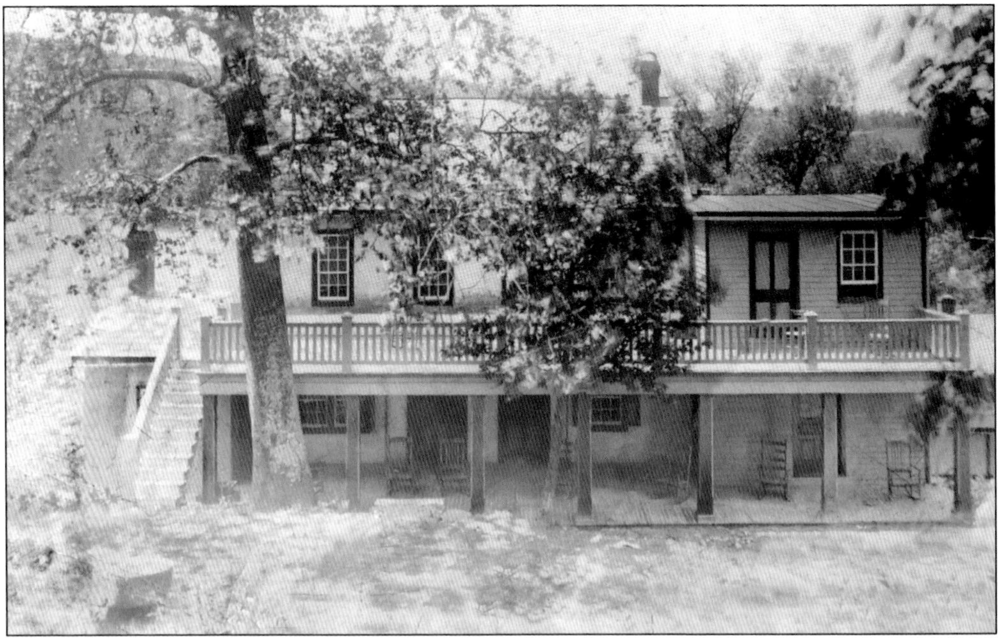

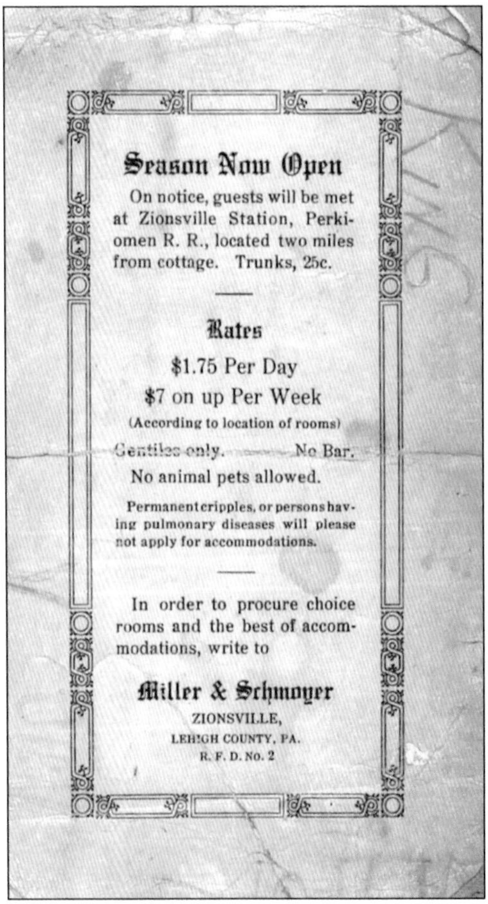

Indian Creek Cottage at the top of Sell Road in Powder Valley was a well-known summer boardinghouse in the early 1900s. Vacationers from Philadelphia came by train to the Zionsville Railroad Station, where they were picked up by horse and buggy and delivered to the resort. The cottage also once served as a general store and had a post office. The Powder Valley Band practiced there. Reported to have been built in 1775 by ? Heimbach, it was originally a two-family dwelling and has been returned to that use today. (Courtesy of Harriet Palomba.)

This advertisement for a stay at Indian Creek Cottage provides potential guests with pertinent information and the rules that accompanied their accommodations. The limitations included no pets, no bar, no permanent cripples, and Gentiles only! Such restrictions were allowed in a different era. The room rates and other services mentioned are also only memories of the past. (Courtesy of Irene Frederick.)

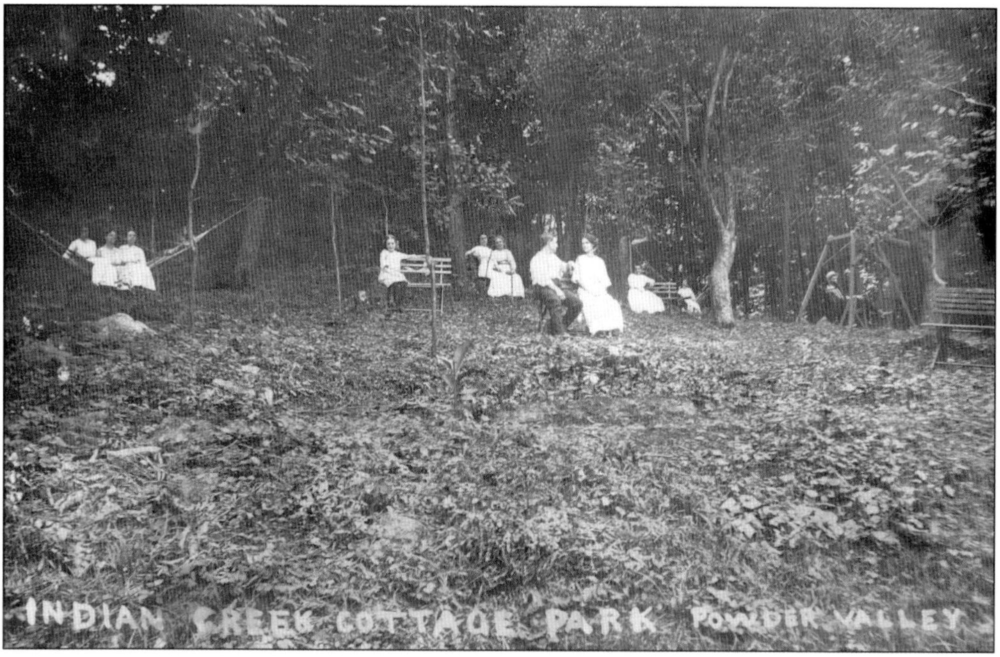

Vacationers at Indian Creek Cottage in Powder Valley had a small park next to the cottage where they could relax and enjoy the pleasant scenery and each other's company. The photograph serves to emphasize the hill on which the cottage is located on Sell Road. That incline undoubtedly enhanced the view of the landscape below. (Courtesy of Beulah Miller.)

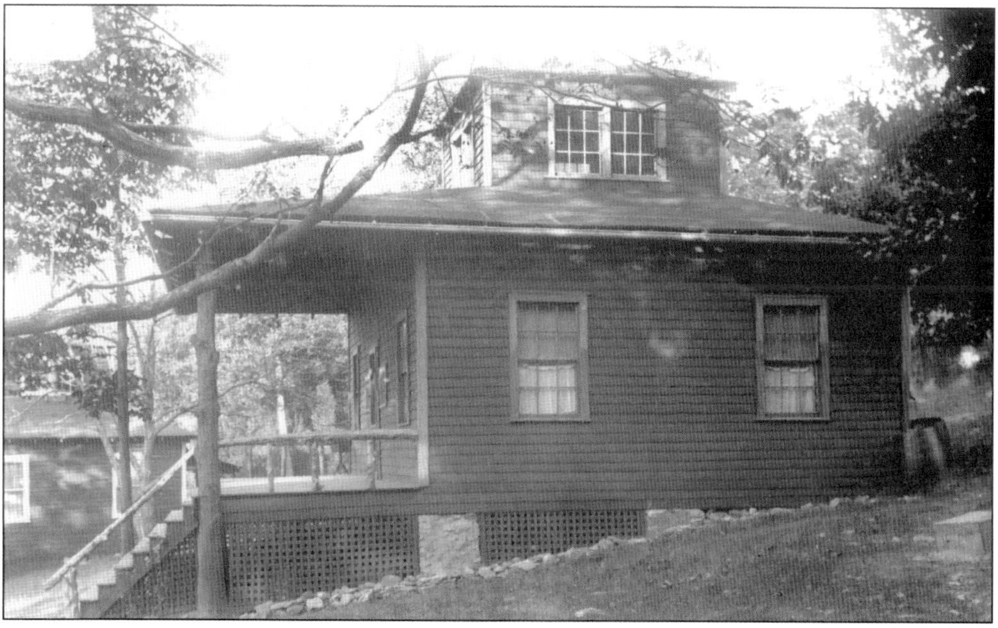

Pictured is one of the cottages that dotted the hills along Powder Valley Road where city dwellers came to spend summer vacations. In the days before air conditioning, these cool retreats nestled in the Powder Valley woods, along with similar retreats of the "hill colony" in Corning, brought welcome relief to visitors from the hot summers in the Philadelphia area. Most of the cottages are gone, but a few have been turned into homes. (Courtesy of Beulah Miller.)

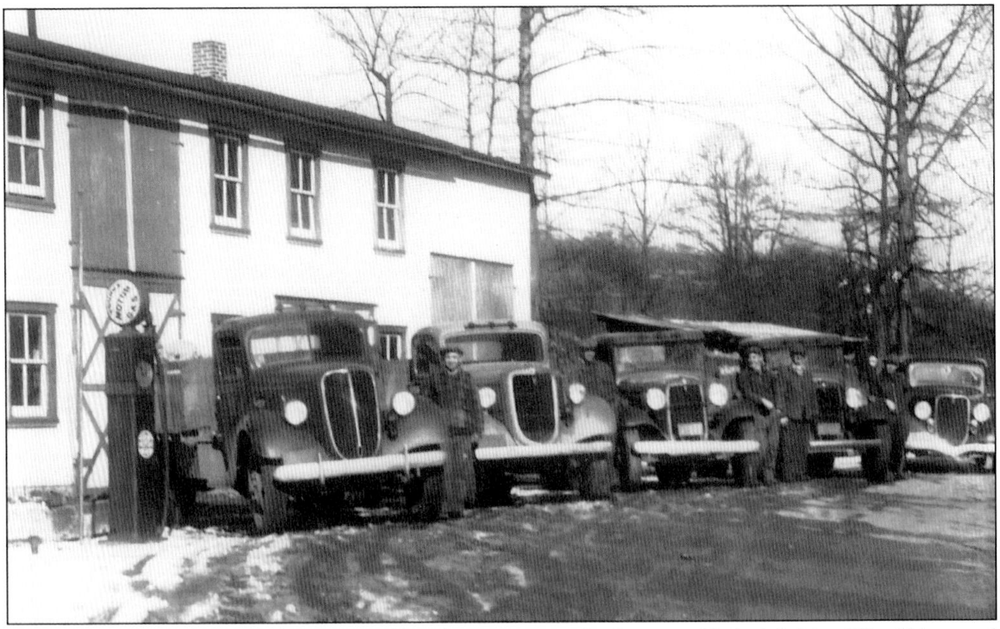

Elton Miller conducted a business of hauling corn and wheat to Philadelphia. The Diamond T trucks would return to Powder Valley with fertilizer and seed for local farmers. Miller had a fine fleet of trucks for his business. Two of his drivers were Ray Mohr and Paul Bartholomew. Mohr went by train to Chicago to pick up one of those trucks at the factory and drove it back to Pennsylvania to join the fleet. (Courtesy of Barbara Heist.)

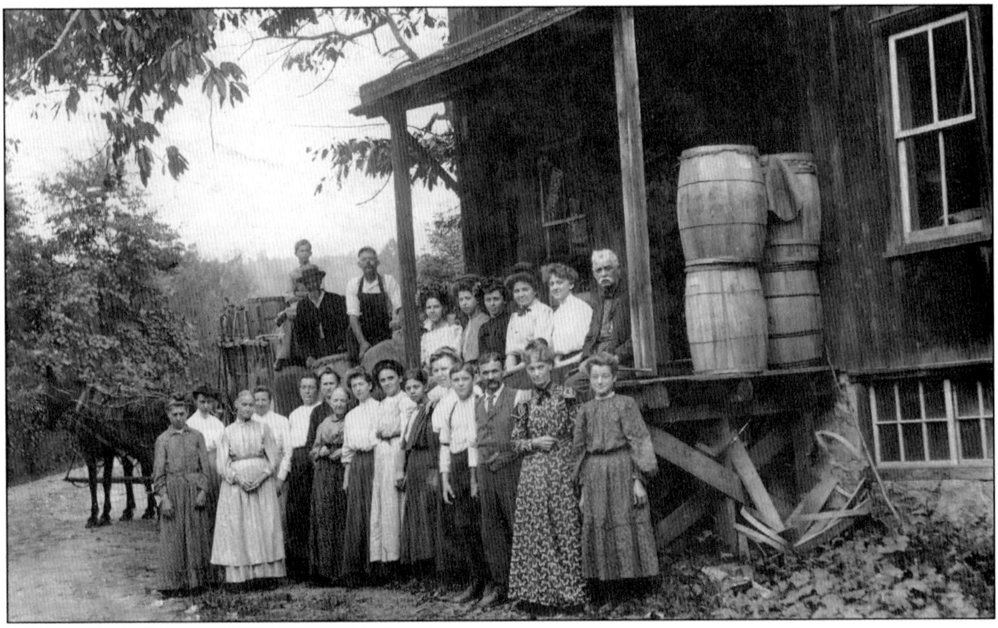

This building on Powder Valley Road had been a paint factory for many years before it was turned into a tobacco factory. The owner of the tobacco factory was Thomas Stahl, of the pottery business, pictured on the left wearing a bib apron. Employees in the picture had surnames proudly imprinted in Powder Valley history: Doney, Hallman, Heil, Jacobs, Koch, Krauss, Miller, Ortt, Renninger, Rosenberger, Schlicher, and Wieder. (Courtesy of Richard Zacharda.)

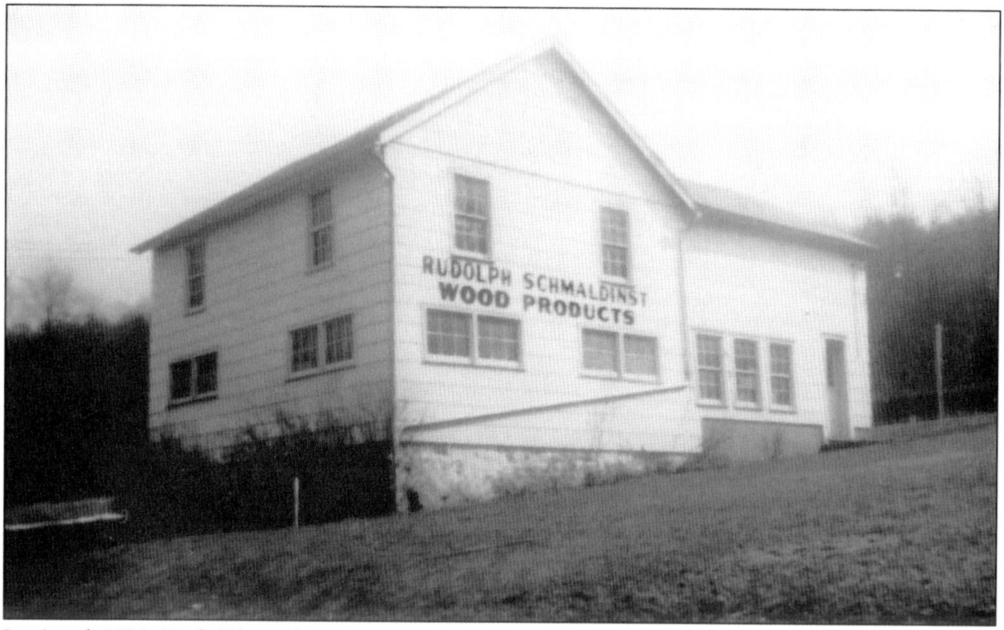

In April 1931, Rudolph and Rose Schmaldinst moved to Woodlawn Drive in Powder Valley. Pictured above is the furniture-making business that he opened in 1947 next to his house. It was the realization of Schmaldinst's dream to have his own factory. Most of the furniture produced by the 12 employees consisted of custom bedroom and dining room sets. Furniture was made on a contract basis with the customer's interests and satisfaction of utmost importance. Below, Schmaldinst is posed beside his delivery truck. The factory was in operation until 1963. (Both, courtesy of Barbara Rohrbach.)

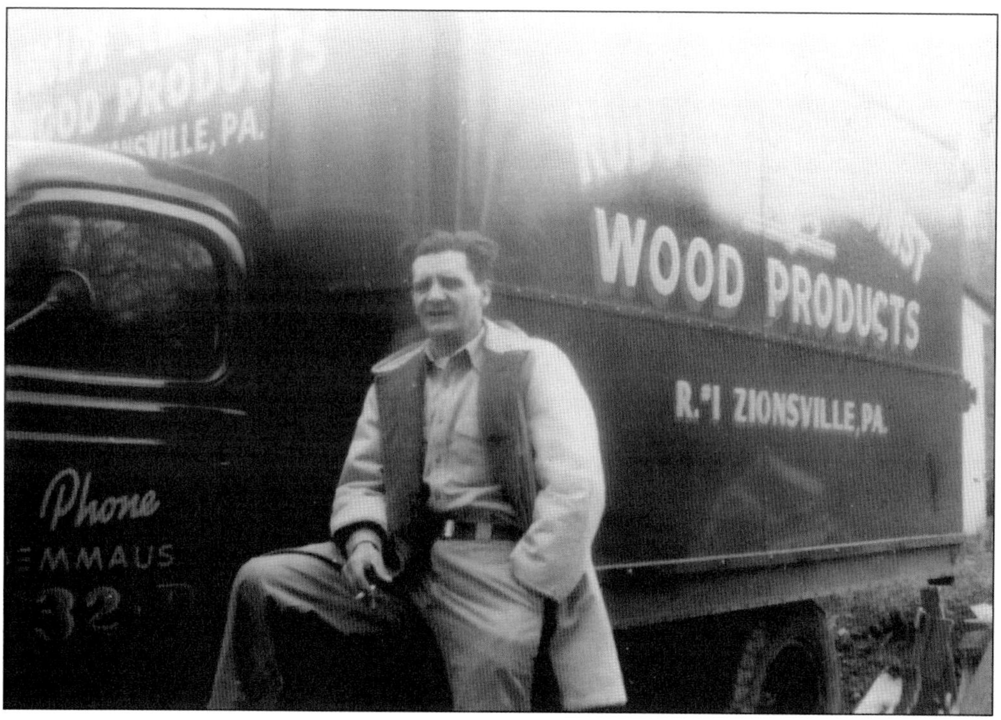

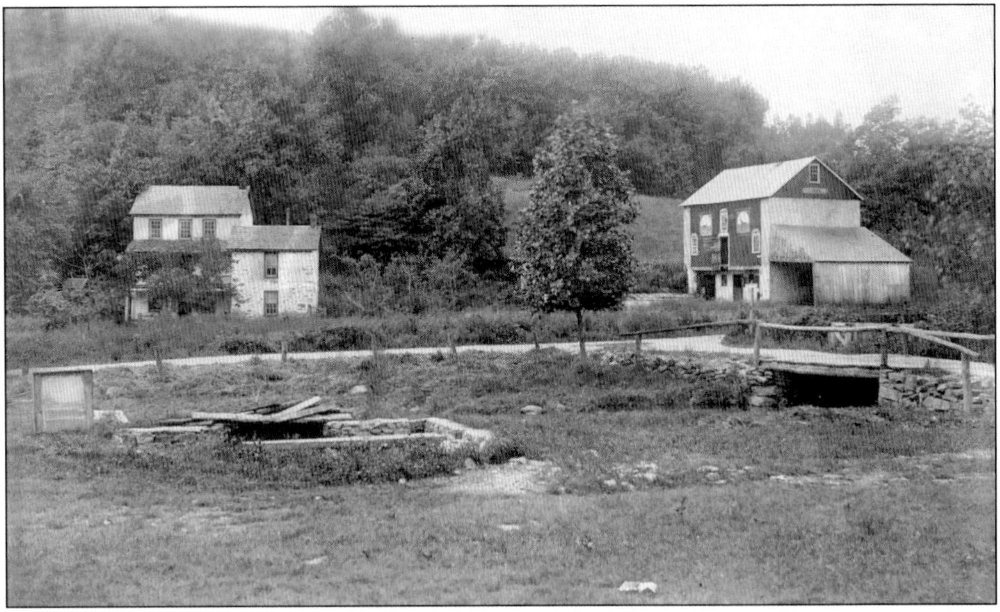

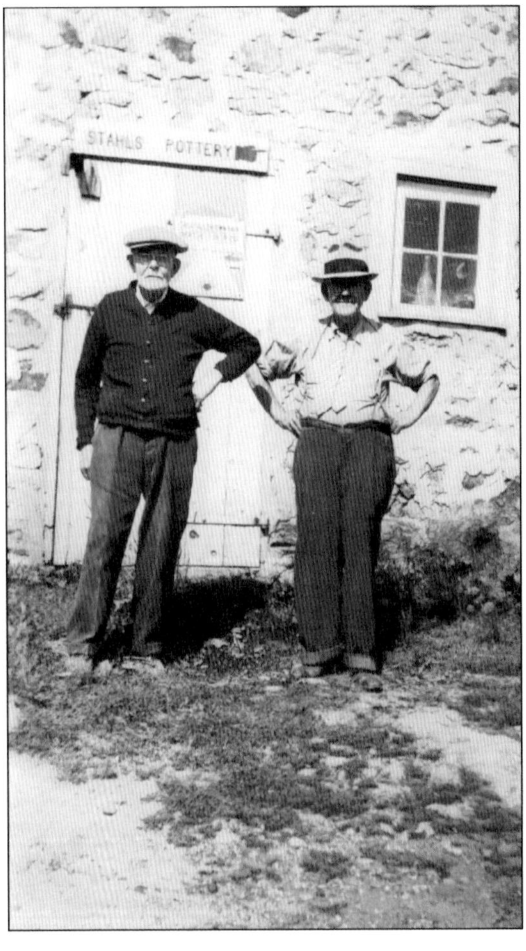

Charles Ludwig Stahl's Pottery began at this location on Powder Valley Road in the mid-1800s. When Stahl died in 1896, sons Thomas and Isaac kept the pottery in operation until about 1901, producing mostly useful, everyday redware items. The barn was made into a house, but the original house also remained. After the property passed from the Stahls' ownership, Frank Rice and Howard Hillegass operated a tannery here for a time. (Courtesy of Barbara Heist.)

In the early 1930s, brothers Thomas, on the left, and Isaac Stahl, on the right, revived the Stahl's Pottery business after they found that Pennsylvania German pottery had become very collectible. A kiln was built on Thomas's property about a half mile from the original Stahl's Pottery, shown above. The Stahl brothers worked together until Thomas died in 1942. Isaac closed the pottery from 1943 to 1945 due to World War II. He resumed in the fall of 1945 with his son Russell's help. Isaac died in 1950, and with Russell's death in 1986, work at the pottery ceased. (Courtesy of John Schultz.)

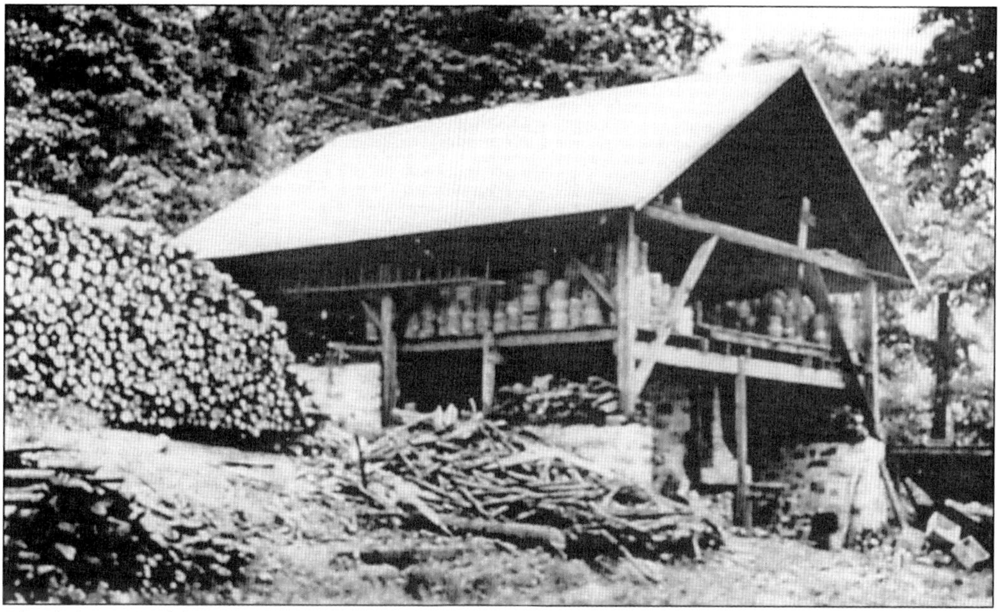

The kiln at Stahl's Pottery in Powder Valley was built by brothers Thomas and Isaac with the help of the third brother James in 1933 and was fired for the first time in 1934. Most of their work was carefully marked and decorated with a variety of Pennsylvania German motifs in slip and sgraffito techniques. In 1987, the site was purchased by descendants of Thomas Stahl as the Stahl's Preservation Society Inc., which preserves their heritage and the integrity of the redware pottery through annual festivals and events. (Courtesy of John Schultz.)

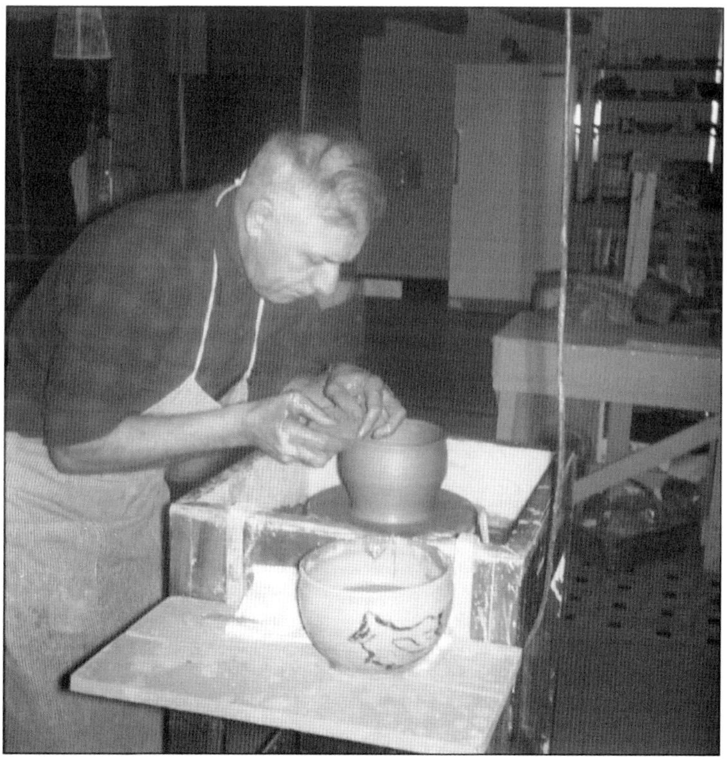

Walter Shunk had a pottery-making studio in his barn that dates to 1822 along Kings Highway North going into Macungie. He was a civil engineer by profession, but his passion was creating classically simple pottery pieces and conducting classes in the art of pottery making. Since his wife, Mabel, was a ceramicist, the Shunks made full use of three kilns. Both were members of the Lehigh Valley Pennsylvania Guild of Craftsmen. (Courtesy of Sidney Unser.)

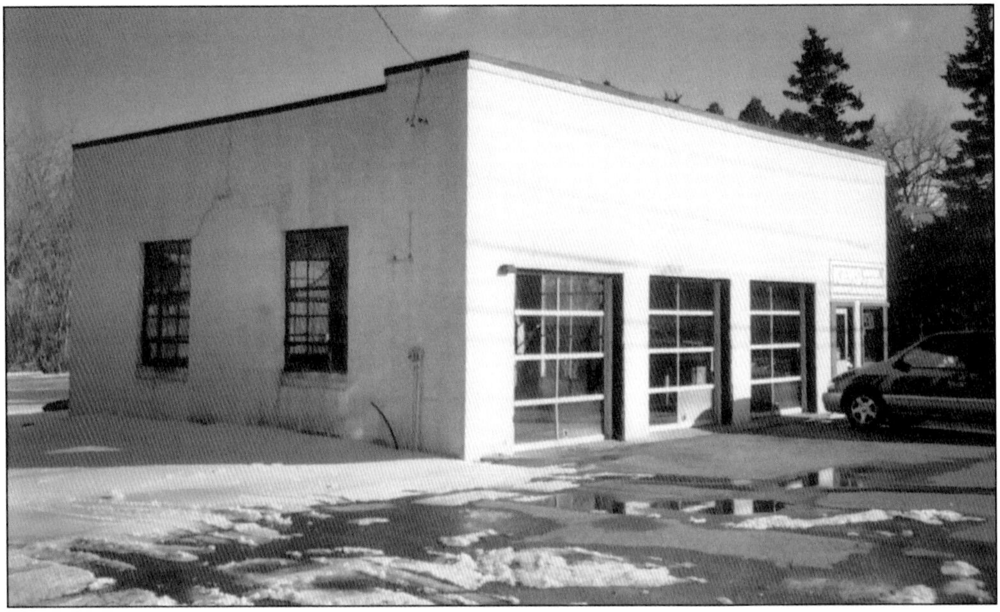

Melvin Kehs and his family built this garage of Hollywood block and opened it for business in 1948. The building had four bays. Kehs specialized in rebuilding car engines. He also built about six tow trucks using Mack engines and sold Sinclair gasoline. After Kehs died in 1991, his son Bruce ran the business until his retirement in 2007. Dean Bachman is the current owner of the garage business. (Courtesy of Charlene Kehs Reinhart.)

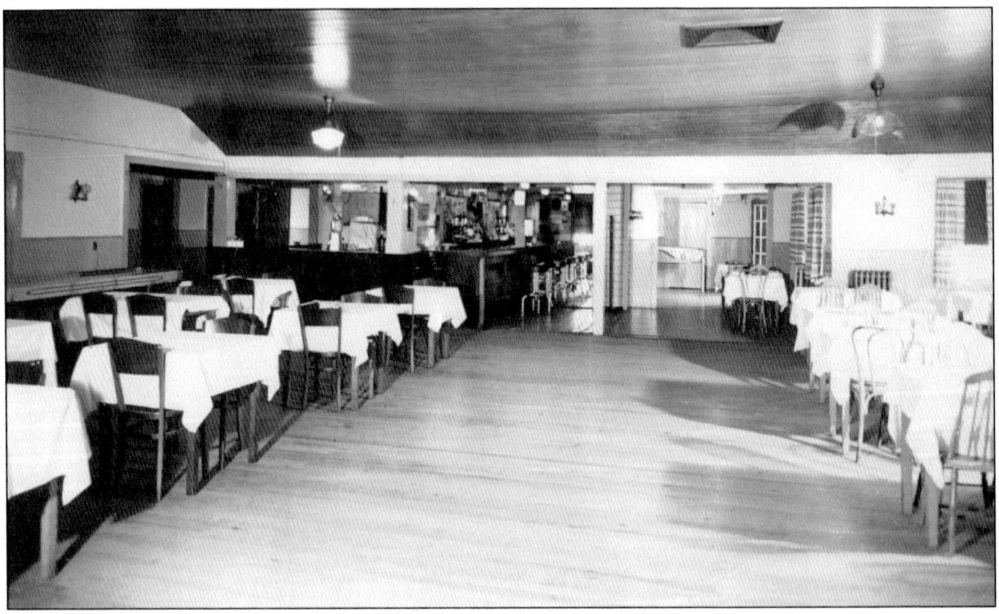

This building on Route 100/29 across from Herbein's Garden Center has had many different occupants, one being John Herbein's garden business that started here but soon outgrew the small space. The garden center moved across the highway. This spot was also home to Raymond and Helen Keeler's restaurant from 1948 to 1960. Keeler was known to serve groundhog to hunters who brought it to her to be cooked. Other businesses in this building were Mae's Place, Victory Fitness Center, and, today, a well pump company. (Courtesy of Ralph Keeler.)

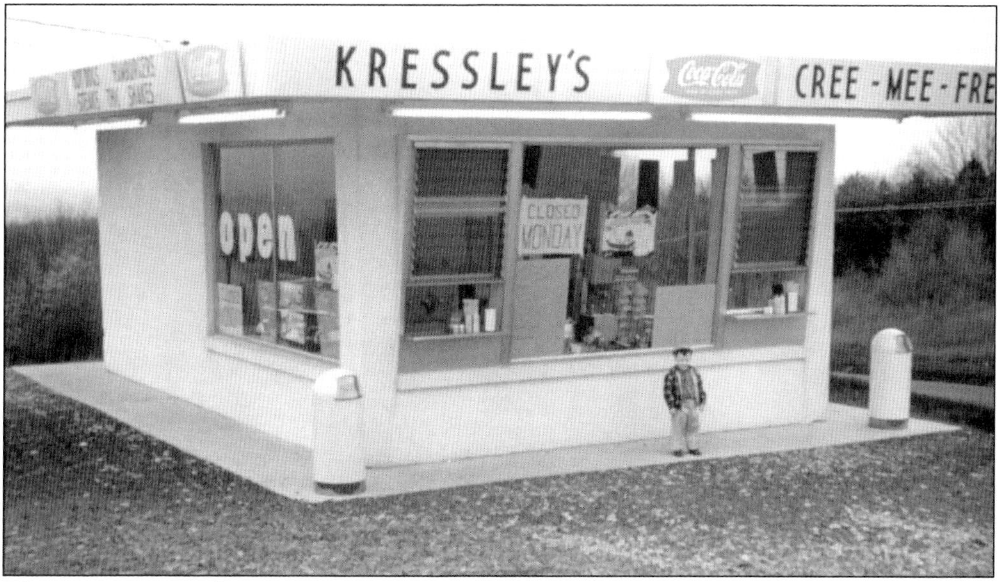

The ice cream served at Leo and Wilma Kressley's Cree-Mee-Freeze in Shimerville, where Routes 29 and 100 meet, was known as some of the best in the area. The small building opened in 1958, as seen in the photograph above, and expanded over the years both upward and outward, as seen below. As many as 15 flavors of ice cream and other frozen treats were offered. First grandson, Michael Ritter, shown above, is ready for his favorite cone! After the entire Kressley family had put in 16 years of hard work, they sold the flourishing business in 1974. The marvelous panoramic view of Lehigh County from Kressley's at the crest of the Shimerville Hill can be appreciated in the picture below. The view added immeasurably to the enjoyment of an ice cream treat. (Both, courtesy of Neil Kressley.)

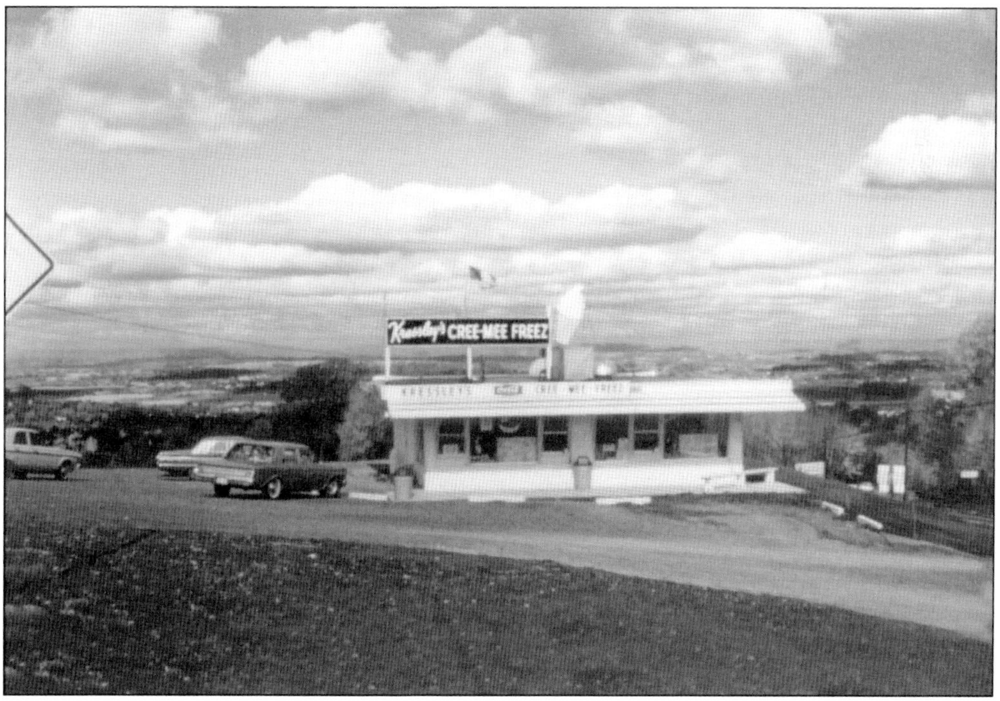

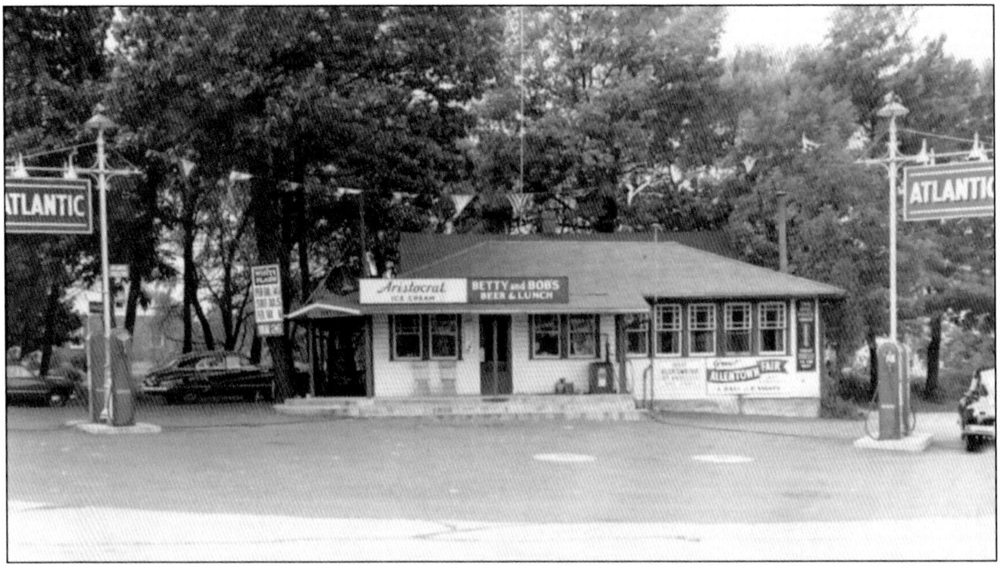

The building at the intersection of Buckeye Road and Chestnut Street (Route 29/100) has had several owners over the years. At one time, it was Betty and Bob's Beer and Lunch, shown above, and at another time, Roy C. Wieder's Luncheonette. Customers could fill up the car with Atlantic gas as well as their stomachs with, as the slogan suggests, "hearty and hot food that hits the spot!" For a time, it was also Burdan's Ice Cream. The eatery has gone through structural renovations, transforming it into the popular Trivet restaurant of today. (Both, courtesy of the Trivet.)

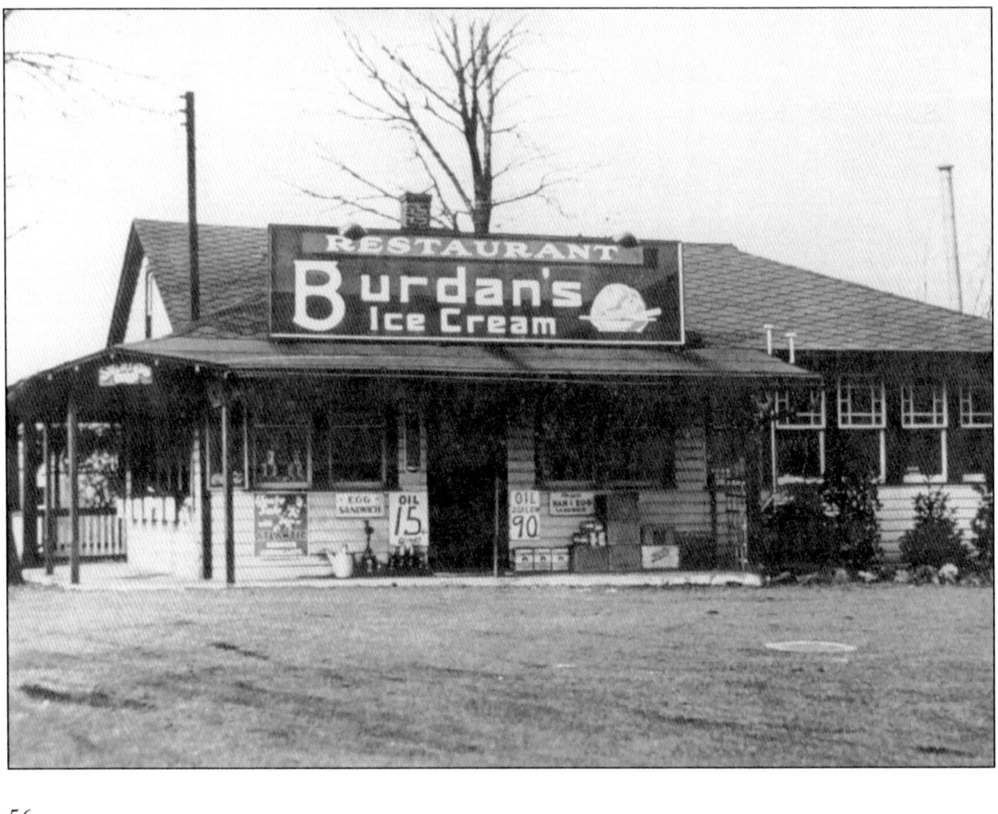

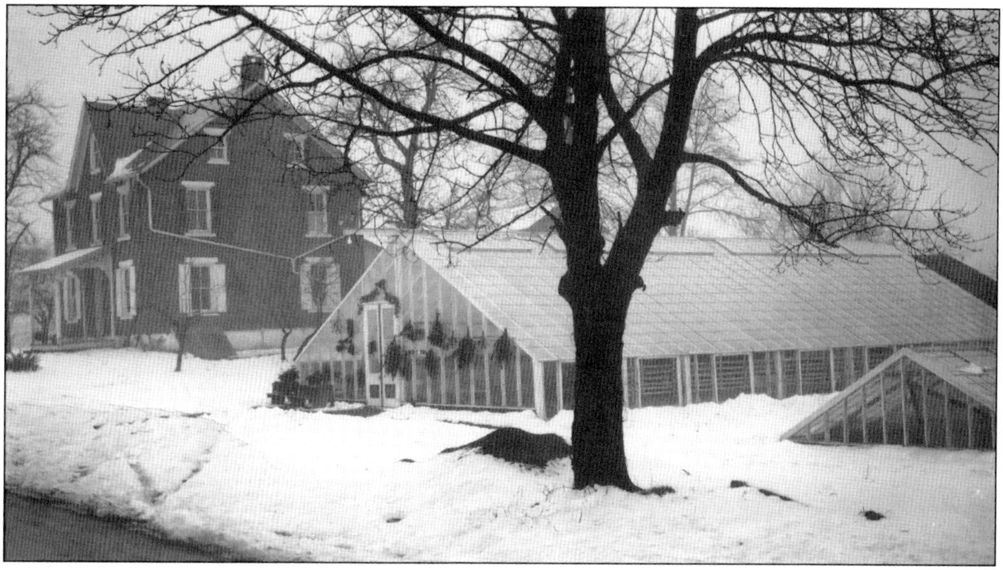

Martin Buss, father of Asher, opened the original Buss greenhouses for growing and selling flowers along Route 100 in Macungie. The small business, shown above, was eventually sold to Pondelek's Flowers, now located in Hellertown. Martin's son Asher Buss followed in his father's footsteps and opened his own flower business in Old Zionsville. The greenhouse has been removed. (Courtesy of Marian Buss.)

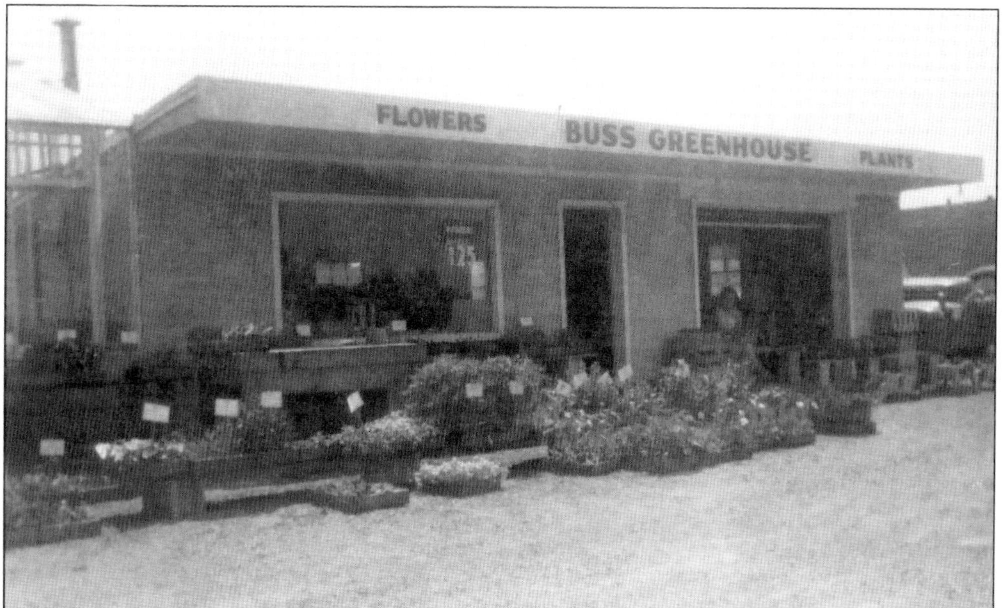

The Buss Greenhouse Business was owned and operated by Asher and Marian Buss on Route 29/100 in Old Zionsville from 1953 to 1989. Their original three greenhouses were glass, but the other 11 were plastic. Conveniently, the Buss home was built right next to the greenhouses. Growing and selling plants, longtime faithful employee Roger Reinhard helped make this a very successful gardening business. Joseph Benner laid the block for this building. (Courtesy of Marian Buss.)

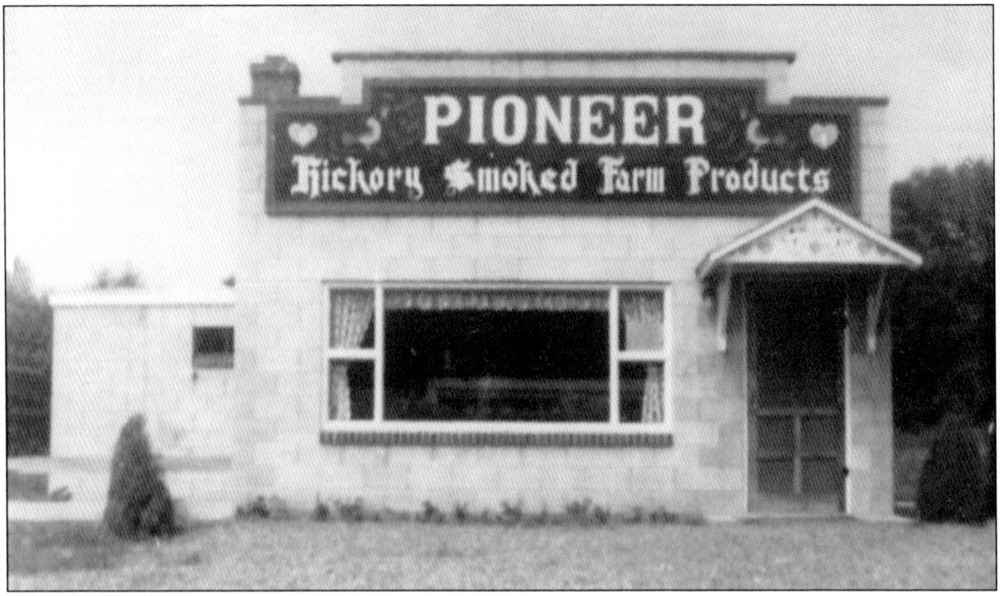

The building that is Vito's Pizzeria on Route 29/100 in Old Zionsville has been many different types of businesses since it was built in about 1952. It was once a hickory smoked meats business (pictured), an antique shop that was run by Frances Ziegler, a print shop, and now a pizza shop. When Joseph Ruffino bought the place as a pizza business in 1986, it was called Vito's. He thought it best not to change the name again. Hence, Ruffino's pizza shop is still known as Vito's. (Courtesy of Joseph Ruffino.)

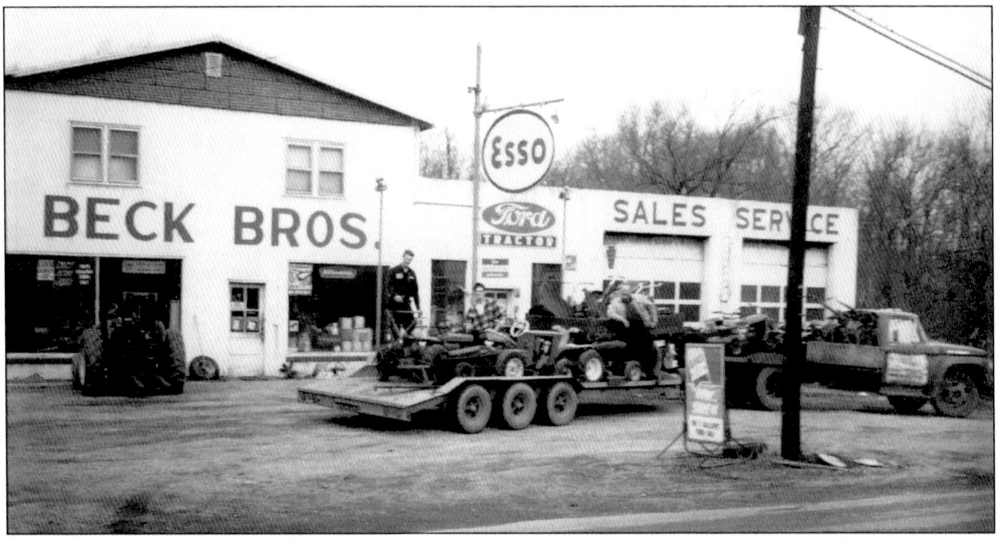

Beck Brothers' auto and truck repair business started in a garage on Paul and Anna Beck's property on Beck Road in the 1920s. After Route 29 was built in the 1930s, the elder Becks gave sons Oliver and Frank property along the new route in 1947 to build the shop pictured. At various times until 1989 when the brothers sold the business, their services included repairing and racing stock cars along with selling gasoline, farm equipment, and light industrial equipment. The Pennsylvania Power and Light Company housed equipment nightly in this garage until 1952, and Oliver's son Larry sold lawn and garden equipment here from 1980 to 1989. Today it is Robert Sentner's auto business. (Courtesy of Larry Beck.)

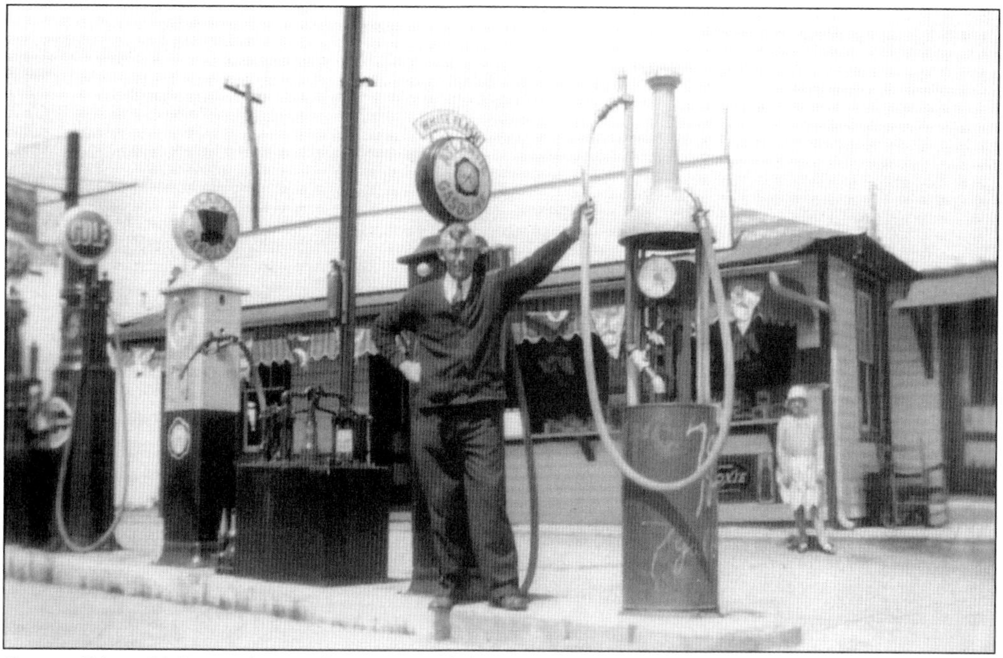

Owner Edward Montz, shown above, started the gasoline/luncheonette business in Old Zionsville called the Hilltop Service Station. He pumped Gulf and Atlantic gas at the time of this early photograph when the building was only one story without a portico. The girl in the background is Montz's daughter Ruth. The picture below shows the station after the building was expanded by a second story. The enterprising Montz also did blacksmithing, welding, and soldering. He conducted that portion of his business in a garage beside the station, not visible in the picture, and via a milk truck he converted into a shop on wheels, which he drove on call to customers. (Both, courtesy of Ronald Montz.)

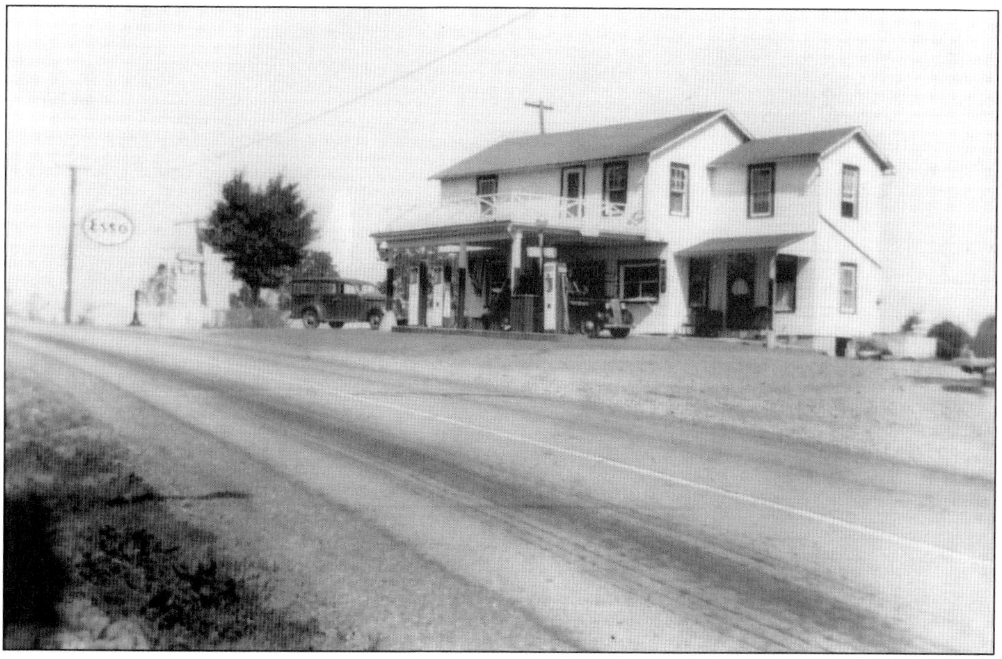

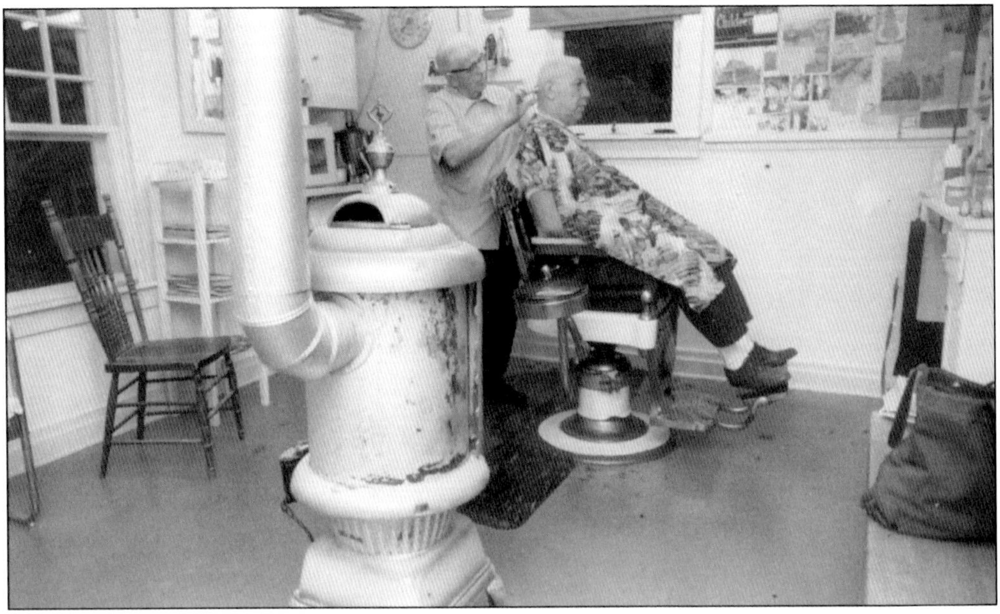

Warren Treichler was granted a barber's license in 1931 and set up a shop behind his home on Route 100/29 in Old Zionsville. His first customer was Horace Beitler, and his last one was his neighbor Earl Scherer, pictured. The cast iron and enamel potbellied stove in the picture burned coal but was converted to kerosene. Treichler also worked as a cutter at the Emmaus Pajama Factory for 35 years. (Courtesy of Barbara Bailey.)

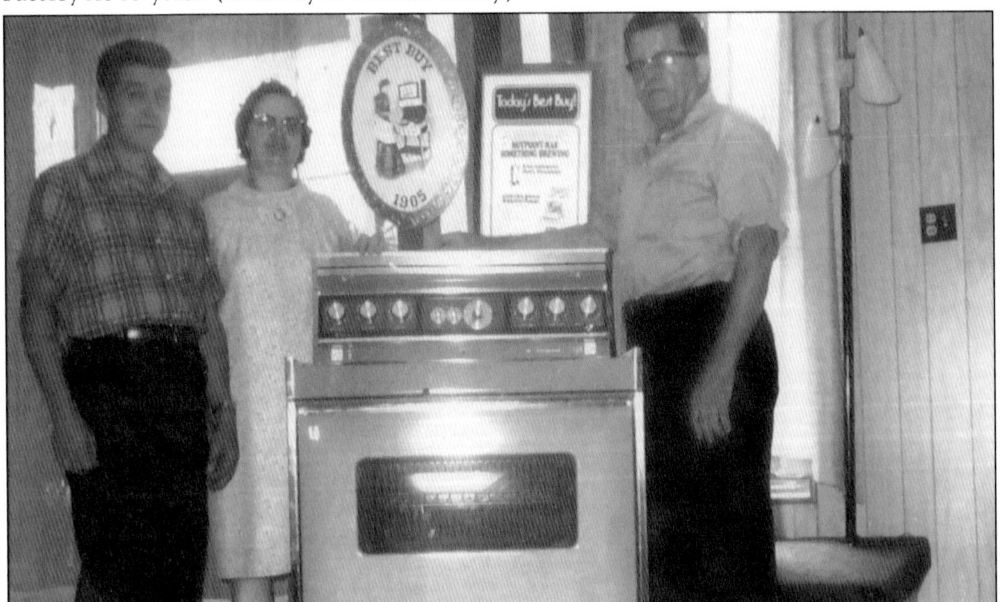

Schultz Appliances was started in Zionsville in 1946 and moved to its present location on Route 29/100 in 1947. Fred Schultz sold lawn mowers and major appliances. Schultz was also a justice of the peace and an insurance agent. In 1971, Fred and Ruth Schultz put an addition on the building and brought sons William and Jeffrey into the business. The elder William Schultz retired in 1979, and Schultz Electric Inc. has been operated since 1989 under Jeffrey Schultz's ownership. (Courtesy of Jeffrey Schultz.)

Four

Homes and Families

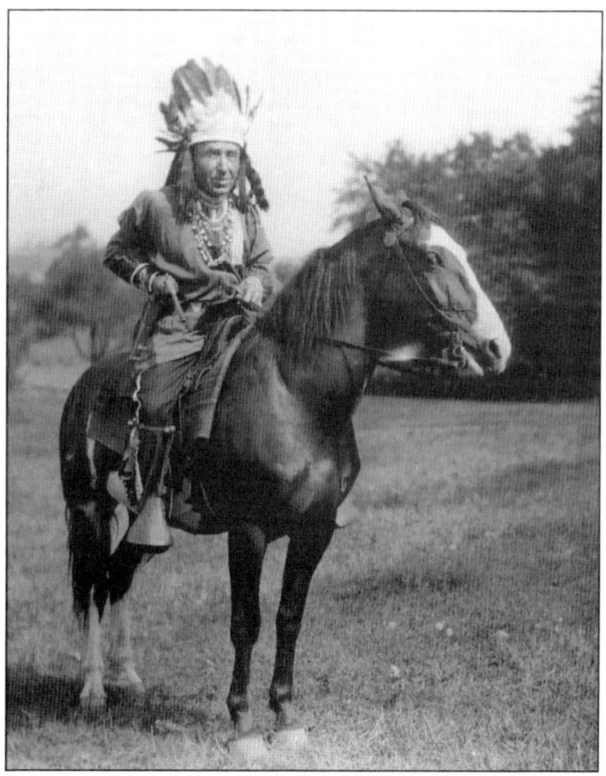

A descendant of the Rosebud Tribe in the Sioux Nation, Henry Kniep was born in 1862 in South Dakota. At 22, he joined Buffalo Bill's Wild West Show and dressed as seen here. Kniep was a cultured gentleman fluent in seven languages, a world traveler, an orator, an artist, a photographer, and an accomplished musician on the saxophone. For a time in the 1920s, he and his family lived in Old Zionsville and Powder Valley and traveled the area performing as the Knippappoo Wild West Indian Company. In 1929, he moved to Red Hill where he died in 1932. (Courtesy of Beulah Miller.)

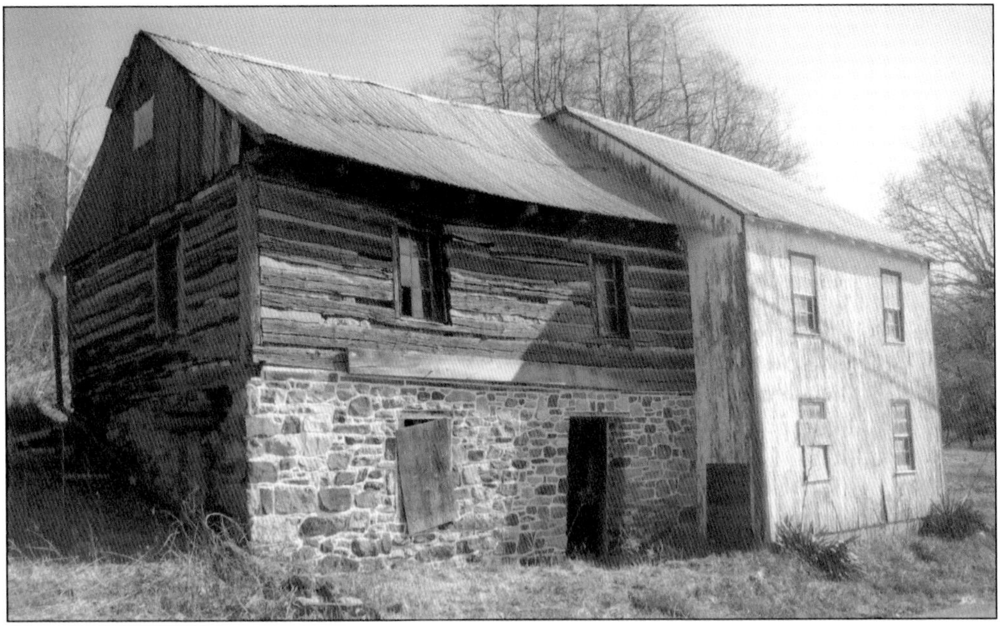

The Schubert/Graber cabin in Powder Valley was built by a Schwenkfelder cooper named Melchoir Schubert around 1760. The log and stone portion has corner posts with mortise and tenon joinery and is dug into a hillside on the former Elmer Graber farm on Powder Valley Road. Once used as a dwelling, it is the oldest existing home in the township. The Hivel und Dahl Preservation Society is working to stabilize and preserve it. (UMHS.)

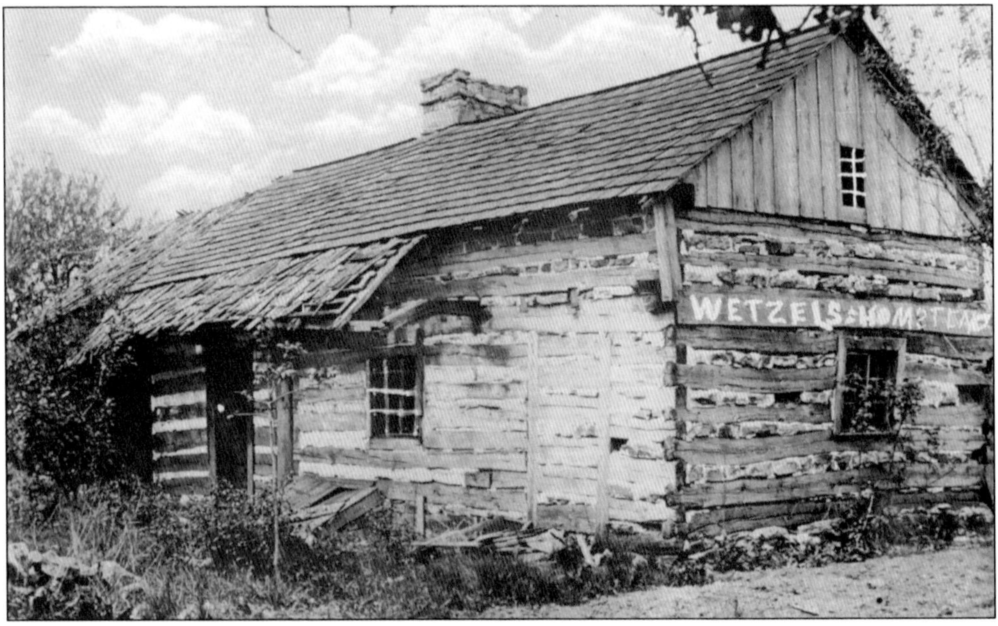

The old Wetzel family homestead, pictured, was on St. Peter's Road near the line between Berks and Lehigh Counties. It was built in 1740 of logs and was occupied until 1900. Of the many Wetzels listed in the 1790 census report, the data indicates that John Wetzel and his sons Henry, Peter, Daniel, and Hans Georg were the occupants of this home. The building no longer exists. (Courtesy of C. Edward Mosheim.)

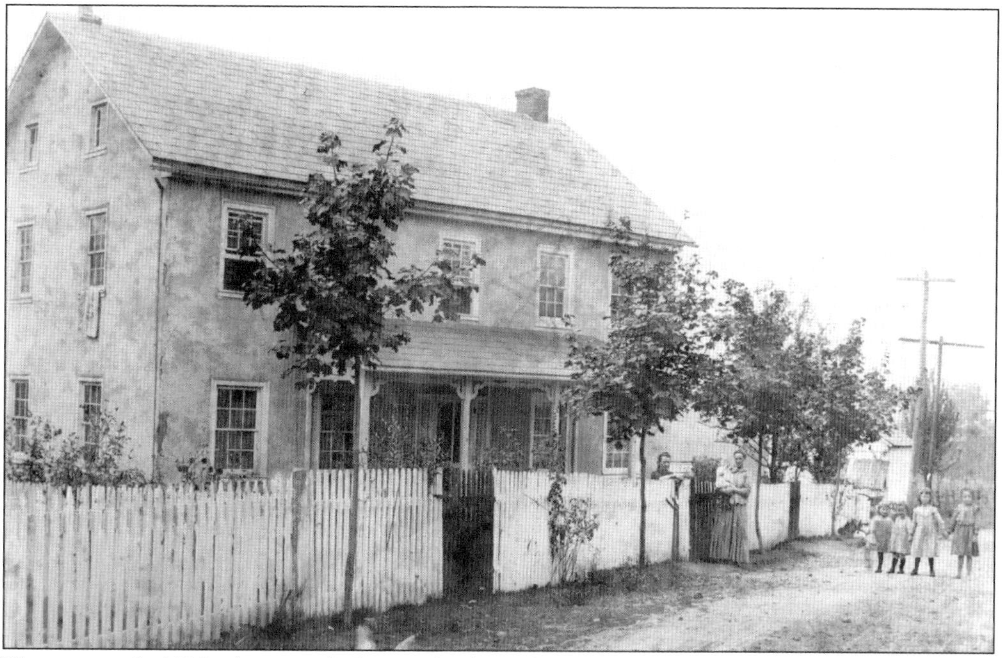

This very early 1900s photograph shows Charles and Katie Yoder at their farmhouse along the old Hereford Turnpike, now Route 29/100. In those days, children could safely walk in the dirt road and chickens could wander freely. Notice the blanket airing outside the upstairs window. The house remains but without a front porch or a white picket fence. (Courtesy of Ruth Yoder-Taylor.)

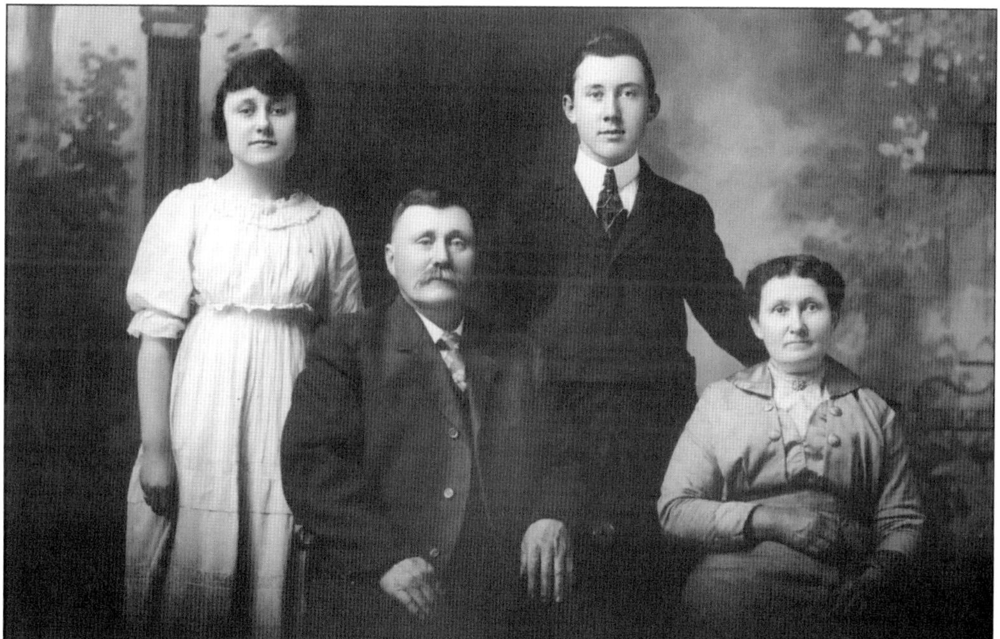

The Charles Yoder family of Zionsville posed for a formal portrait at the Walp and Boyer Studio in Allentown about 1920. Pictured are, from left to right, daughter Verna, father Charles, son Roman, and mother Katie Yoder. This is the respected teacher Roman Yoder found in many photographs throughout this book. (Courtesy of Ruth Yoder-Taylor.)

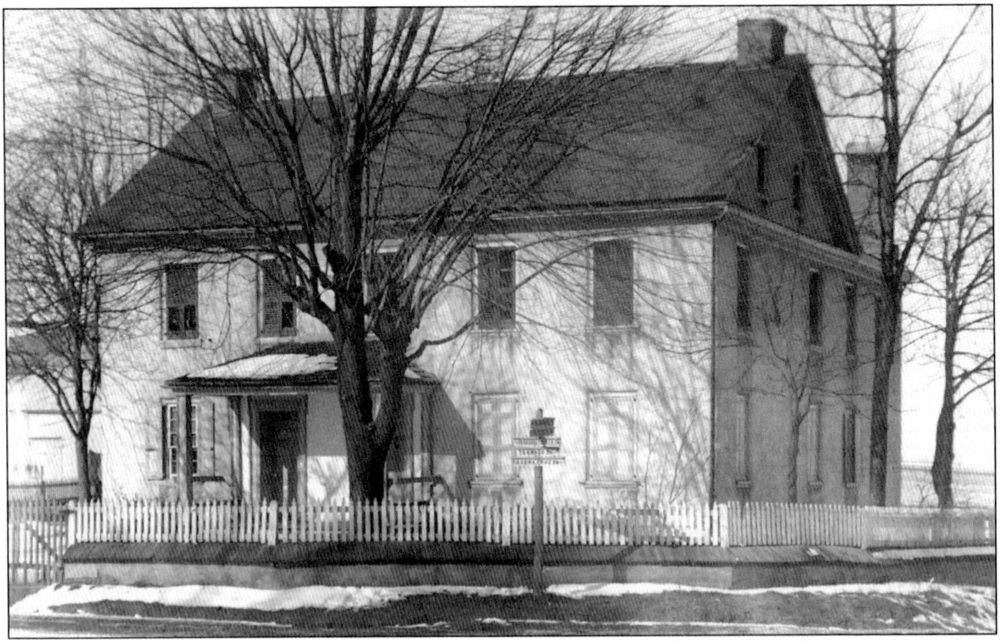

In 1792, John Shimer purchased over 200 acres from Jacob Miller in what became the village named after him, Shimerville. Shimer was a successful farmer, landlord, justice of the peace, and innkeeper for the 35 years he lived here. At the intersection of St. Peter's Road and Route 100/29, the house had a barn across St. Peter's Road that burned in a spectacular fire in 1905 when the Harry Schreiber family occupied the farm. (Courtesy of Jean Iobst.)

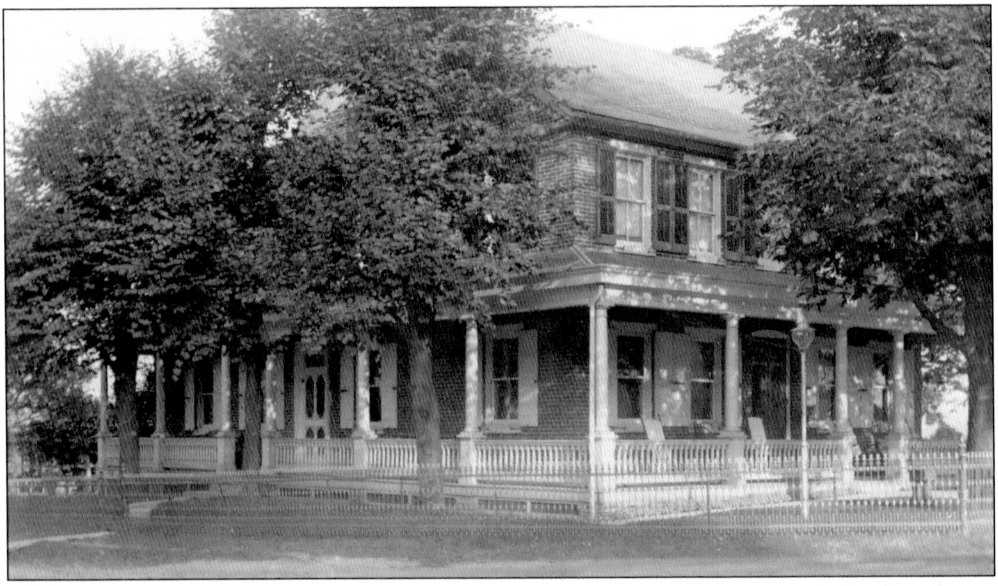

Another Shimer home at the intersection of route 100/29 and Shimerville Road, this large home was built by Charles Shimer between 1834 and 1850. Later, it was also home to Harry Shimer and Llewellyn Shimer. The porch and the fencing are gone, but the smokehouse in back remains, as does the large stone bank barn. It was at the side of this barn that one of the last stone mile markers along the Kings Highway was positioned informing travelers of the number of miles to Philadelphia. Today, this is the business known as "aunt daisy's." (Courtesy of Jean Iobst.)

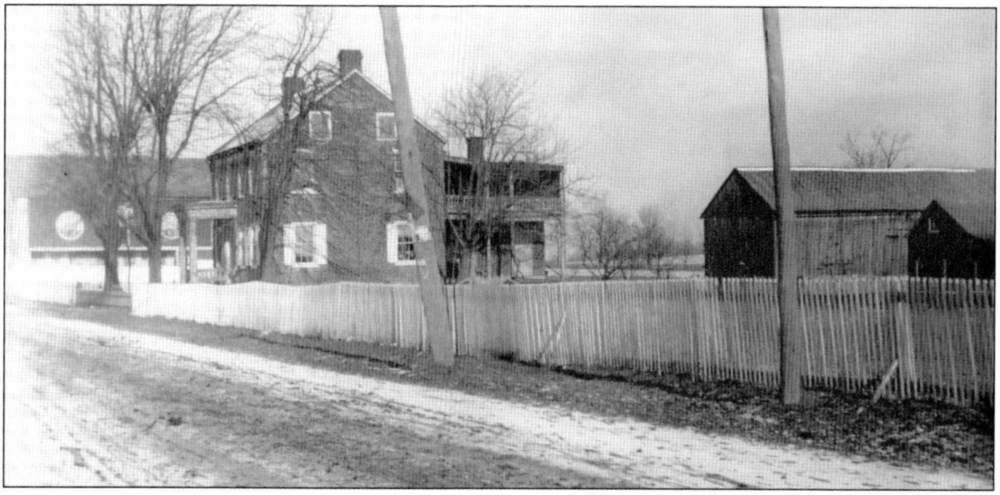

A window designer for Hess Brothers in Allentown, John Gabellini and his family once lived in this stately home on Route 29/100 in Shimerville. Gabellini also designed the lobby area of the first Holiday Inn East in Bethlehem. The barn in the distance is on the property of "aunt daisy's" business, pictured at the bottom of the previous page. The fence has been replaced by a high hedge, and the house has had several additions. (Courtesy of Jean Iobst.)

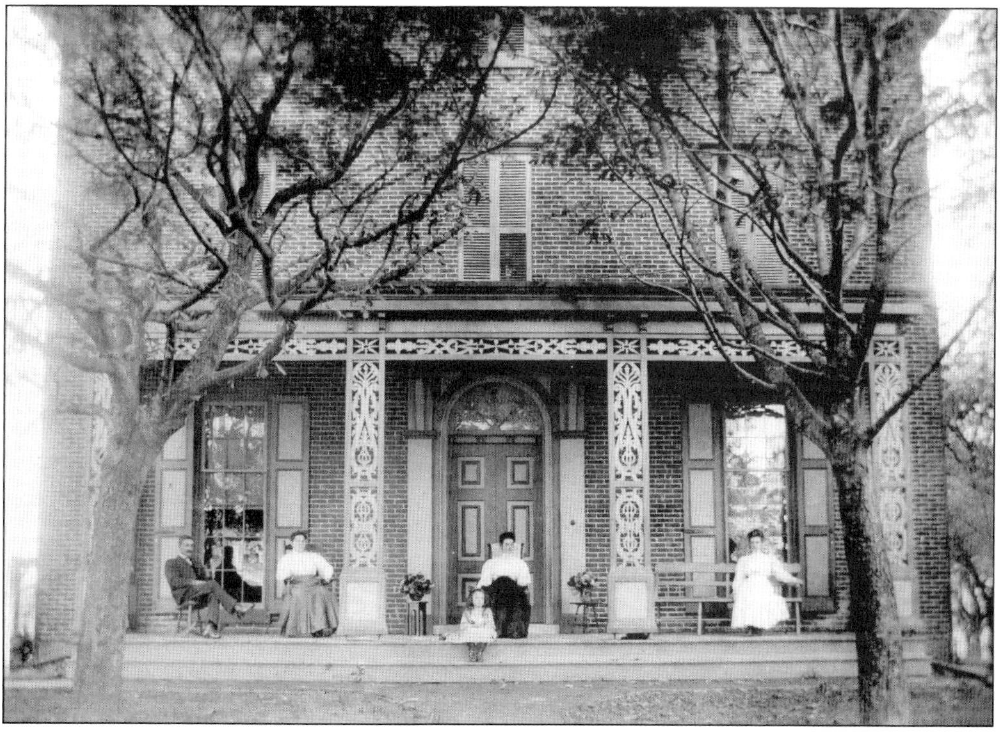

This was the elegant John Schreiber residence along Route 29/100 in Shimerville around 1900–1910. Seated on the front porch, on the left, are Edward and Agnus Schreiber, and on the right is Sallie Schreiber. John Schreiber was a farmer in his early life, a veteran of the Civil War, a county commissioner, and a member of the state board of agriculture. He served as postmaster in Shimerville from 1872 to 1885 and died in 1902. It is still an elegant home with white walls, white columns, and lush landscaping. (Courtesy of Palmer Schreiber.)

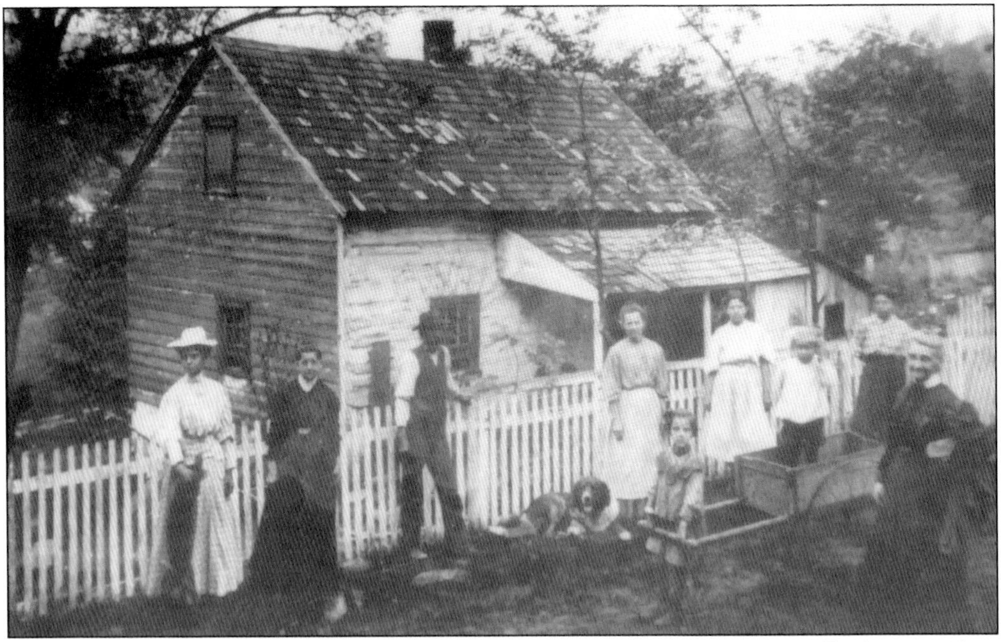

Drive to the top of Sell Road in Powder Valley to find the original Solomon Miller home. When this picture was taken, it was the home of the Milton Miller family. The Millers pictured are, from left to right, Mary, Carolina, Milton, Susan, Esther, Belva, and Rebecca in the foreground. James is sitting on the cart, and Verna is pulling the cart. The family dog, Major, joined in the picture, too! (Courtesy of Beulah Miller.)

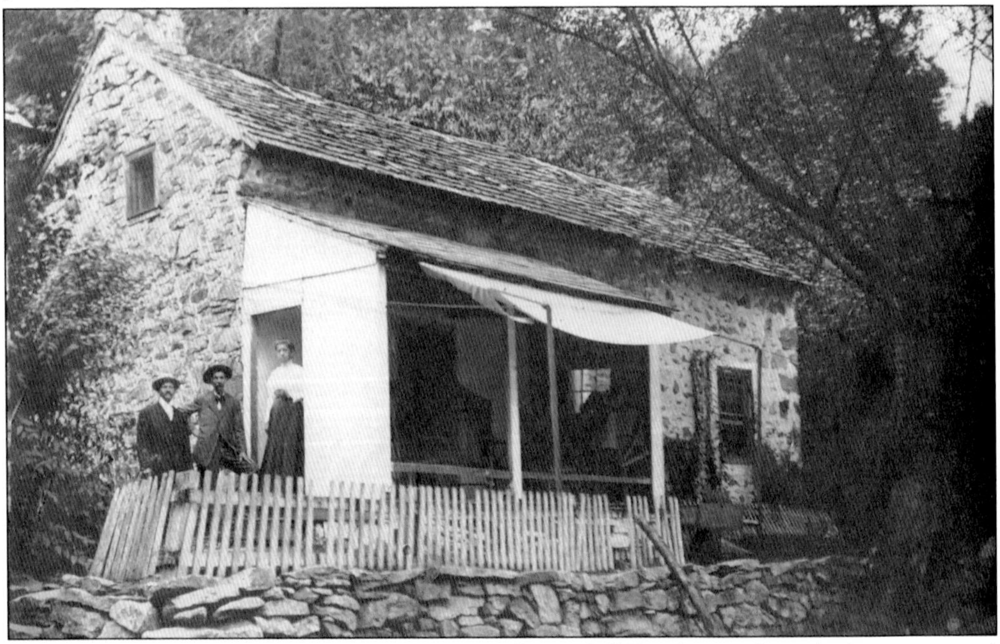

This was another home belonging to Solomon Miller on Sell Road across from the home pictured above. The appearance of this house changed in later years when dormers were added, but a portion of the original log structure still remains. At one time, the James Sell family lived here, giving Sell Road its name. (Courtesy of Beulah Miller.)

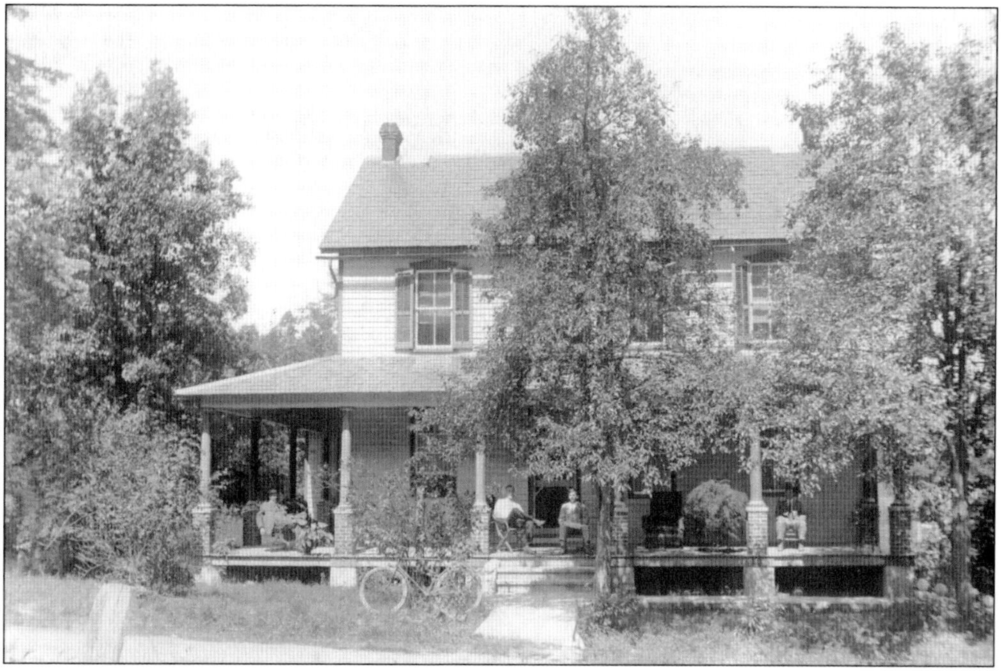

The Amandus Miller home at Woodlawn Drive and Corning Road in Powder Valley was one of the first homes in the area to have a telephone. Miller bought the place in 1910, years after it had been a home and butcher shop belonging to George Bartholomew. Sitting on the porch are Elton Miller on the right and his brother Newton. Today, the home looks much as it does in the photograph, except that the trees have been removed. (Courtesy of Barbara Heist.)

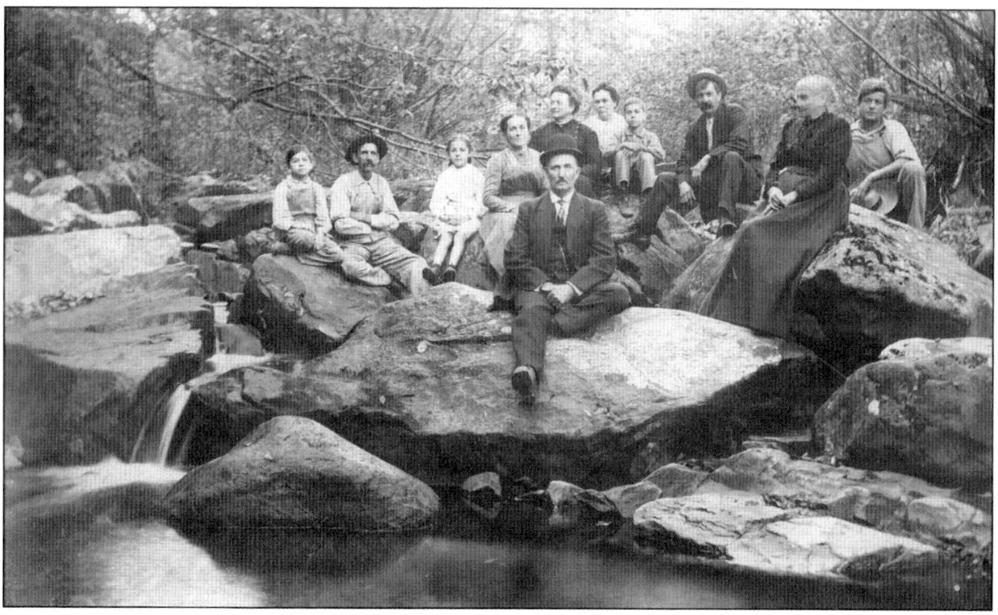

The Amandus Miller family entertained Sunday visitors posed on the huge rocks along Indian Creek in Powder Valley about 1910. Miller is the man with the mustache, Grandma Sarah Yeakel is on the right, Newton Miller is on the left, and Annie Miller is dressed in white. Amandus Miller was an influential Powder Valley businessman in the early 1900s. (Courtesy of Barbara Heist.)

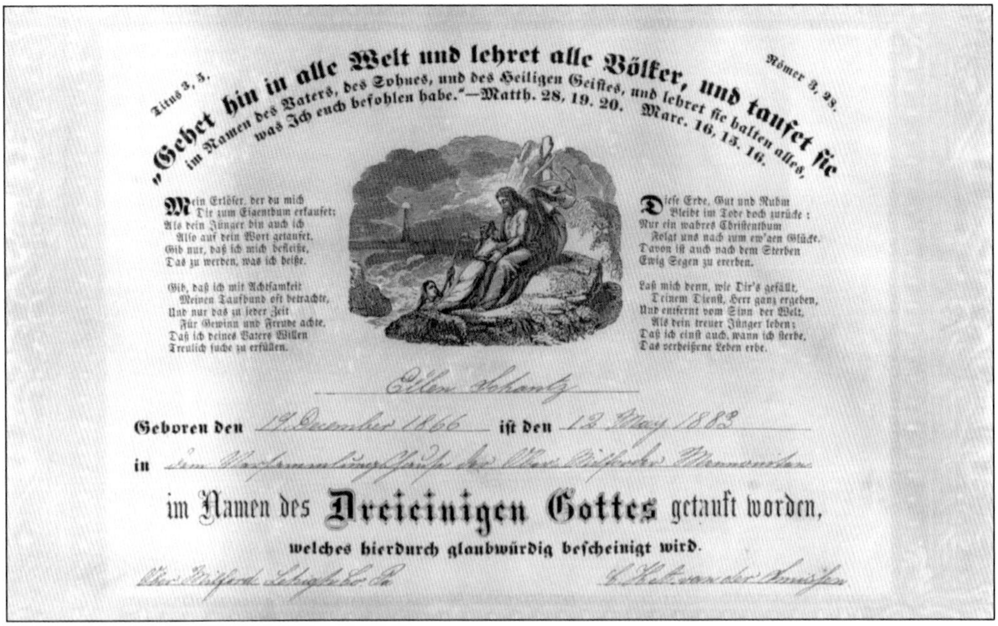
Titus 3, 5.

„Gehet hin in alle Welt und lehret alle Völker, und taufet sie im Namen des Vaters, des Sohnes, und des Heiligen Geistes, und lehret sie halten alles, was Ich euch befohlen habe." — Matth. 28, 19. 20. Marc. 16, 15. 16.

Römer 3, 28.

Mein Erlöser, der du mich
Dir zum Eigenthum erkaufet;
Als dein Jünger bin auch ich
Also auf dein Wort getaufet.
Gib nur, daß ich mich befleiße,
Das zu werden, was ich heiße.

Gib, daß ich mit Achtsamkeit
Meinen Taufbund oft betrachte,
Und nur das zu jeder Zeit
Für Gewinn und Freude achte,
Daß ich deines Vaters Willen
Treulich suche zu erfüllen.

Diese Erde, Gut und Ruhm
Bleibt im Tode doch zurücke:
Nur ein wahres Christenthum
Folgt uns nach zum ew'gen Glücke.
Davon ist auch nach dem Sterben
Ewig Segen zu ererben.

Laß mich denn, wie Dir's gefällt,
Deinem Dienst, Herr ganz ergeben,
Und entfernt vom Sinn der Welt,
Als dein treuer Jünger leben;
Daß ich einst auch, wann ich sterbe,
Das verheißene Leben erbe.

Ellen Schantz

Geboren den 19 December 1866 ist den 12 May 1883

in

im Namen des Dreieinigen Gottes getauft worden,

welches hierdurch glaubwürdig bescheinigt wird.

Ober Milford Lehigh Co. Pa

Thanks to Renate Schneider Plank, this old German baptismal certificate has been translated. Ellen Schantz was born December 19, 1866, and baptized May 12, 1883, in the Meetinghouse of the Upper Milford Mennonites, Lehigh County. The signature of the presiding minister is not deciphered. Matthew 28 and Mark 13 and 16 are quoted. One portion reads, "Therefore, go and make disciples of all the nations." (Courtesy of Ruth Yoder-Taylor.)

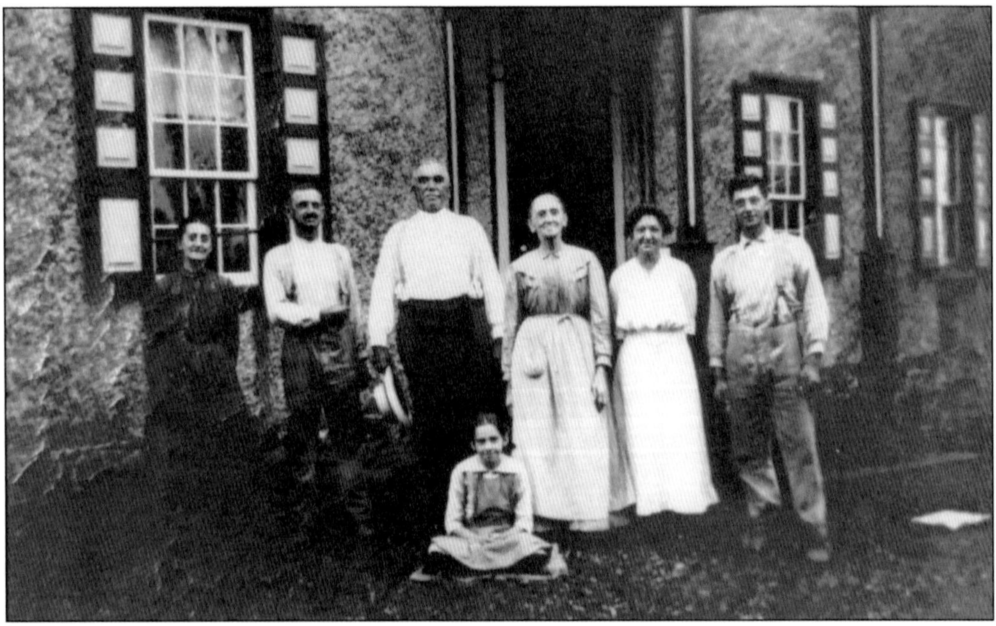

Marie Moyer Yoder, last woman on the right, is standing with her Schantz relatives in this photograph about 1914. The girl seated in front is Esther Shelly, daughter of Albanus Shelly, owner of Shelly's sawmill in Vera Cruz. Standing are, from left to right, Sallie Shelly Schantz, a sister to Albanus, uncle Daniel Schantz, Daniel Meyer, grandmother Sarah Meyer Schantz, and Norman Schantz on the end. (Courtesy of Ruth Schantz.)

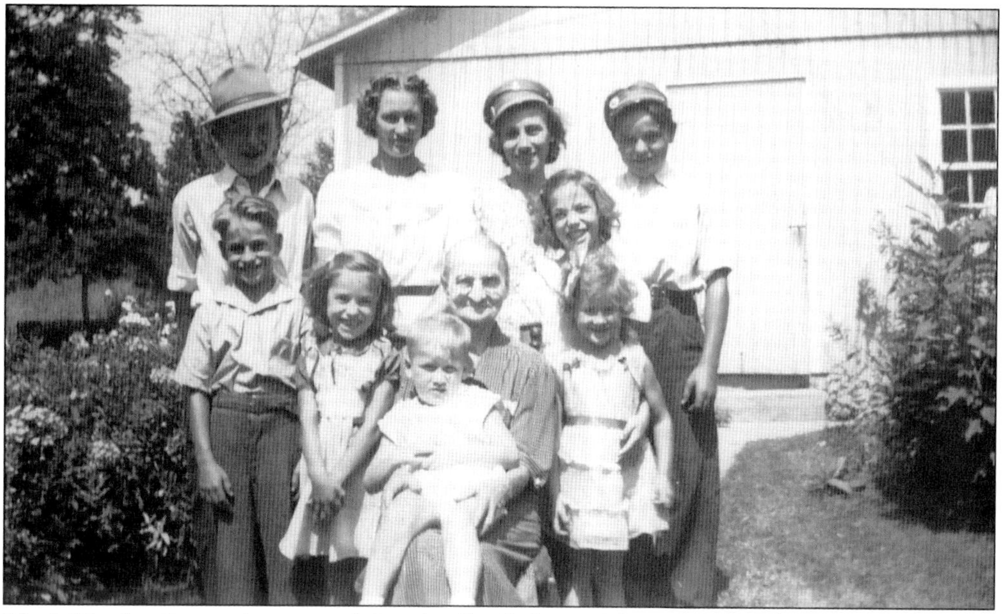

The Miller family members visited their landlord's farm in Corning around 1941. The landlords, Allen and Abbesina Moll, are the same couple named on the marriage certificate below. Abbesina is holding Willard Miller. The children in the first row are, from left to right, Raymond Eppler, Geraldine Eppler, and Dolores Eppler with her arm around Pauline Miller. In the second row are, from left to right, Linford Schmoyer, Beulah Miller, Dorothy Eppler, and Thomas Hetrick. (Courtesy of Beulah Miller.)

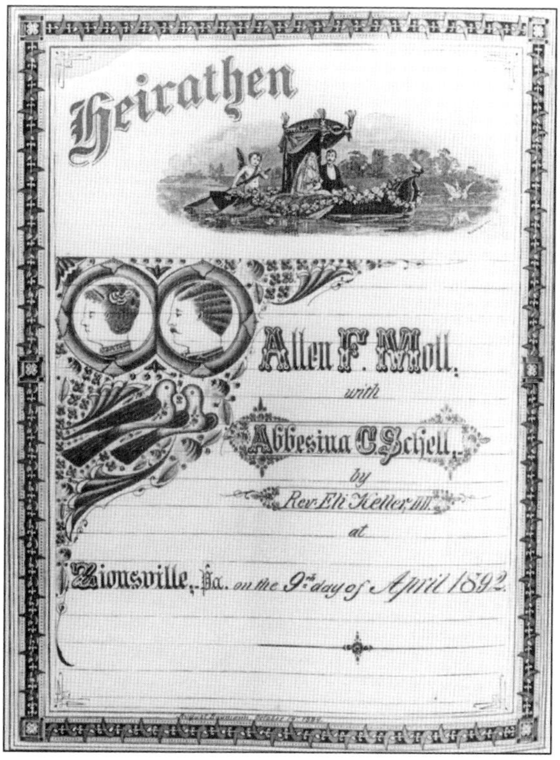

This decorative marriage certificate for Allen Moll and Abbesina Schell is an example of the kind of items that could be bought from the salesmen who traveled the villages in earlier times peddling their wares. Rev. Eli Keller married the pair on April 9, 1892. Abbesina Moll is shown in the image above. (Courtesy of Beulah Miller.)

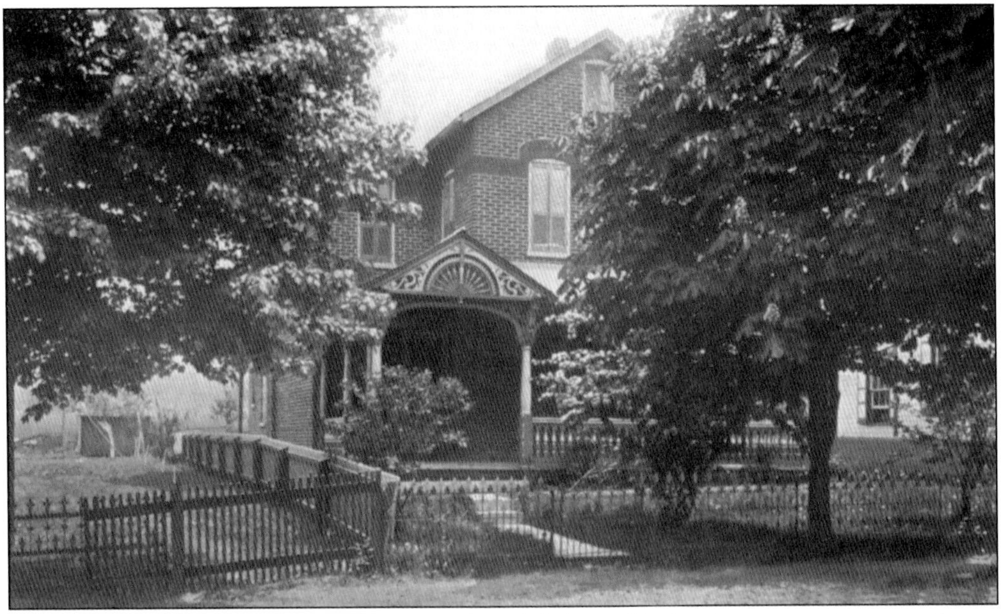

A large home with a decorative front porch and fashionable fencing was only proper for an important resident of Vera Cruz like Amandus Schuler. Such was the home in the center of the village for this store proprietor and farm owner. Schuler was another of the family names very prominent in the early history of Vera Cruz. Amandus joins Jacob, John, Samuel, Uriah, and Wharton with the Schuler name in Vera Cruz history. (Courtesy of Joseph Benner.)

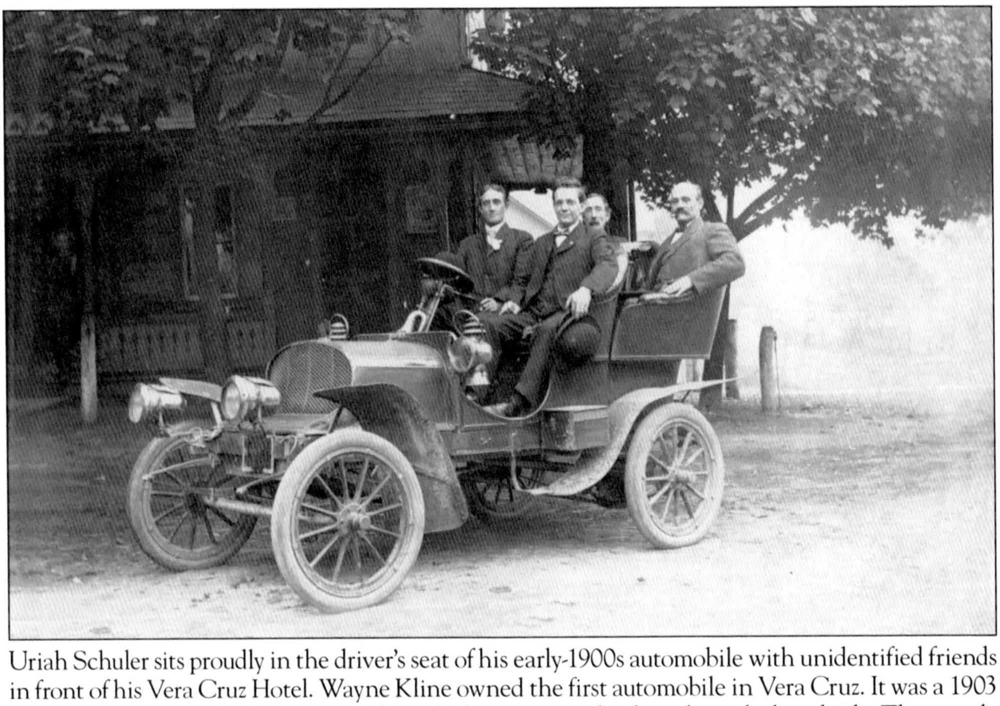

Uriah Schuler sits proudly in the driver's seat of his early-1900s automobile with unidentified friends in front of his Vera Cruz Hotel. Wayne Kline owned the first automobile in Vera Cruz. It was a 1903 chain-driven, one-cylinder Oldsmobile with the steering wheel on the right hand side. These early cars often got a flat tire, which meant lots of work removing the tire, taking out the inner tube, patching the leak, reassembling the tire, and pumping up the flat with a hand pump. (UMHS.)

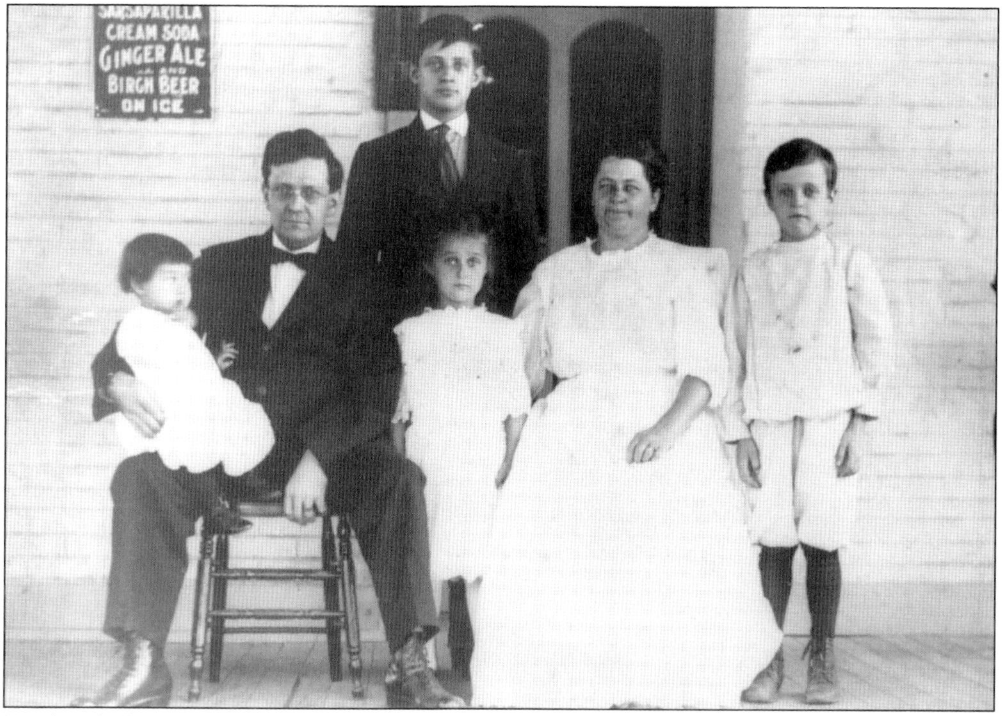

Uriah Schuler, a Vera Cruz store and hotel owner, is shown with his family about 1909. Pictured from left to right are (first row) daughter Janet, Uriah, older daughter Annie, wife Lydia, and son Nevin Schuler; (second row) older son Wharton. (UMHS.)

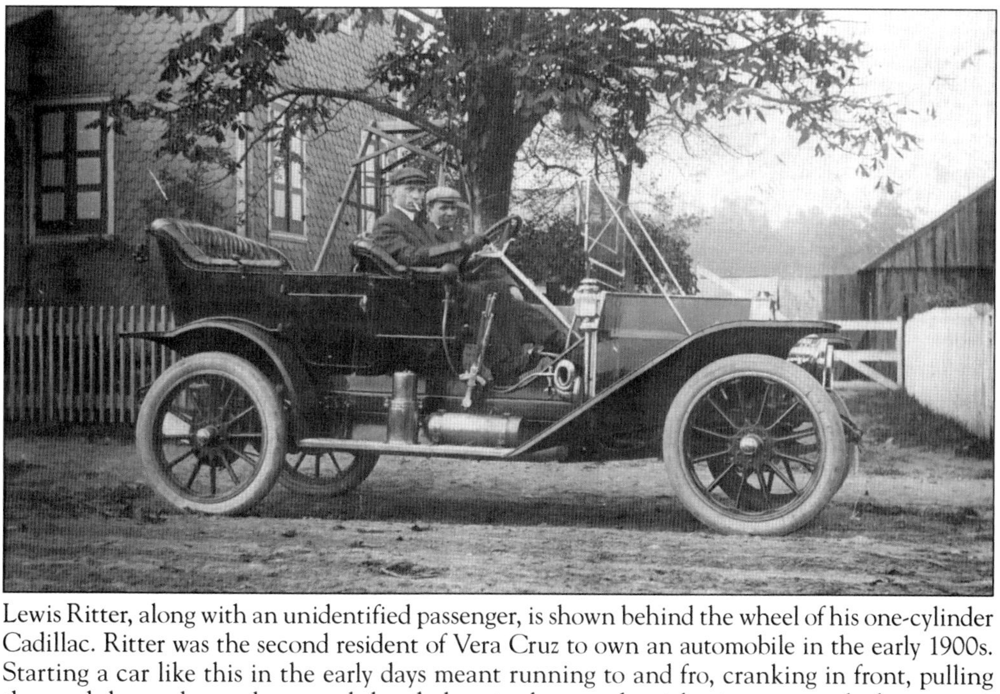

Lewis Ritter, along with an unidentified passenger, is shown behind the wheel of his one-cylinder Cadillac. Ritter was the second resident of Vera Cruz to own an automobile in the early 1900s. Starting a car like this in the early days meant running to and fro, cranking in front, pulling the spark lever, the gas lever, and the choke wire loop at the right times to catch the car as it hopefully "coughed" to a start. (Courtesy of Joseph Benner.)

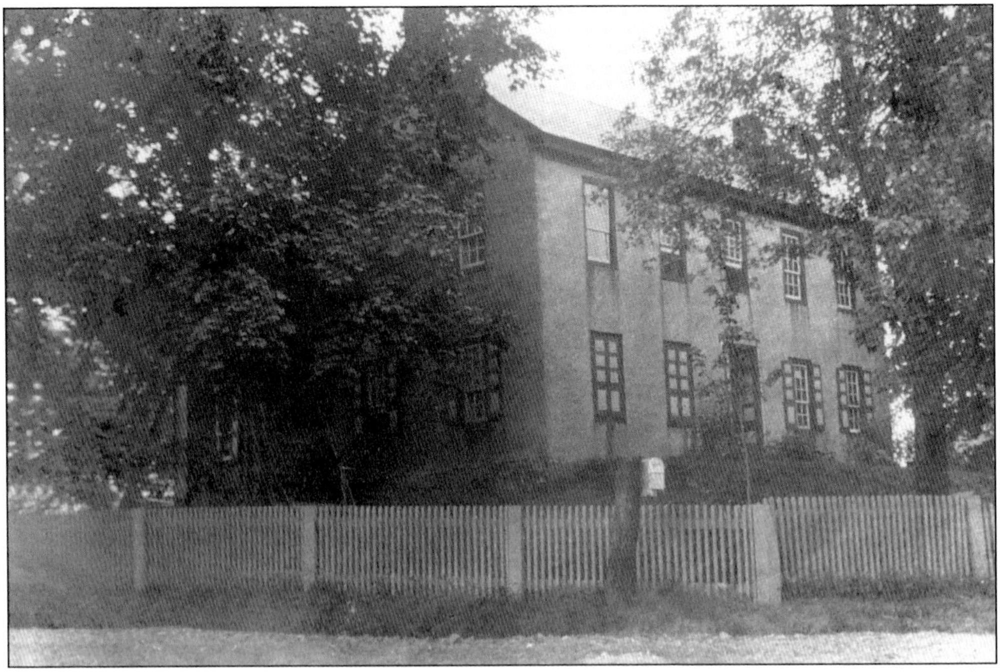

The Schantz homestead, shown above about 1900 and below in the 1970s, is located at the intersection of Vera Cruz Road and Church View Road in Zionsville. Henry and Sarah Schantz's daughter Elizabeth "Lizzie" Schantz (1870–1961) was raised on this farm, as were generations of Schantzes. In 1893, Elizabeth married Harry Schreiber, son of John Schreiber, who later bought this Schantz homestead. He in turn sold it to his son Paul S. Schreiber, who lived here until his death in 1966. The Schantz family reunions took place here for over 20 years. After the death of Schreiber's wife, Ella, in 1985, the farm was sold. (Courtesy of Barbara Harris.)

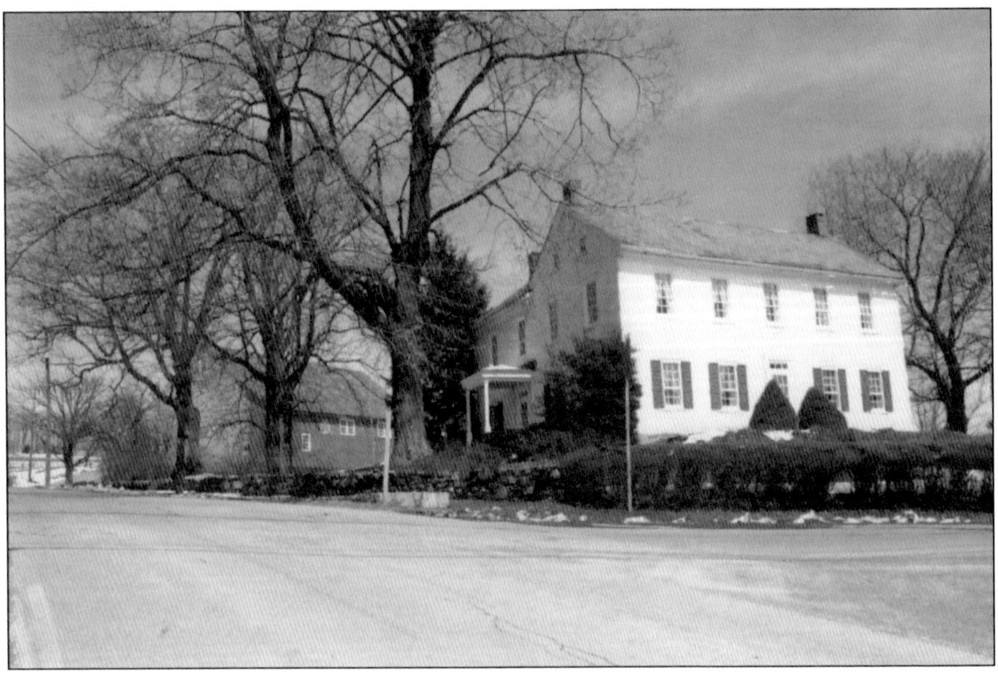

The Schantz reunion was started by Henry (1834–1898) and Sarah (1836–1916) Schantz, pictured right, and held at their farm on Vera Cruz Road, shown on the opposite page. Besides Schantz, this large, wide-ranging relation included the following Zionsville surnames: Benfield, Bieber, Carl, Mohr, Moyer, Schreiber, Stauffer, Treichler, and Yoder. The large gathering below was held in 1946. Mary Schantz Snyder is in the first row, third from the left. Barbara Schreiber Harris is at the far right of the last seated row. The final reunion was held in 1965 upon the death of Paul Schreiber. (Both, courtesy of Barbara Harris.)

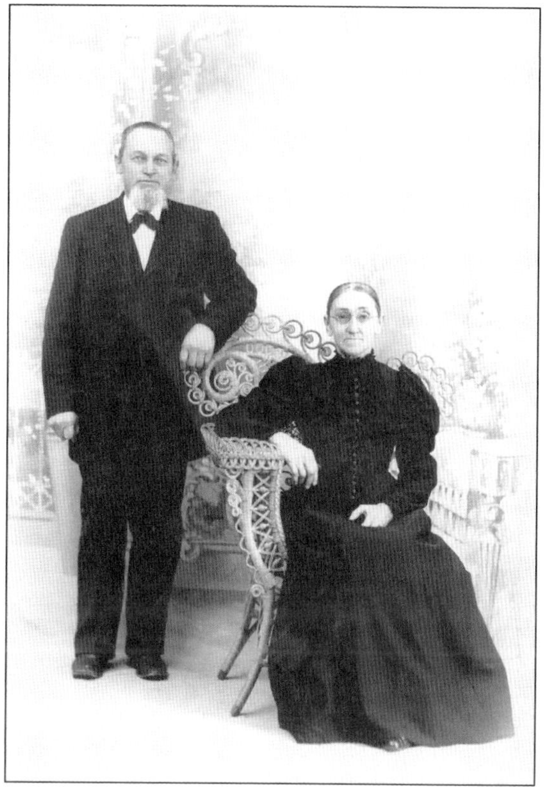

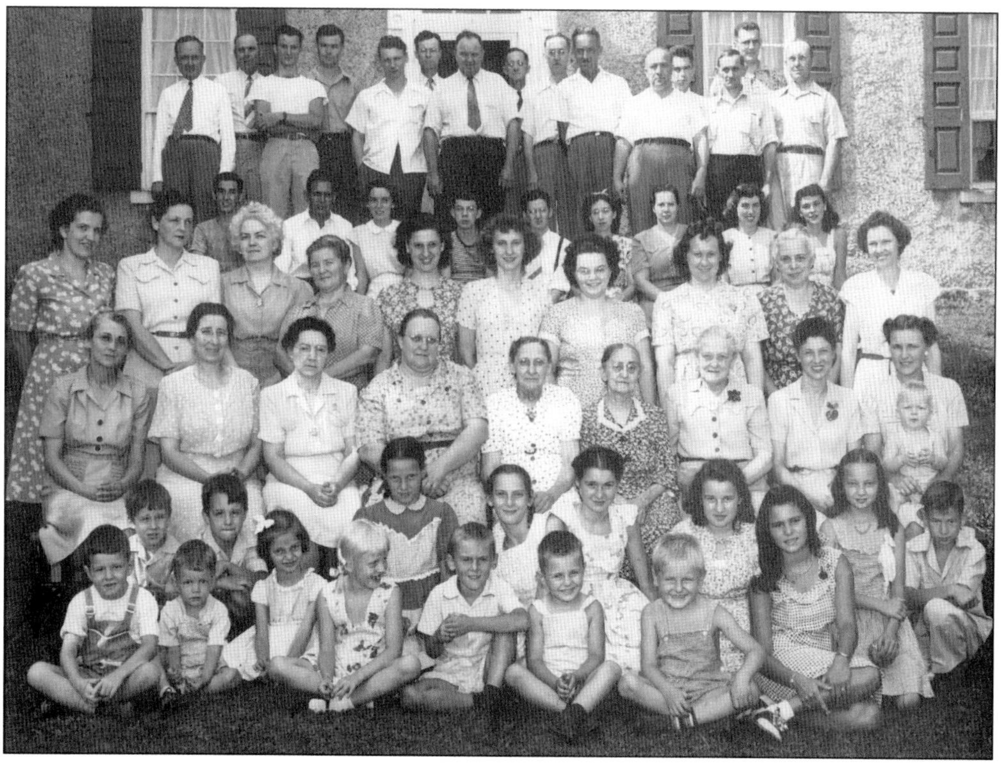

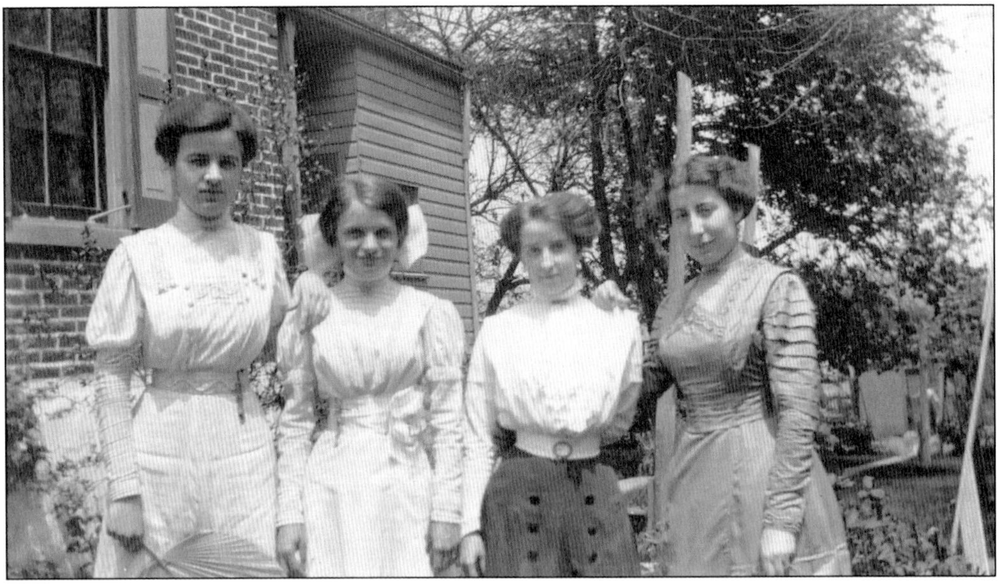

Wearing the fashions of the times, four charming women are pictured at the Miller homestead in Old Zionsville in the early 1900s. Tiny, nipped-in waists and high-necked dresses were in vogue, and they all appear to be wearing a similar hairstyle. Teacher Lulu Miller is on the left, and Ella Reese Schantz is on the right. (Courtesy of Barbara Harris.)

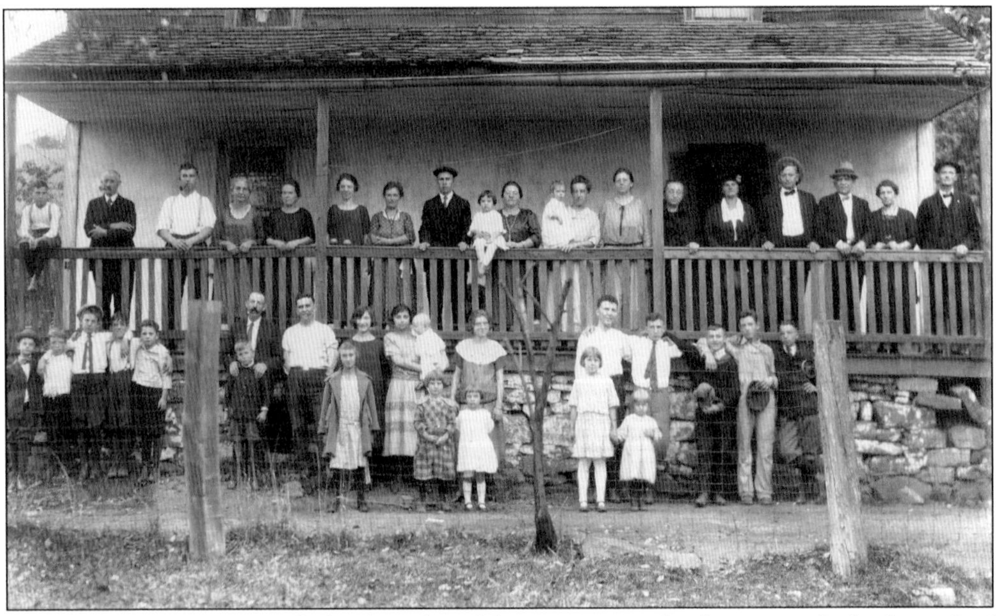

The William and Mary Fegely family gathered for a reunion with relatives on the back porch of the Fegely farm on Church View Road in Old Zionsville. The Fegelys had four children. Son Earl is in the first row on the left with his father's hands on his shoulders. Daughter Helen (Berger) is the next girl in the first row. Lillian (Wetzel) is behind Helen. Baby Warren is being held next to Lillian. Mary Fegely is on the porch, eighth from the left. (Courtesy of Mary Ann Hoch.)

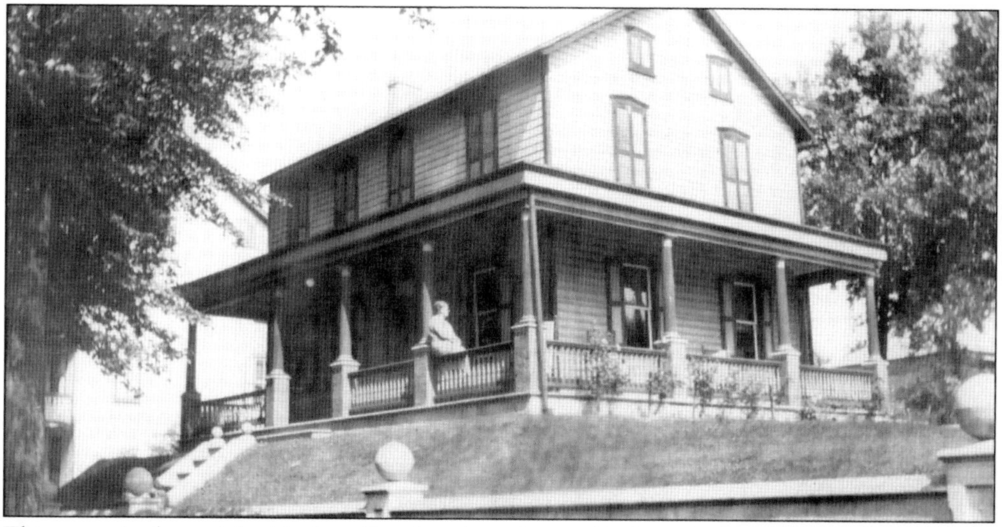

This attractive home is beside the railroad tracks in Zionsville. It was home to Tillie Kuhns Schantz, a graduate of and teacher in the area schools. Much of Schantz's life was closely connected to this house. She married Readen Schantz, who operated the former Anderson Coal Yard across the tracks from the home. Her father was the ticket agent at the railroad station that was a short way down the railroad tracks. Later, she was a part-time clerk at the post office across the street from this house. (UMHS.)

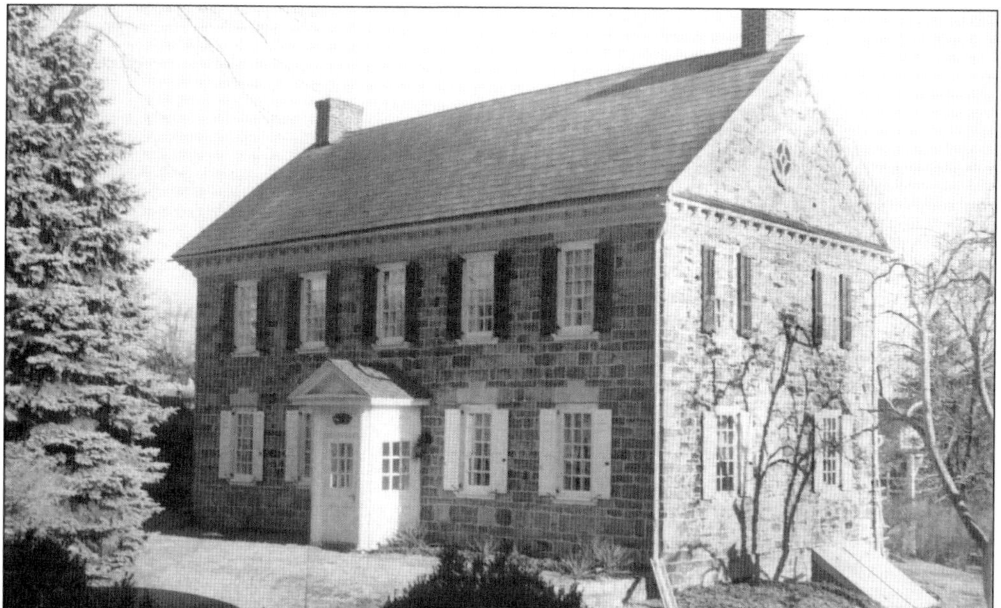

Once considered the oldest and finest house in Old Zionsville, this home was completed in 1799 by the Wieand family, owners of hundreds of acres in and near the village. The original portion of the house is thought to be from the 1760s. It stands at the end of Fountain Road across from the Memorial Fountain and contains five fireplaces and 20-inch-deep stone walls. A brickyard was at the end of the property, which was where Moravian tiles were made for use in constructing other buildings on the premises. At various times, it was home to the Bray, Palmer, Roth, and Smith families, among others. (Courtesy of Phyllis Palmer Vaughn.)

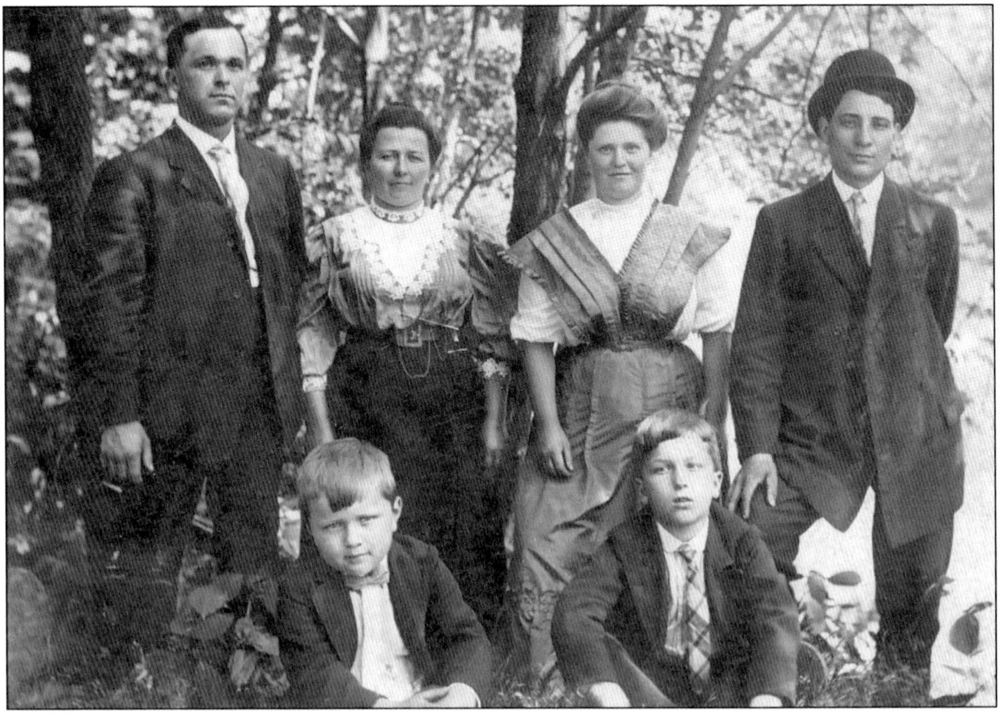

One of many Benners who lived or live in Vera Cruz, Elmer Benner is in the second row above with his wife, Annie. Their sons in the front row are, from left to right, Warren and Elwood. The other two people are unidentified. When grown, Elmer's son Warren and his family lived in a house on Main Road West that had been George Lambert's carriage and body works shop before Benner bought it and made it into his home. Below, Elwood's oldest son, Cornelius, is seated on the hood of a 1927 Maxwell in the driveway of Elwood's home on Main Road West. Elwood and sons Cornelius and Joseph all had long careers as railroad engineers. (Both, courtesy of Joseph Benner.)

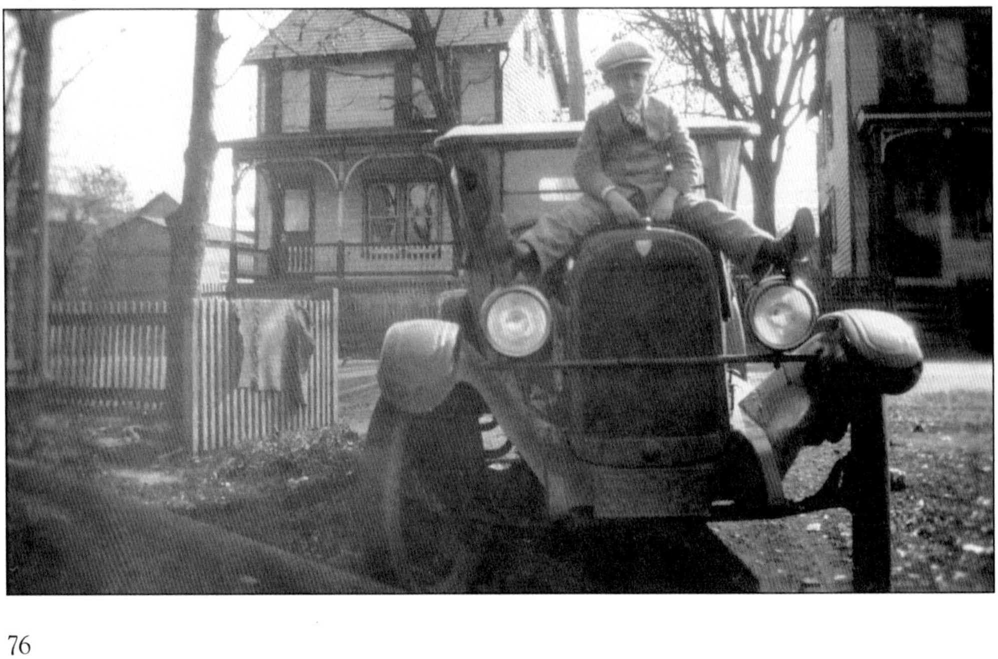

Five

FARMS AND AGRICULTURE

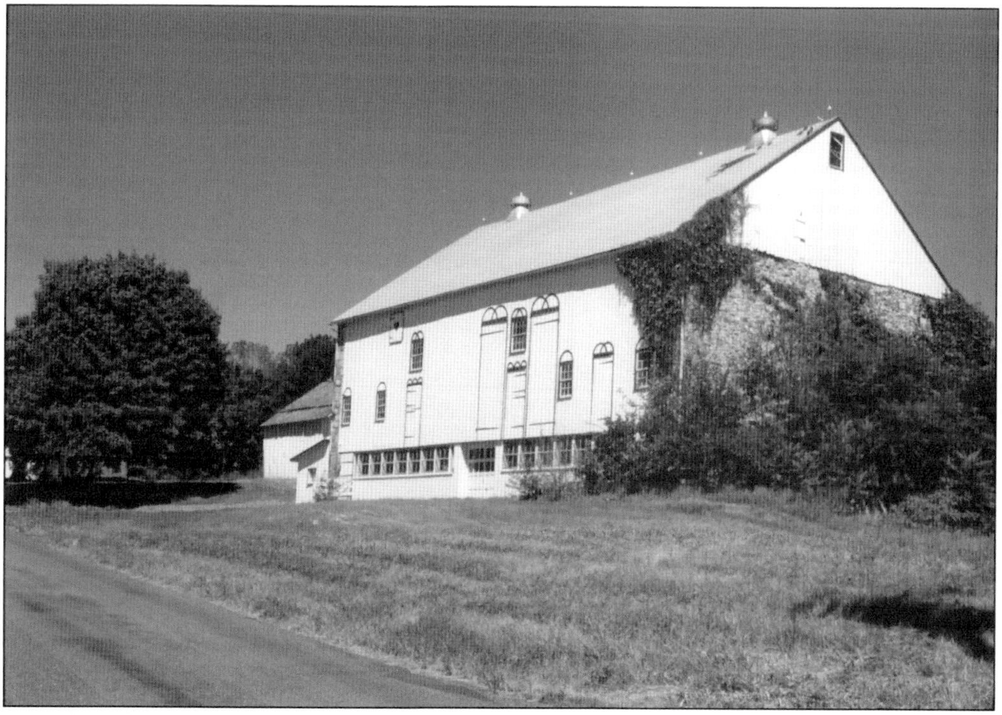

Timothy Schubert built this imposing barn in 1865. When the photograph was taken in 1937, the property was owned by Elmer Graber. A freelance photographer happened to be in the Powder Valley area that year, photographed the picturesque barn on Powder Valley Road, and later in the same year featured it in a *National Geographic* magazine article. The house for the Graber Dairy Farm is on the opposite side of the road, but the beautiful barn was razed to make way for a housing development. The historic Schubert/Graber Cabin is to the far left of the barn beyond the trees. (UMHS.)

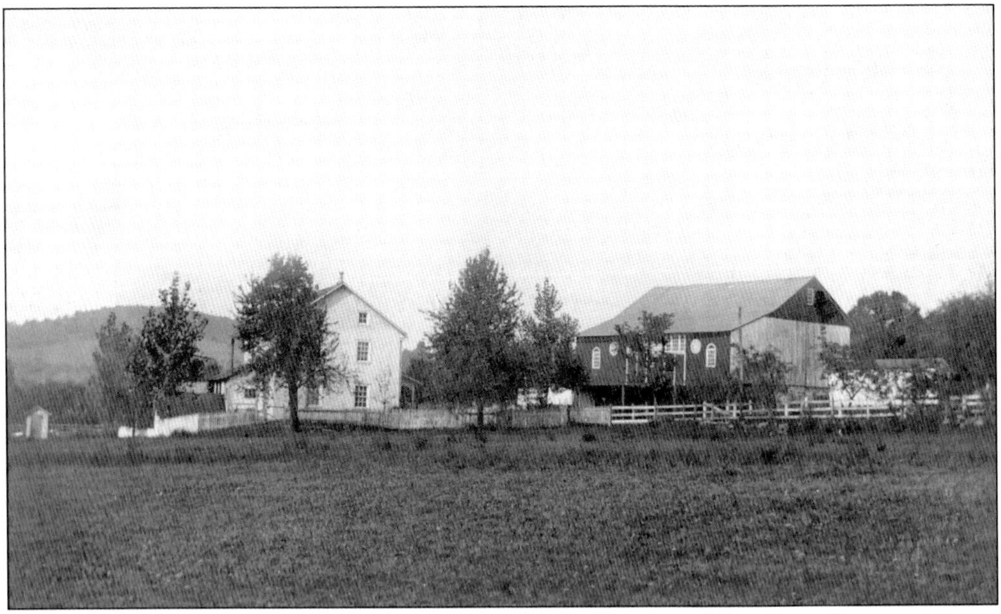

About 1906, the Yoder farm, shown above, was at the intersection of Woodlawn Drive and Route 100 in Zionsville. Known then as Tollgate Road, the road made its way between the house and the barn. The barn was torn down in the 1970s when the newly widened Route 100 came too close to it, but the house remains. As seen below, the Yoder house had front and back porches and was set directly beside the dirt road. Verna Yoder is the girl at the road, and Roman Yoder is sitting on the fence. (Both, courtesy of Ruth Yoder-Taylor.)

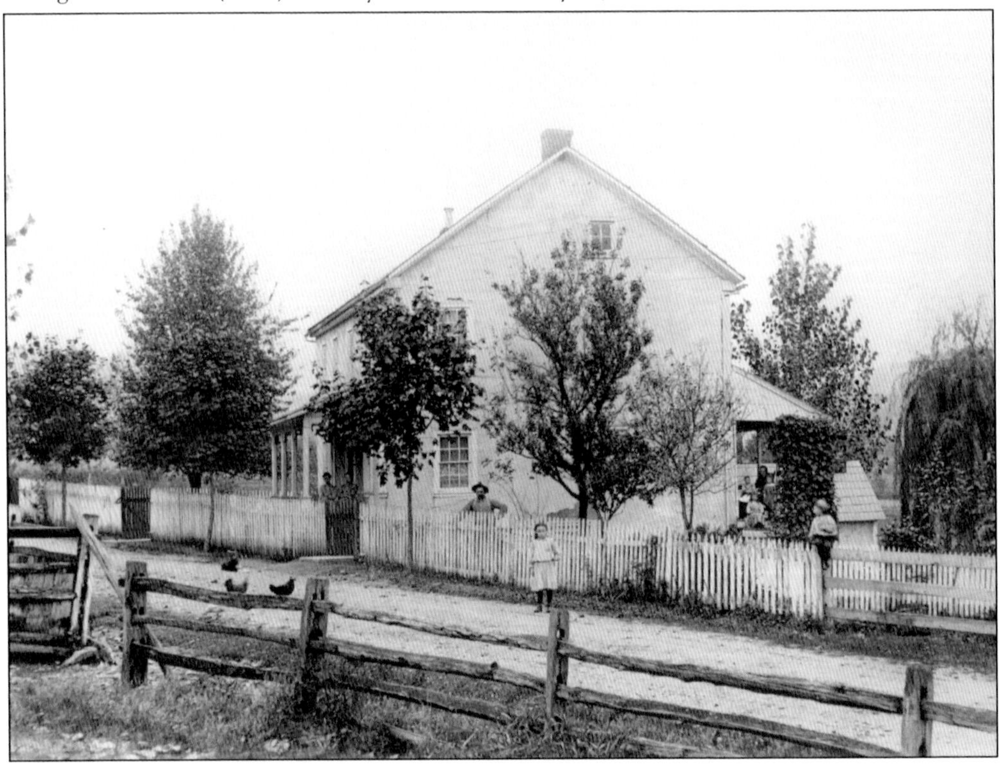

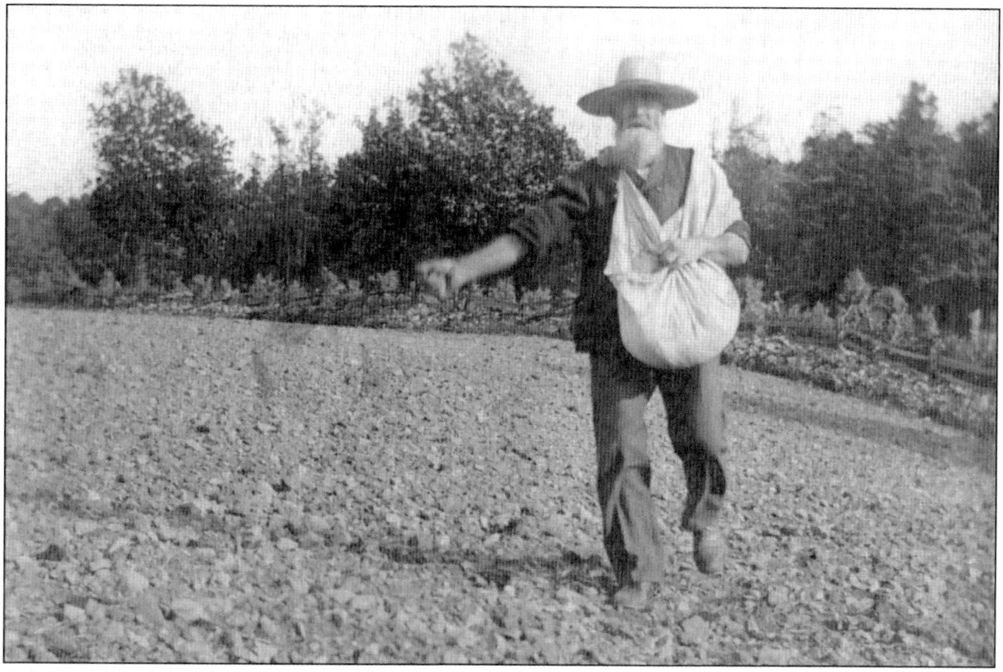

Solomon Merkel is shown broadcasting winter wheat by hand on his Zionsville farm. Wheat was one of the most important agricultural products of these early farmers. The farming techniques brought to the area by German ancestors were the foundation for superior crop production attributed to Pennsylvania farmers. (Courtesy of Ruth Yoder-Taylor.)

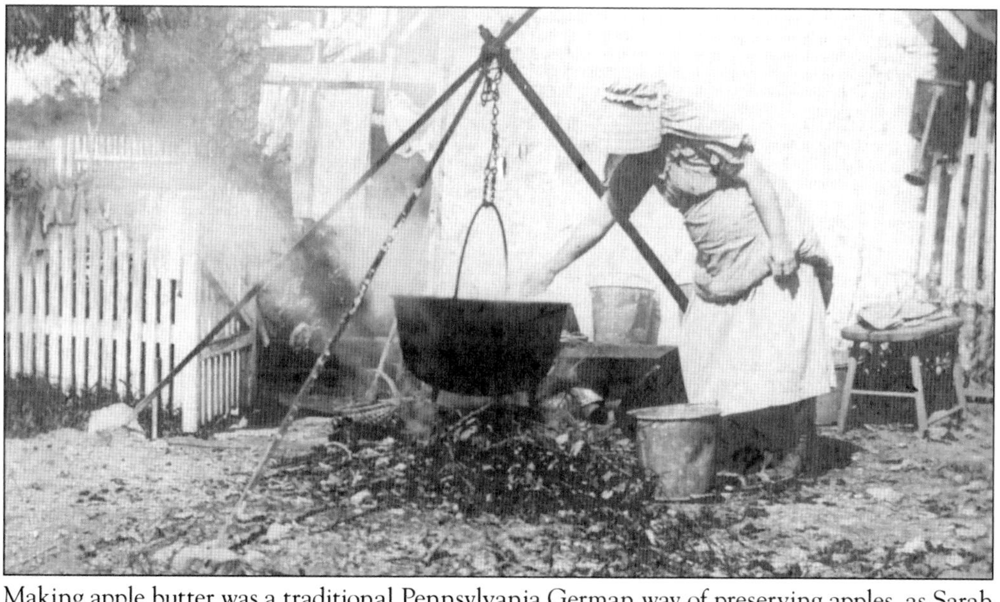

Making apple butter was a traditional Pennsylvania German way of preserving apples, as Sarah Yoder was doing in this photograph. Apple butter had a much longer shelf life than apple sauce, but it required a long, slow cooking down of the apples with cider or water. Many hours of tedious stirring with the long-handled stirrer were required to produce the deep-brown apple butter, one of the "seven sweets and seven sours" offered by Pennsylvania German cooks. (Courtesy of Ruth Yoder-Taylor.)

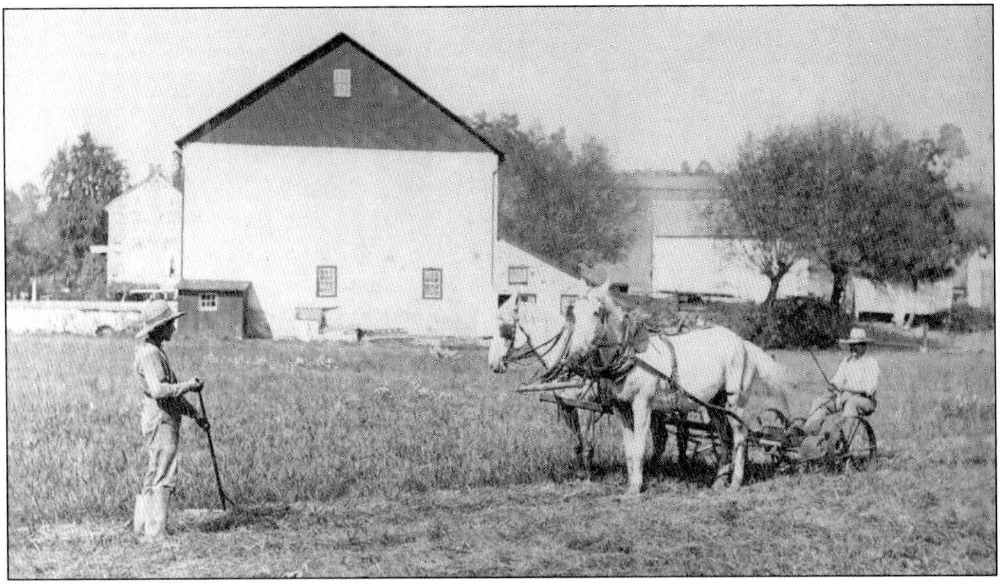

Charles Yoder is working in the fields of the neighboring Treichler farm along Route 100 in Hereford. Horse-drawn mowers were still in use for farmwork at the time of this c. 1906–1910 photograph. The unidentified man with the rake may be a hired hand. Extra hired men were needed in order to harvest enough crops and get enough hay stored in the barns for the winter. (Courtesy of Ruth Yoder-Taylor.)

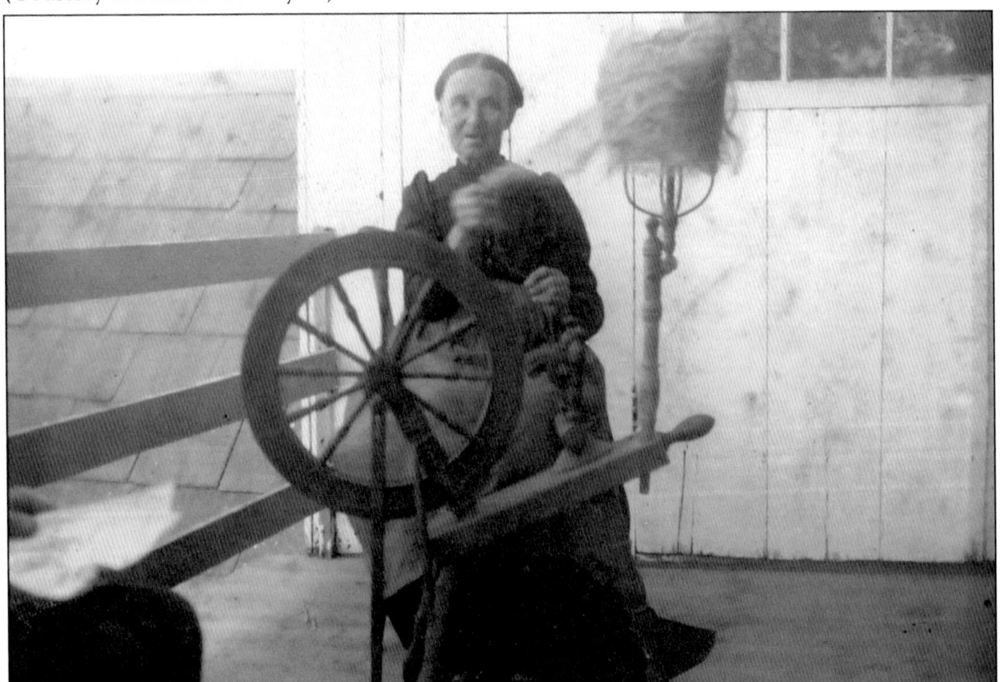

Sarah (Yeakel) Yoder, wife of Benjamin Yoder and mother of Charles Yoder, was doing one of the main chores of an early-1900s woman, spinning. Wives and daughters were kept busy combing, carding, and twisting the wool to prepare it for spinning and, later, making it into clothing for the family. (Courtesy of Ruth Yoder-Taylor.)

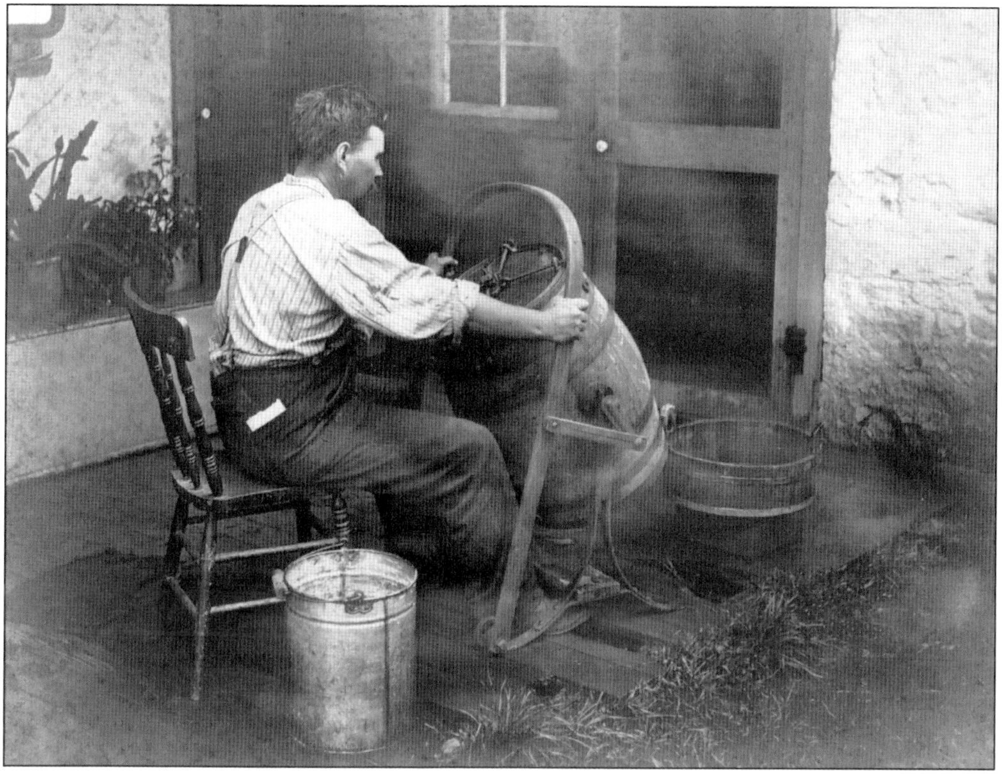

Making butter was one of the tedious but necessary tasks on an early-1900s farm. Much patience was required turning the handle, as the butter did not start to form for several hours. Many farm families made butter for sale and for their own use. Charles Yoder is shown here churning butter on his Zionsville farm. (Courtesy of Ruth Yoder-Taylor.)

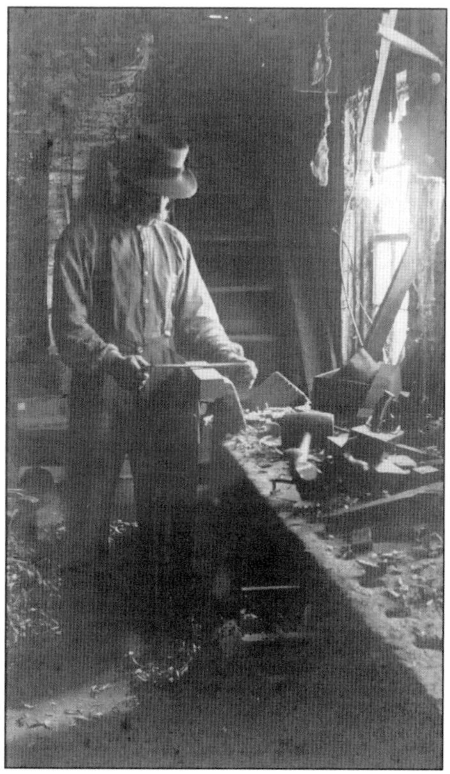

Charles Yoder is working on a vise inside his barn. Farmers spent winter days and rainy times repairing equipment inside their barns and sheds. The many kinds of heavy machinery required to run a farm meant there was always something that needed fixing in addition to the countless other chores. (Courtesy of Ruth Yoder-Taylor.)

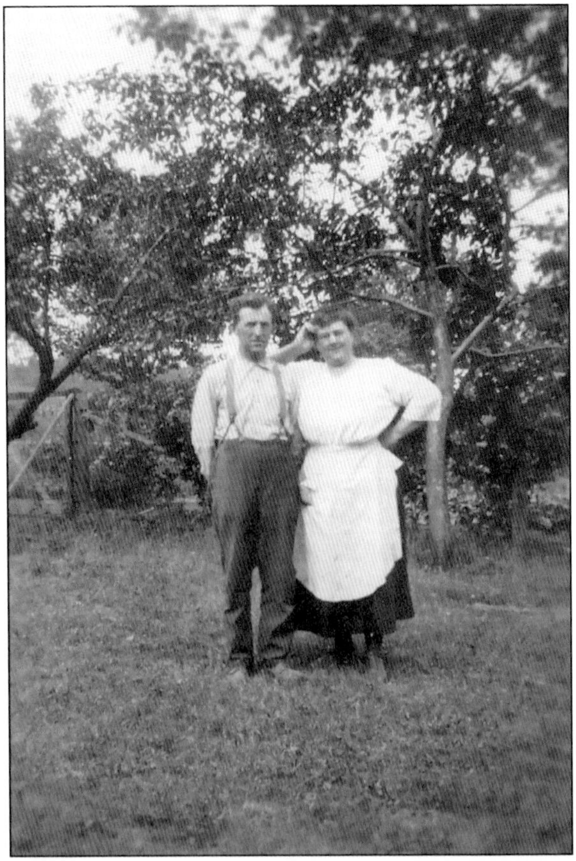

Franklin and Victoria Clauser, parents of the Clauser children below, are posing on their 19th wedding anniversary at their farm on Church View Road in Zionsville on July 2, 1923. Before the Clauser family, the Meyer (Moyer) family had settled this homestead sometime in the mid-18th century and lived here into the early 20th century. (Courtesy of Carolyn Lagler.)

The children of Franklin and Victoria Clauser are standing near the family's barn on Church View Road in Zionsville during the 1920s, which was when the property was a dairy farm operated by the Clauser family. The Clauser children pictured are, from left to right, Paul, Verna, Louisa, and Daniel. This is the same property as pictured at the bottom of page 89. (Courtesy of Carolyn Lagler.)

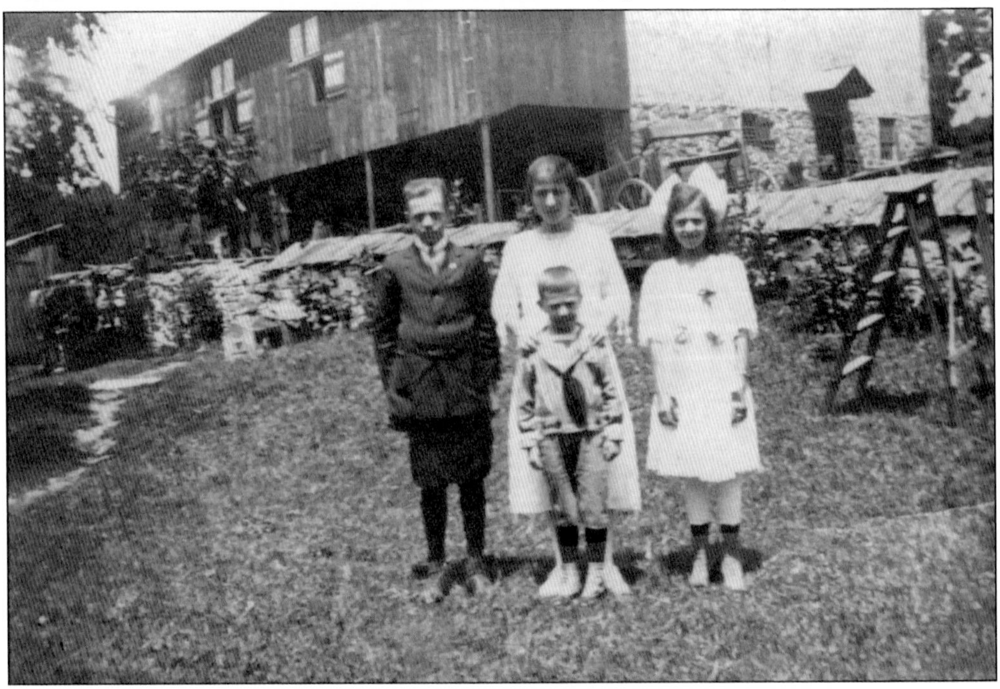

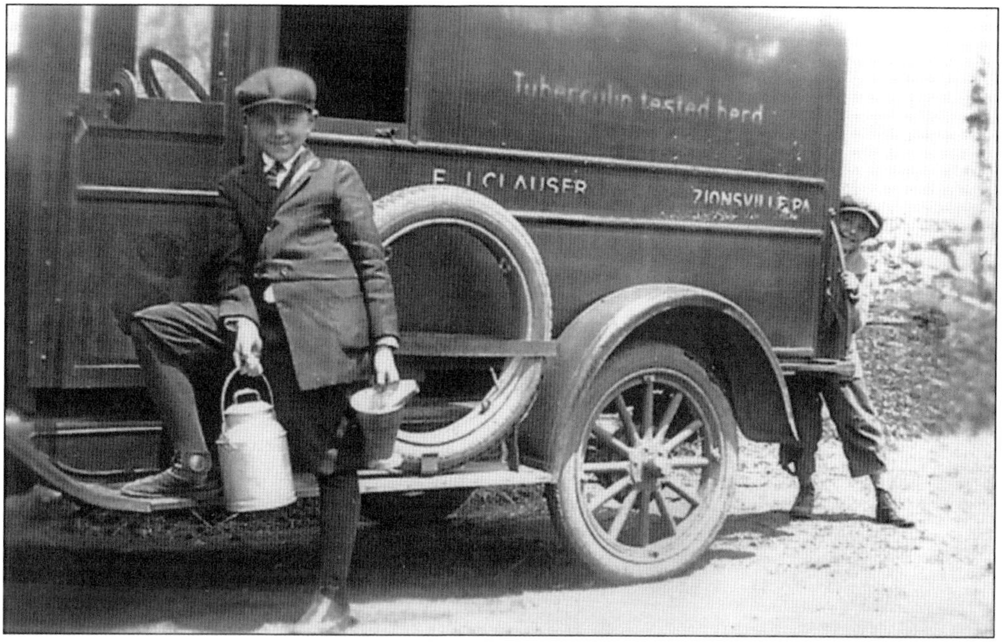

The Seem (now Moyer) farm on Church View Road was owned by the Franklin Clauser family in the 1920s. Pictured above, Daniel Clauser is at the milk truck for his family's dairy, Superior Spring Dairy Farm. The mischievous tyke peeking around the back of the truck is unidentified. Below is Daniel's father, Franklin, showing off one of his dairy cows. (Both, courtesy of Carolyn Lagler.)

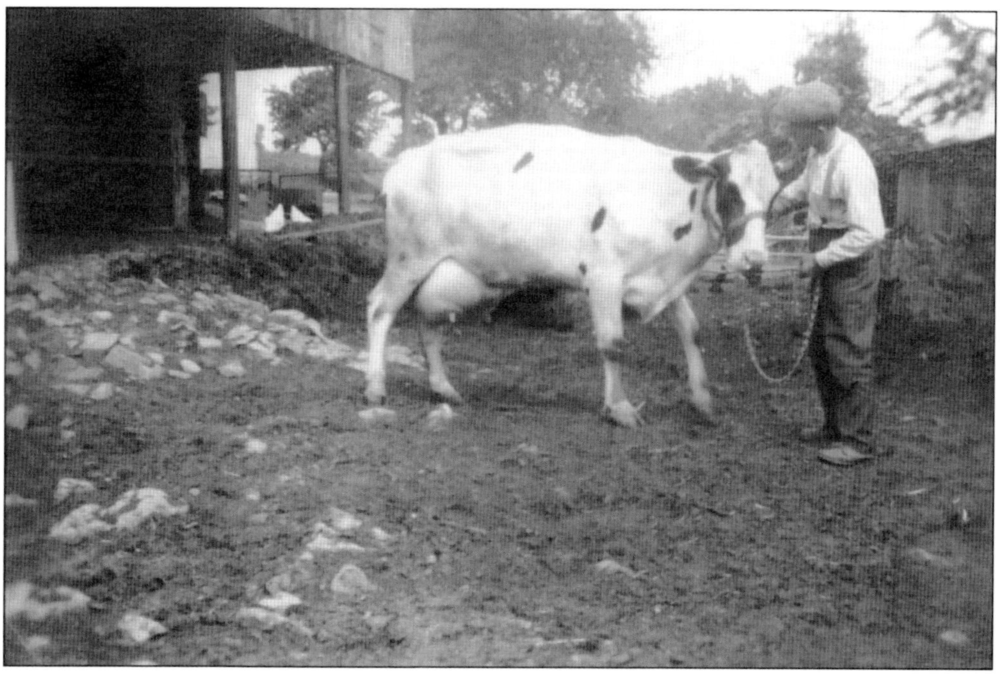

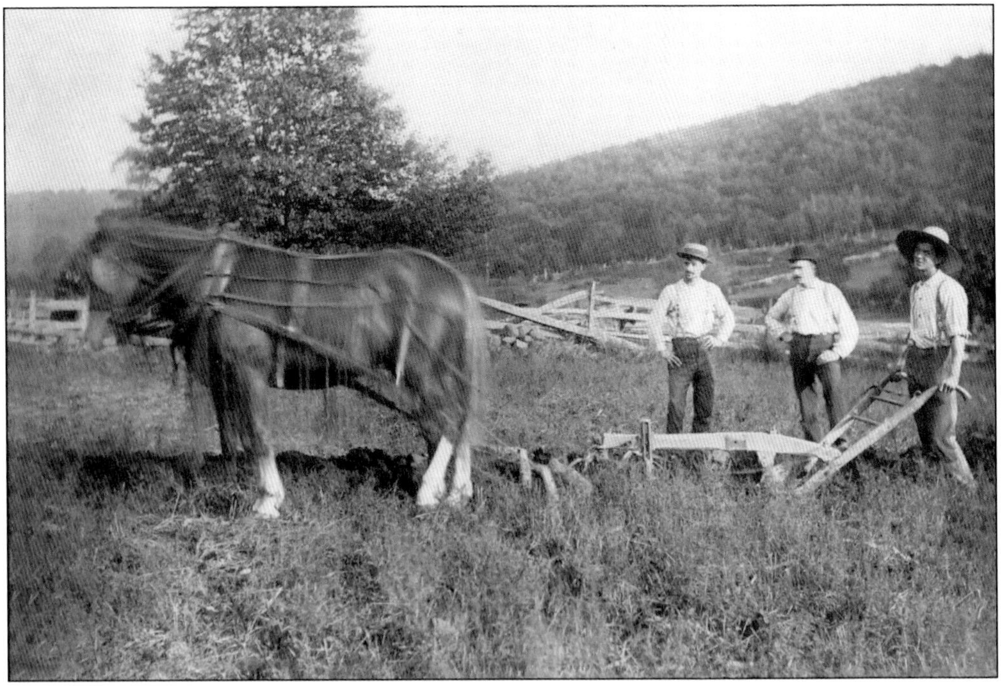

The Miller brothers, from left to right, Amandus, Thomas, and Levi, are shown plowing the fields on their farm in Powder Valley around 1891–1892. Notice the fringes on the horse to chase away the pesky flies. The zigzags or snake fences in the field are typical of the type built by farmers of the time. (Courtesy of Barbara Heist.)

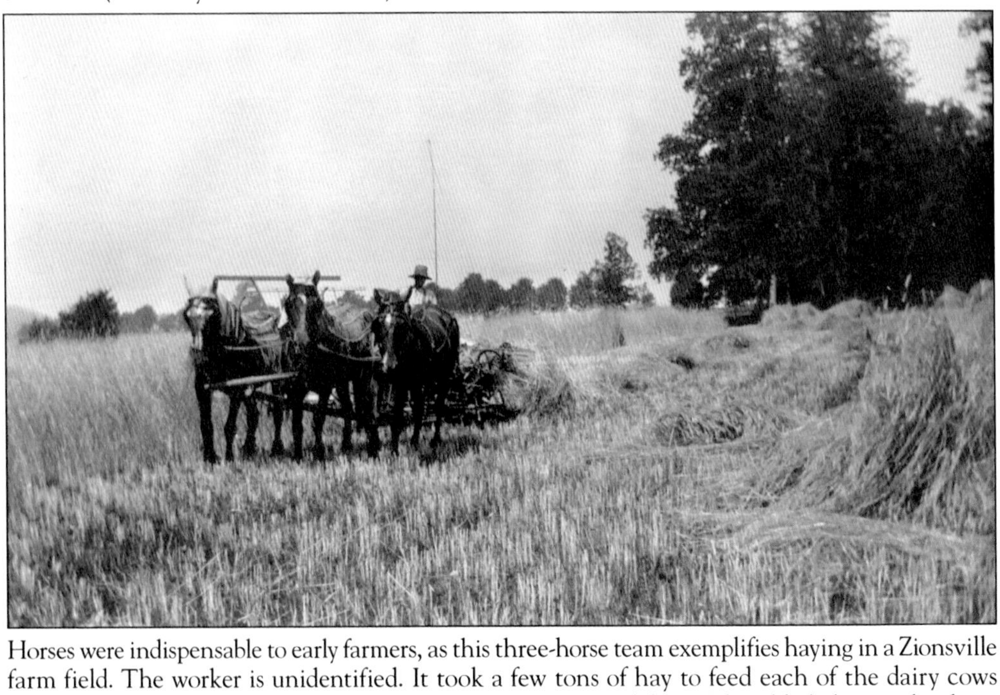

Horses were indispensable to early farmers, as this three-horse team exemplifies haying in a Zionsville farm field. The worker is unidentified. It took a few tons of hay to feed each of the dairy cows and the four to six workhorses during the winter on a typical farm. The old clichés apply: those "workhorses" had to hustle and "make hay while the sun shines." (Courtesy of Barbara Harris.)

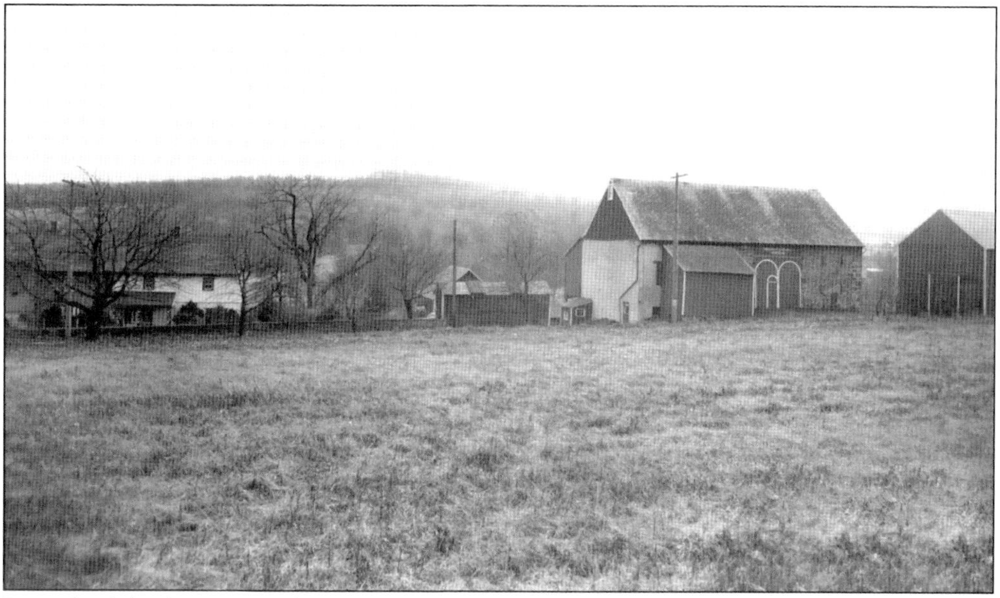

Records of the farm pictured above on Main Road West near Vera Cruz indicate that, in 1835, the land was owned by Charles B. Scheimer of the family after whom Shimerville is named. Readon and Anna (Miller) Frey had the property from 1875 to 1910, and in 1929, Harrison M. and Katie (Frey) Kline became the owners. The Kline family owned the farm for at least 75 years until widowed Katie Kline was forced to sell in 1951. The present-day owner is Vernon F. Goodman. (Courtesy of Larry and Lucille Ackerman.)

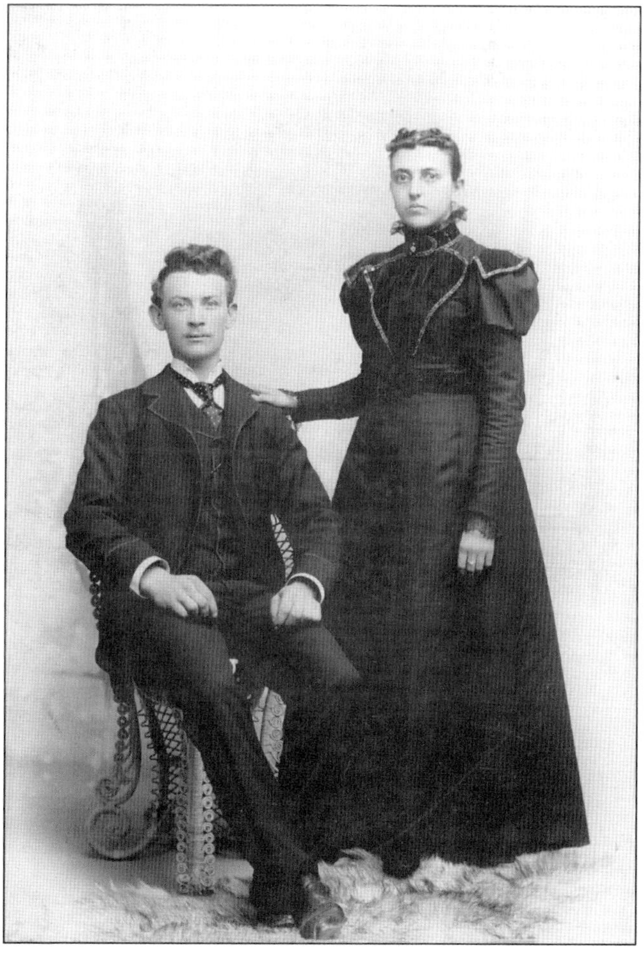

Harrison "Harry" Kline and his wife, Katie, are pictured in their younger years. Katie Kline was the youngest daughter of Readon and Anna Frey and succeeded her parents as owner of the family farm on Main Road West. Their stone English Lake District–style banked barn and rare log-and-stone house still exists. (Courtesy of Larry and Lucille Ackerman.)

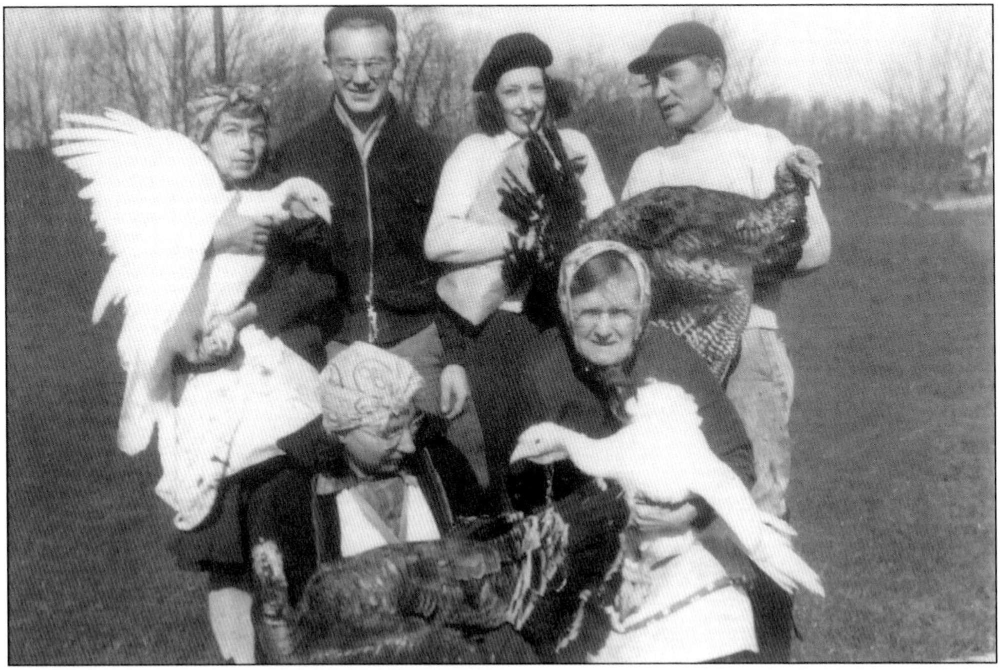

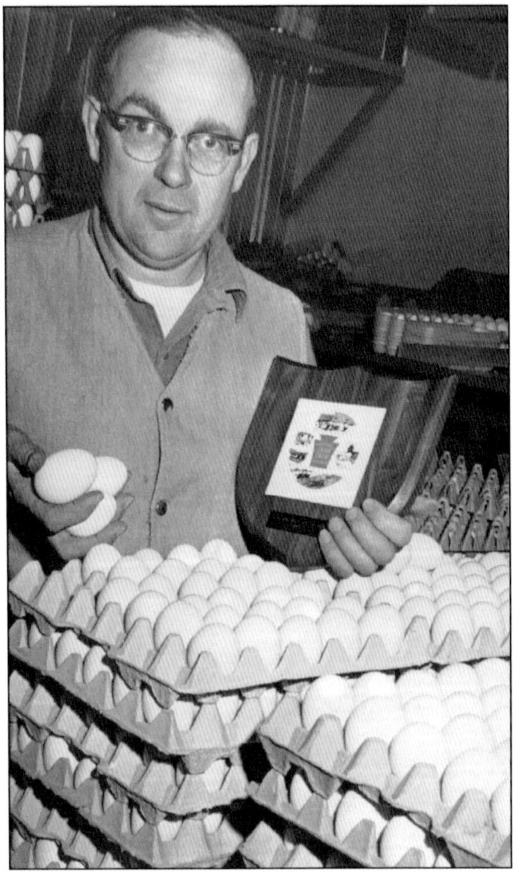

About 1949, Stanley and Edna Helfrich bought property along Church View Road and built a house on it along with six large turkey pens. They began a family business of raising turkeys for market, largely at Thanksgiving and Christmastime. Members worked in the basement of the home to clean the turkeys and ready them for sale. Eventually, all of the buildings were torn down, and the land became the property of the township. Edna Helfrich, on the left in the second row, and Stanley Helfrich, on the right in the second row, are pictured with a few of their unidentified helpers. (Courtesy of Charlene Kehs Reinhard.)

Schell's Egg Ranch in Vera Cruz on Vera Cruz Road South started as a family farm operated by Carl and Ruth-Ann Schell in the 1950s. Shown here proudly displaying his prizewinning eggs, Schell won first place for a dozen white eggs in the 1973 Farm Show in Harrisburg. There were three chicken houses by 1977, with approximately 50,000 chickens on the job. Most customers were local groceries, restaurants, smaller commercial chains, and, of course, area residents. The business closed in 1993. (Courtesy of Richard Gaal.)

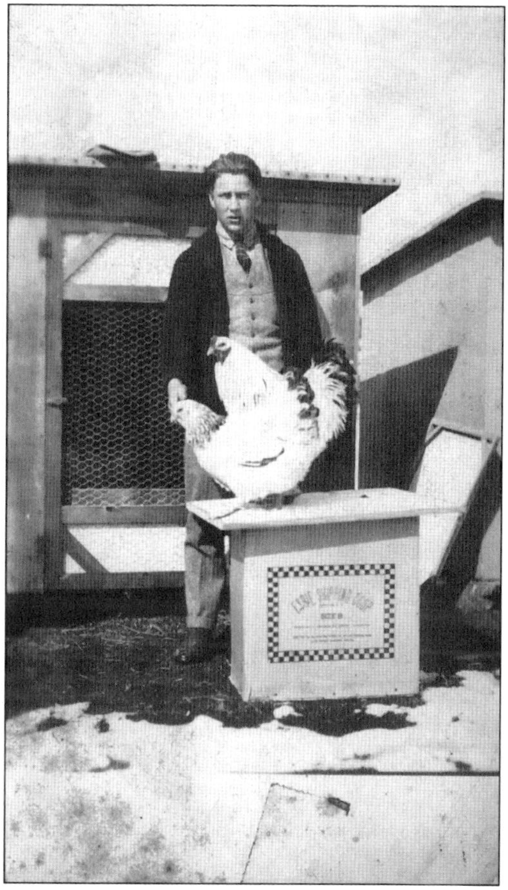

Basil Smith moved from New York to Old Zionsville when he was 12 years old. He lived and worked at Jake Kuhn's poultry farm on Church View Road. Smith's involvement in the poultry business led him into the "expensive hobby" of exhibiting fancy Bantams at fairs throughout eastern Pennsylvania. His highly successful pastime earned him so many champions and so many blue ribbons that he became known as the "Bantam King." (Courtesy of Irene Frederick.)

By 1798, tax records in Upper Milford Township listed 70 barns of various types, such as this Pennsylvania German four bay bank barn on Geissinger Road in Zionsville. It is the type of plan brought to America by the German and Swiss settlers whose first priority was to build a barn for their animals even before a house for the family. Constructed to be functional, long-lived, and bargain-priced, these barns were not meant to be pretty. But some, like this barn, outlived other parts of the farmstead and remain examples of rustic beauty. (Courtesy of Sidney Unser.)

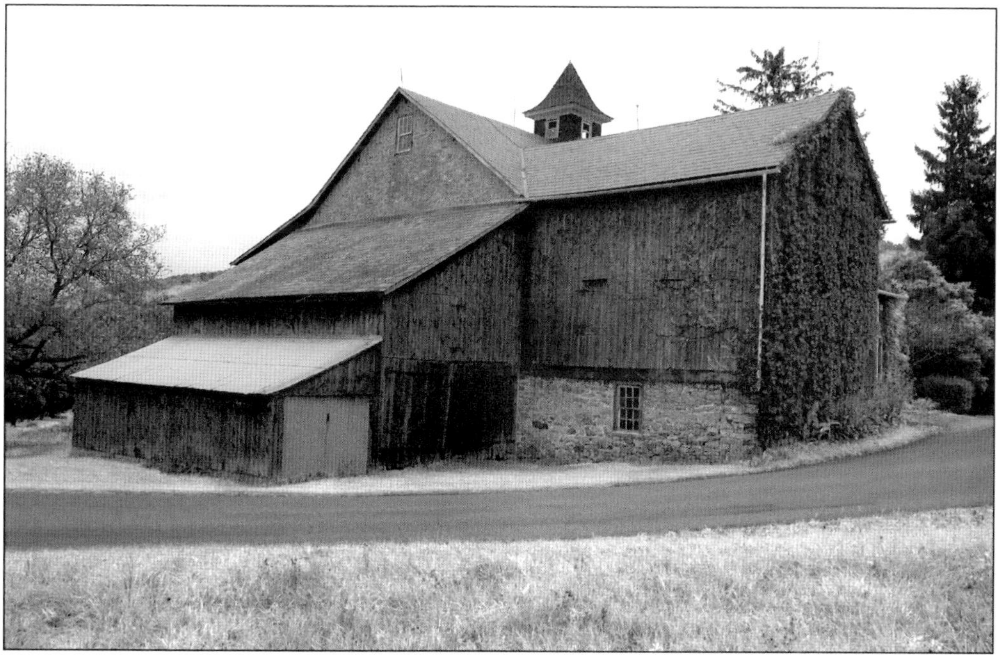

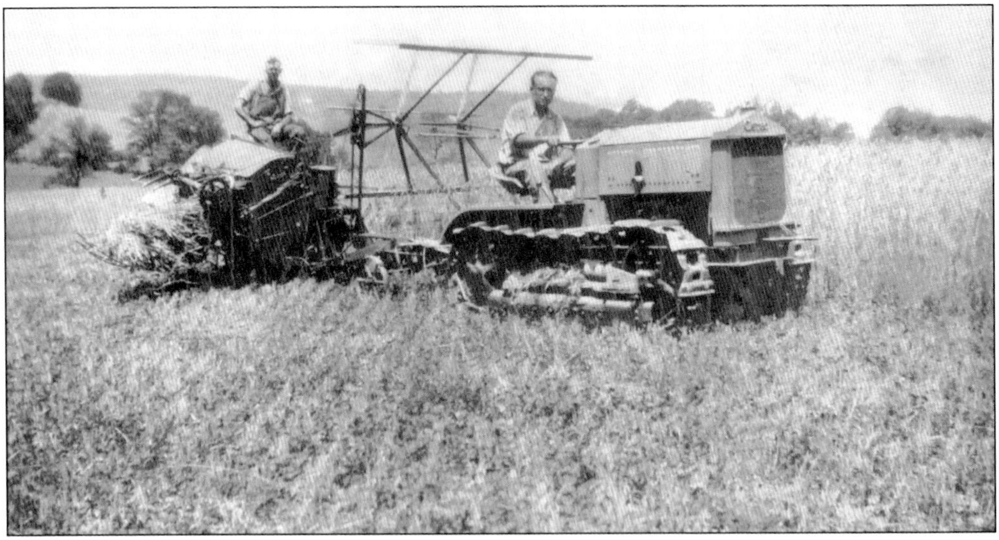

Paul Eschbach worked with Horace Beitler on the Mechling farm on Kings Highway South in Hosensack, now in Lower Milford Township. Eschbach is driving a cleat tractor, and Beitler is riding the wheat binder. The farm produced potatoes, corn, apples, and wheat. Later, this was the picturesque Bradbury farm, often the subject of newspaper photographs featuring beauty spots in rural Upper Milford Township. (Courtesy of Pauline Greulich.)

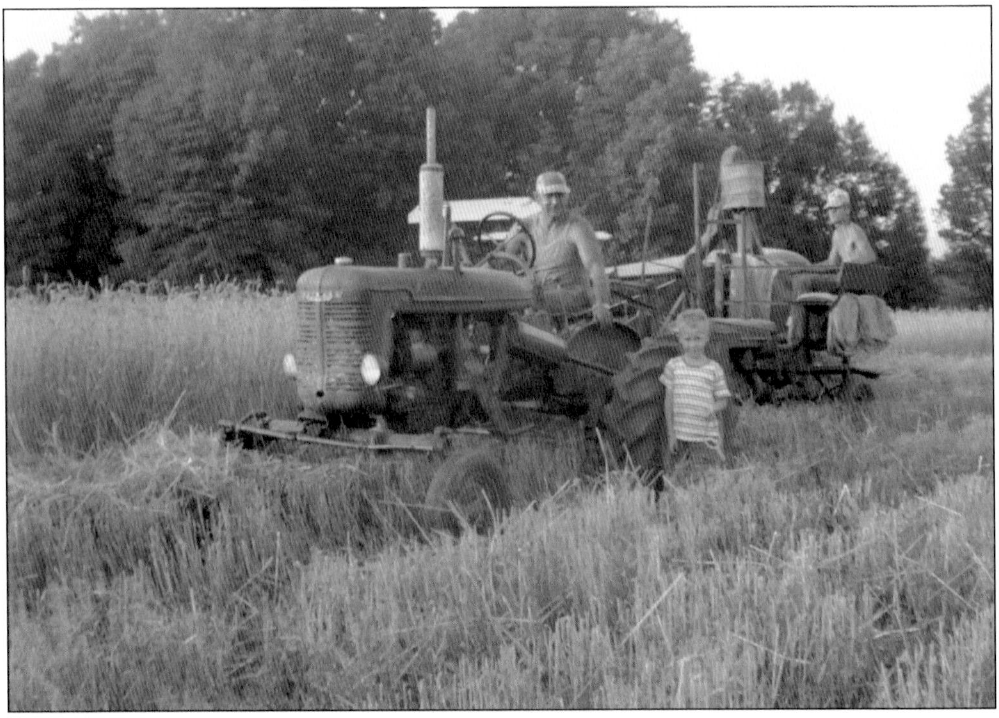

Walter Lichtenwalner is cutting one of the fields on the Thomas Unser farm on Kings Highway North, Route 100. Besides farming, Lichtenwalner also operated a sawmill at his farm in Vera Cruz until his 89th birthday. He was elected an Upper Milford Township supervisor and served as road supervisor. The little boy with the slingshot is Sidney Unser. Today, these fields hold many lovely homes. (Courtesy of Sidney Unser.)

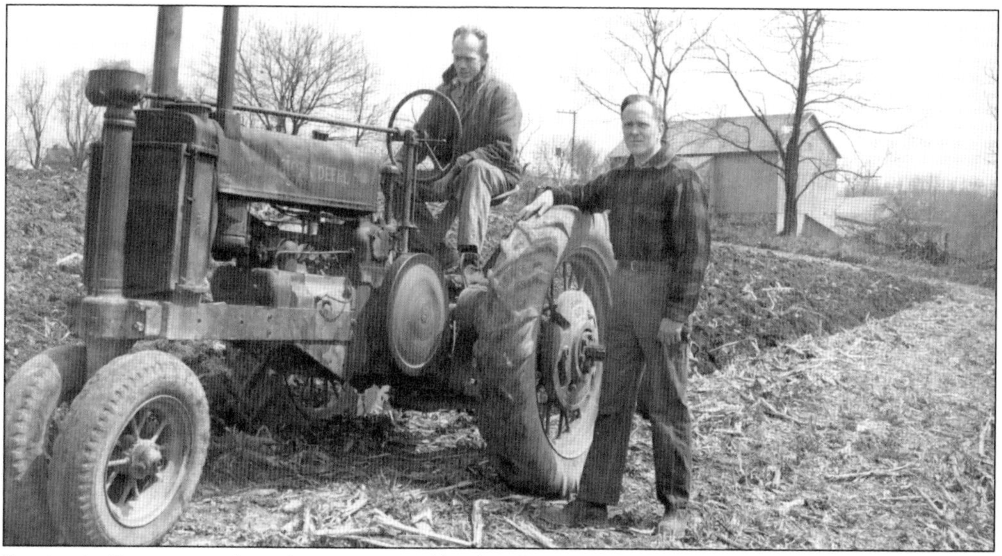

Benjamin Seem, seated on the tractor, and his brother Joseph Seem (standing) operated the Seem Seed Farm on Vera Cruz Road. Benjamin Seem and his wife, Sally, bought the 301-acre farm with five ponds, which were used in their business of raising seed corn. Seem's parents, Charles and Ada, were earlier owners of the property seen below on Church View Road. (Courtesy of Joseph Seem.)

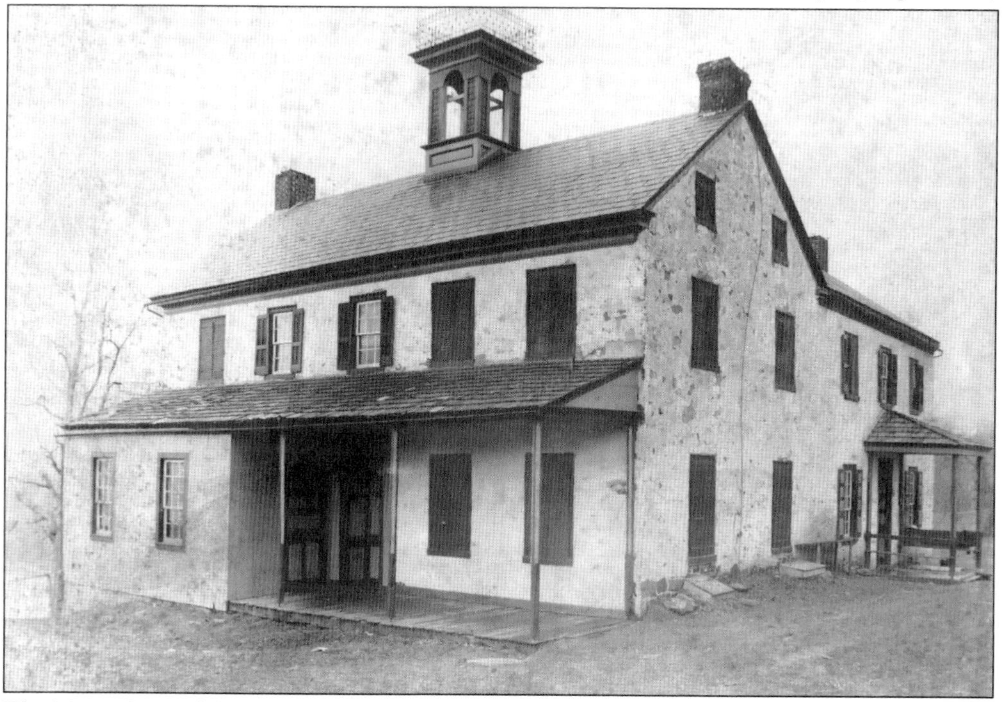

The Meyer (Moyer) family settled on this farm on Church View Road in Zionsville sometime in the mid-18th century and lived here into the early 1900s. Moyer erected a tower on the roof of this house, installed a bell rejected by the local Mennonite group as too worldly, and rang the bell each Sunday before going to church. This property was also once home to the Clauser dairy farm, Charles Seem, and Joseph Seem. Dennis and Linda Moyer currently own it. (Courtesy of Dennis and Linda Moyer.)

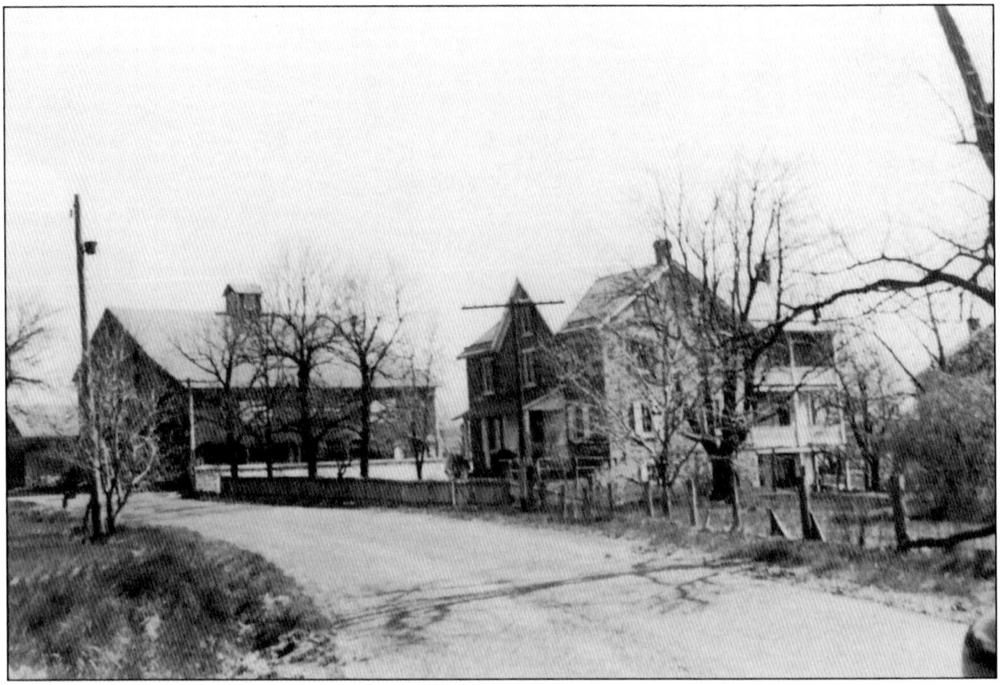

Pictured in the 1920s or 1930s is the Heintzelman farm, the first farm after the railroad tracks on Vera Cruz Road South. The Victorian farmhouse was home to oral surgeon Dr. Richard Covert. When he lived there, he put an addition onto the house. (Courtesy of Barbara Harris.)

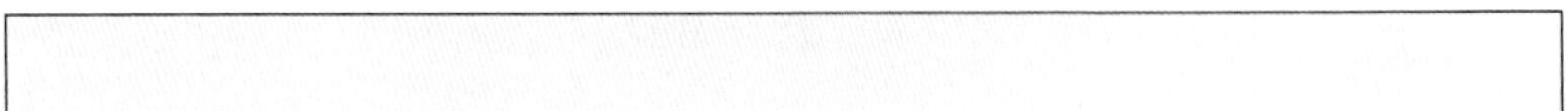

The Amandus R. Schuler farm in Vera Cruz was at the intersection of Main Road West and Vera Cruz Road, the hub of the village. The property is the location of Otterbine Barebo Pumps today. The Schulers were prominent landowners in the early 1900s with this very productive farm as well as the creamery business next to the barn. Years later, when Edward Reichenderfer owned the farm, he did butchering on the property. (UMHS.)

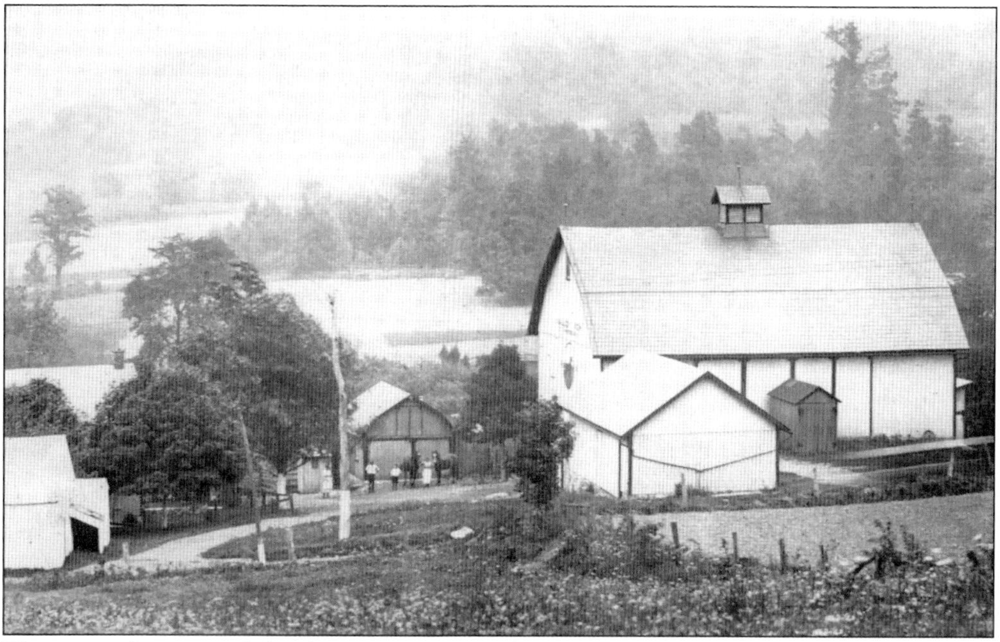

The original owners of this farm on Main Road West in Vera Cruz were Elmer and Almeida Hinnerschietz. The farm passed down to son John Hinnerschietz, his wife, Lillian, and their children John, Terry, and Diane until 1956, when it was sold to Ray Losch. On their farm, Hinnerschietz family members raised cabbage, which was made into sauerkraut using wooden barrels. Much of the sauerkraut was sold at the family food tent at the Great Allentown Fair, along with pork and mashed potatoes, a Pennsylvania German staple. (Courtesy of Diane Hinnerschietz.)

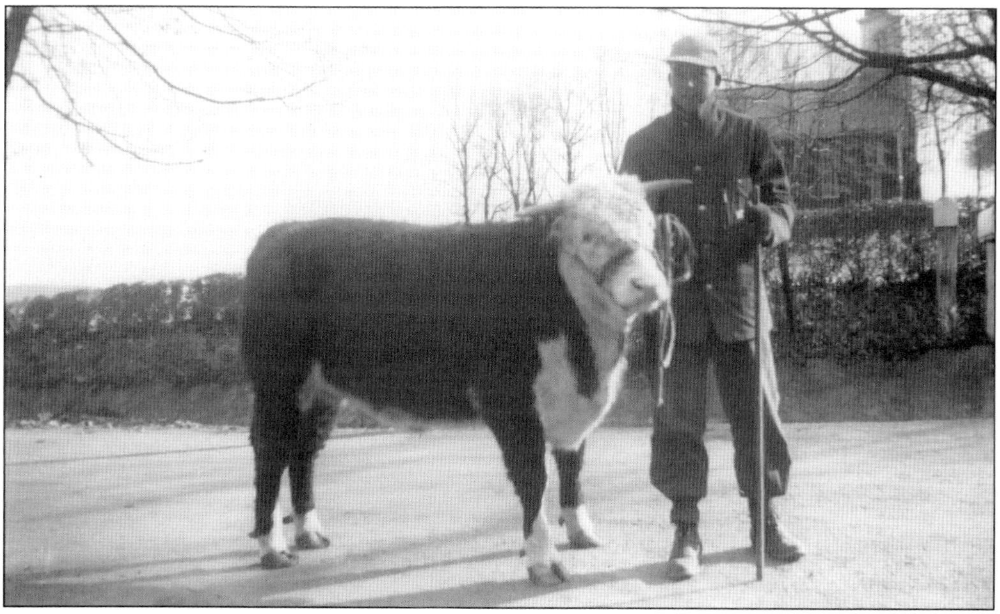

Phillip Geissinger is walking his Hereford bull Jake on Church View Road in Old Zionsville. Bought as a calf from a farmer in Catasauqua, the bull was his 4-H project in 1948. Jake was well fed on corn mash and trained for show. He was eventually taken to the Hatfield Round-Up and sold. (Courtesy of Phillip Geissinger.)

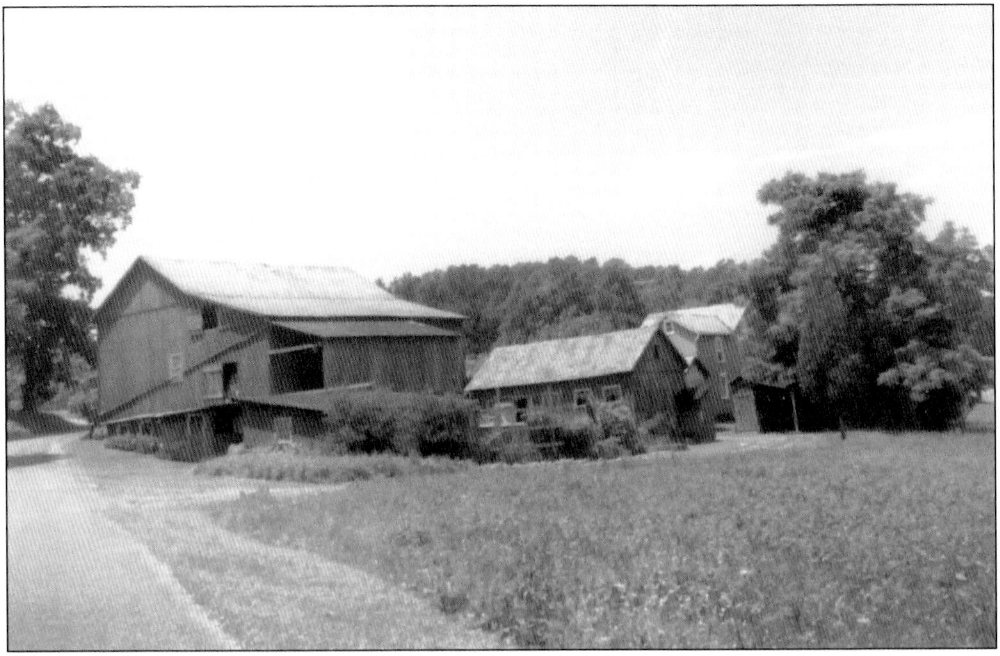

At the age of 30 in 1923, Joseph and Elsie (Kulp) Batman bought the 32-acre farm in Zionsville along Batman Road, which had been built by Howard Layton. There, they operated a successful dairy business. The pictured barn no longer exists, nor does the original log cabin where Batman stored ice in the cellar for his business. (Courtesy of Beulah Miller.)

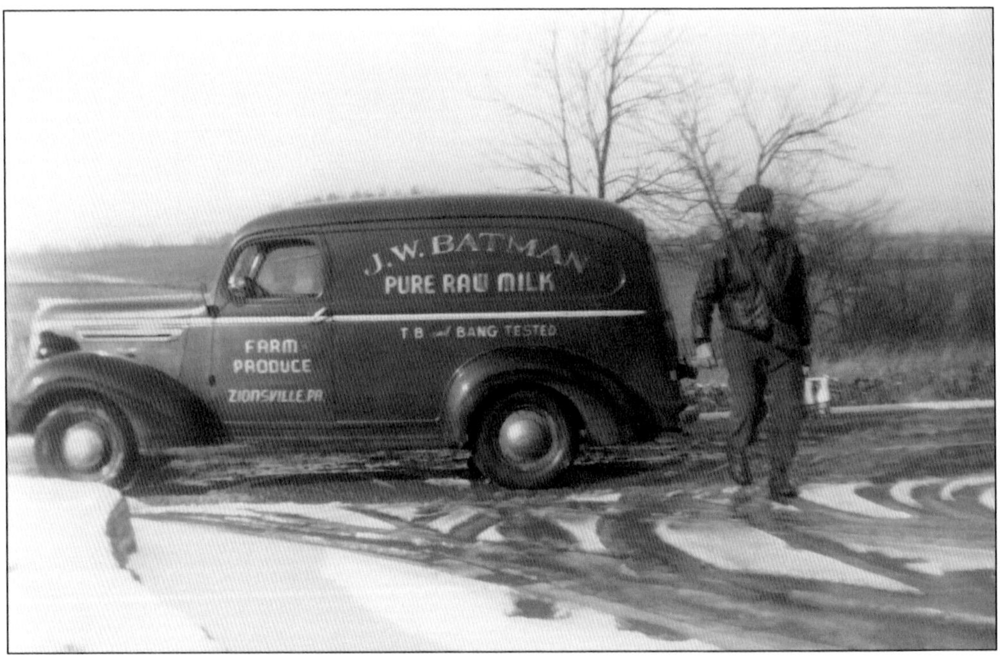

By 1930, Joseph Batman began delivering fresh raw milk via horse and wagon to customers in the Zionsville area. He later purchased the truck pictured to travel his daily route. At the peak of his business, Batman was selling 20 crates of milk per day. He sold the business to Longacre's Dairy in 1953. (Courtesy of Beulah Miller.)

Six

Public Service and Transportation

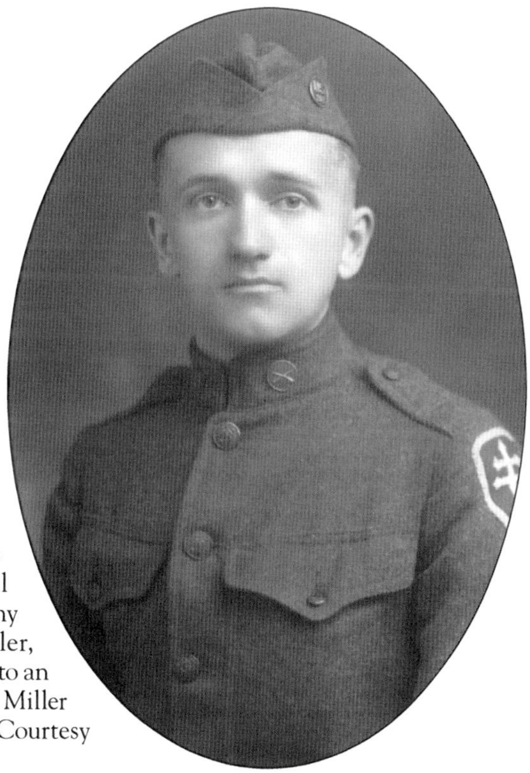

Harry S. Miller took a leave of absence from his responsibilities at the Old Zionsville Post Office from May 1918 to March 1920 to serve in the US Army. During the World War I Meuse-Argonne Offensive, he sustained wounds that kept him in the hospital for 17 months. During that hospitalization time, he was reported to be missing in action. His obituary was published at home and a funeral was held. However, there had been an Army mix-up with Miller names, and this Miller, though scarred, recovered and returned home to an overjoyed family. He went on to continue the Miller family hardware business in Old Zionsville. (Courtesy of Barbara Harris.)

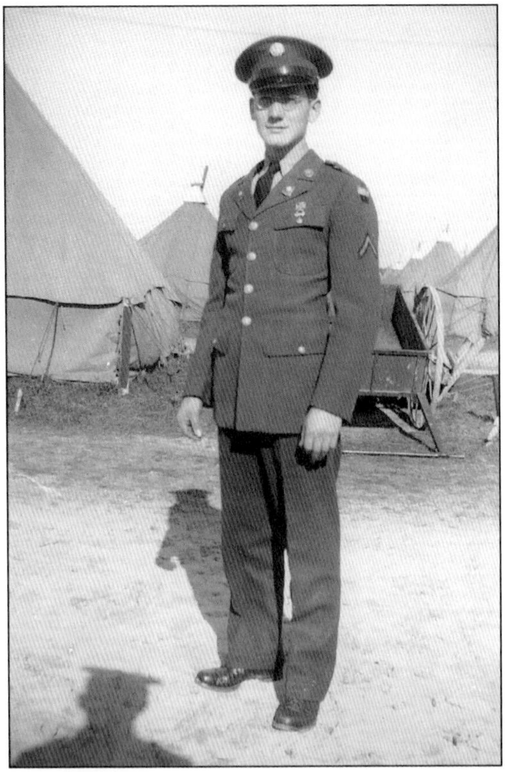

Wallace Worth of Powder Valley joined the Army in 1940 and, by the time he returned to civilian life in 1945, had fought many battles in Germany and sustained a serious head injury. His service earned him many commendations, among them a Purple Heart and eight Combat Stars. In 1950, he returned to service as a platoon commander in the Korean War until 1952. After he finally ended his military service, Worth graduated from Dickinson Law School in 1953 and opened his own law firm. Later, he served as township solicitor for many years. (Courtesy of Eileen Worth.)

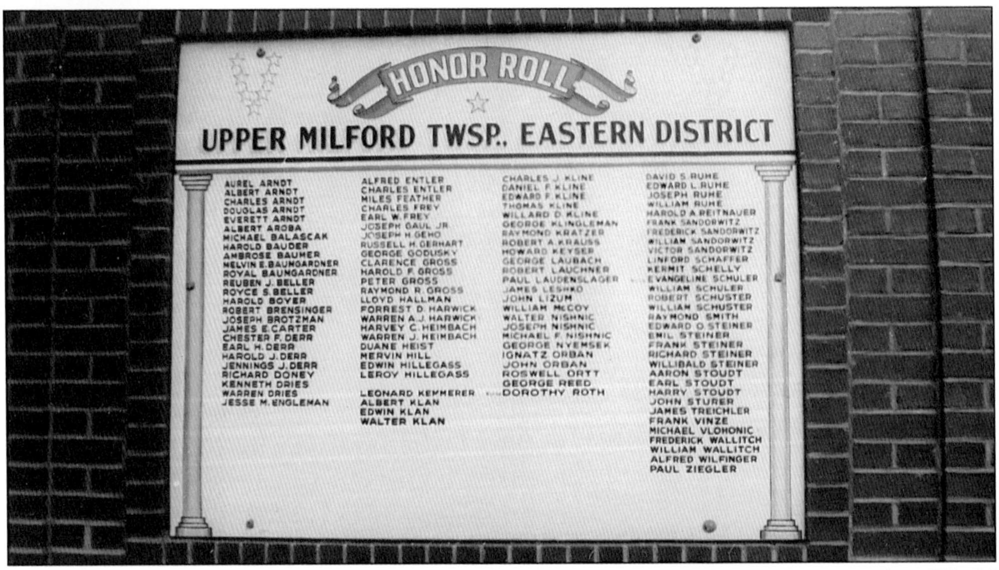

The original Honor Roll listing the names of 107 Vera Cruz residents who served in World War II has disappeared, but fortunately, this photograph of that plaque remains. Just to name a few, Arndt, Derr, Gross, Kline, Nishnic, Ruhe, Sadrovitz, and Steiner are representative of the many sons and two daughters, Evangeline Schuler and Dorothy Roth, who answered the call to serve their country. Notice the large number of families that had more than one member in the military. The community continues to salute these patriots for their service! (Courtesy of Ernest and Kathy Stoudt.)

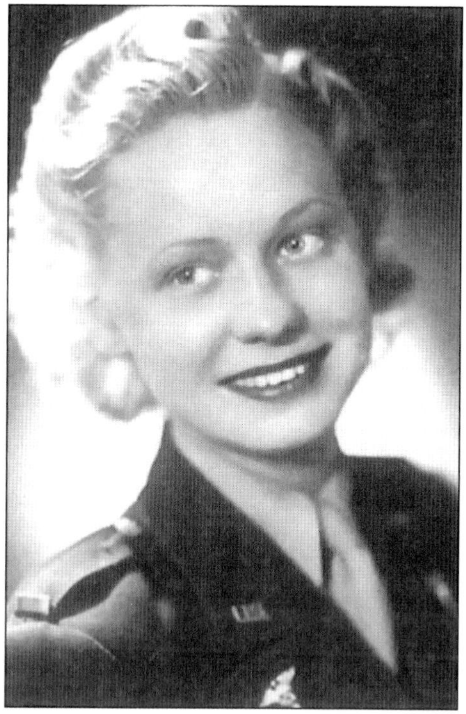

Born in Vera Cruz, the daughter of Wharton and Gertrude Schuler, Evangeline Schuler Coeyman graduated from St. Luke's School of Nursing in 1941. She joined the World War II Army Nursing Corps in 1942 and was assigned to the 59th Field Hospital of the 90th Infantry Division, a mobile unit. 2nd Lieutenant Coeyman served behind the front lines in the European Theater, treating wounded soldiers as the hospital followed General Patton's army across Europe. She witnessed the horrors of two concentration camps, Gosen and Mauthausen. After her discharge in 1945, Coeyman received a master's degree in education at Temple University and a bachelor's degree in nursing from the University of Pennsylvania all the while continuing her career with St. Luke's Hospital in Bethlehem as an instructor in medical/surgical nursing. Coeyman retired in 1989 after 40 years of nursing. (Both, courtesy of Evangeline Schuler Coeyman.)

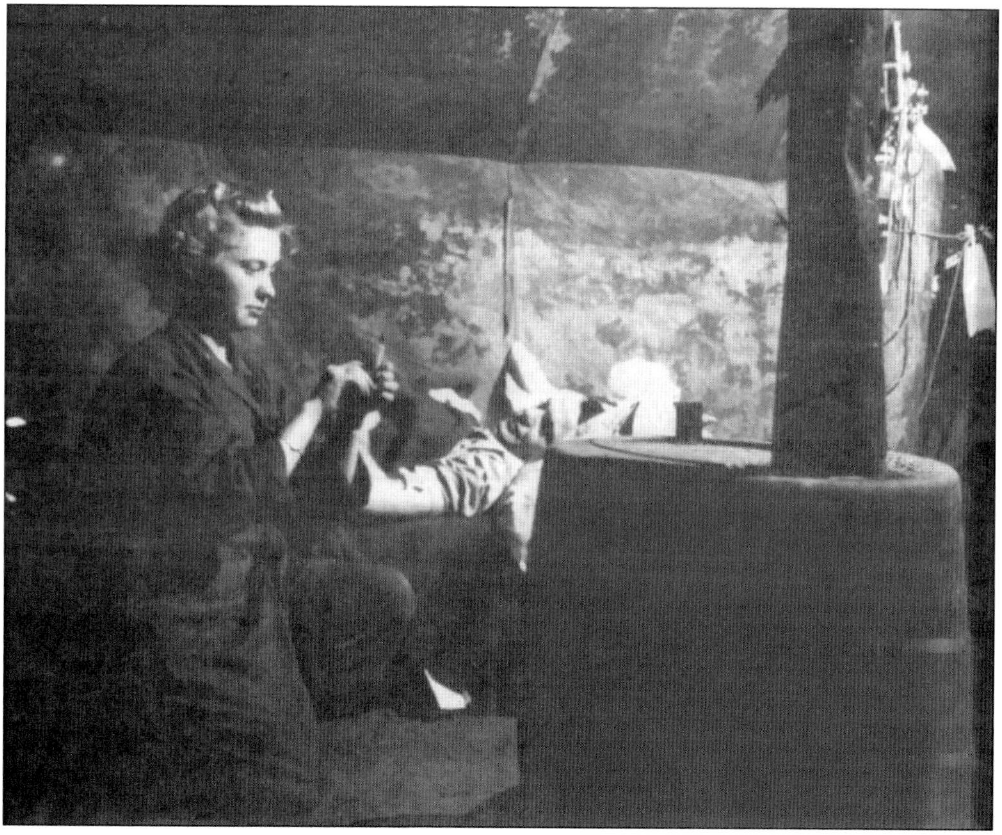

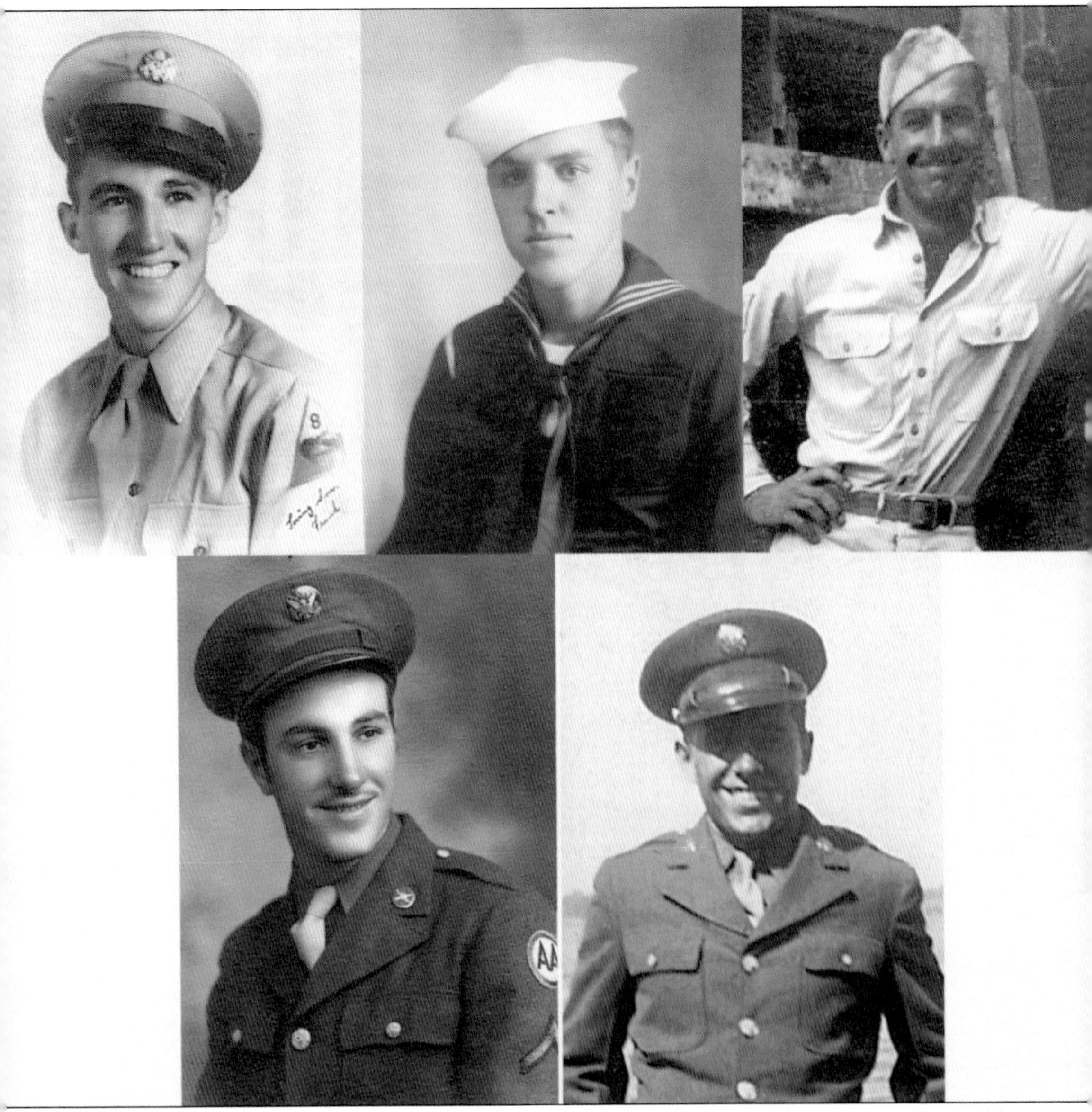

Victor and Angela Sadrovitz of Vera Cruz had five sons who served their country honorably in World War II, giving Angela the rare distinction of being a "Five Star Mother." Clockwise from upper left, Frank was with the 8th Armored Division, 3342 Quarter Master Division, 49th Armored Infantry in the European Theater, 1943–1946; The only Navy man, Seaman 1st Class Walter was on ships in the Pacific Theater, 1944–1946; Frederick was a construction machine operator in the Philippines and Luzon, 1942–1945; Victor Jr. was a medical aid serving in the European Theater, 1943–1946; and Staff Sergeant William served in Battery A, 559th Coast Artillery Battalion in France and Central Europe, 1943–1946. All of the brothers earned many medals during their service. (Courtesy of Frank Sadrovitz.)

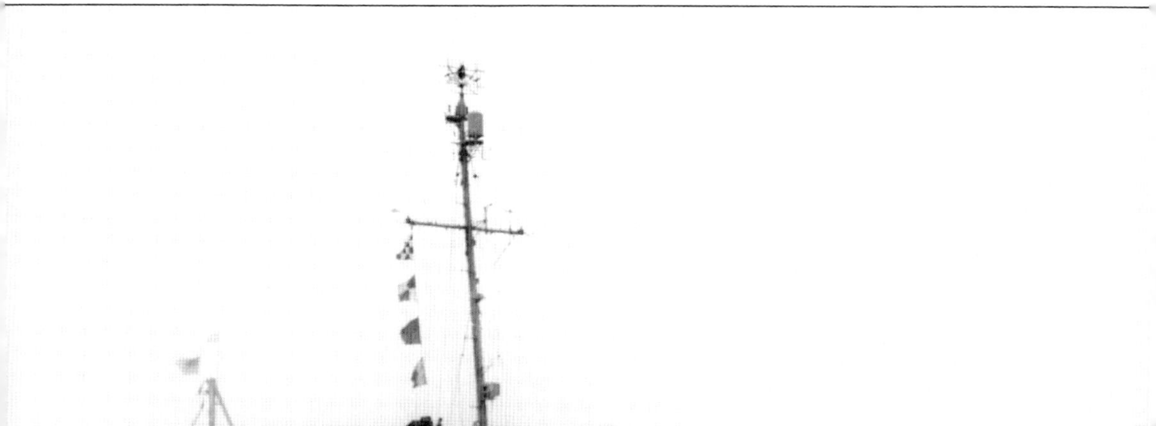

Charles Kleinsmith was born September 28, 1904, to Quinn C. and Emma (Doney) Kleinsmith of Old Zionsville. He first enlisted in the Navy on October 26, 1922, and reenlisted at five different times over more than 17 years. During the Battle of Midway, June 4, 1942, Chief Water Tender Kleinsmith and his crew maintained auxiliary power on the USS *Yorktown* despite stifling fumes, intense heat, and the imminence of explosion resulting from a bombing attack. His devotion to duty enabled the aircraft carrier to continue fighting and to launch its own attack. At the end of the battle, the *Yorktown* sank, and Kleinsmith went missing. To recognize his heroism, this Old Zionsville native was awarded the Navy Cross posthumously, and the Crosley-class high-speed transport pictured was named the USS *Kleinsmith* (APD-134). Launched January 27, 1945, in Michigan, the ship was decommissioned May 16, 1960, and transferred to the Republic of China until its final decommissioning about 1997. The *Kleinsmith* was used in the making of *The Frogmen* film with Dana Andrews and Richard Widmark. (Courtesy of Edward Zajkowski, NavSource.)

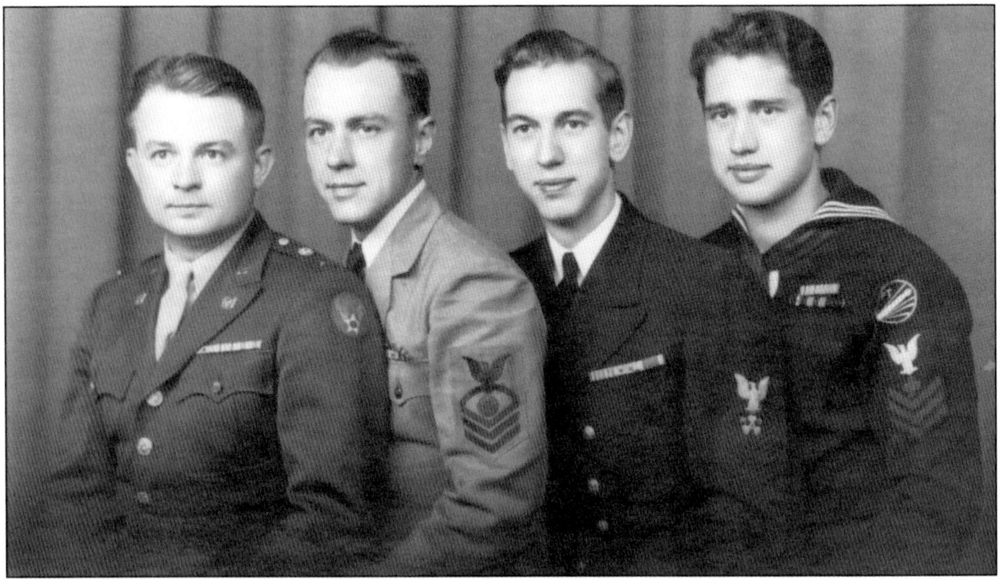

Oscar and Agnes Stauffer moved to Upper Milford Township in 1916 beginning a long line of Stauffers in the area. Four of their son Howard's children from Old Zionsville served in the military. From left to right, Richard E. Stauffer had a distinguished career in the Army Signal Corps and in the Air Force as chief warrant officer, communications specialist, 1934–1958, and among his many decorations was a citation from Pres. Harry S. Truman "for difficult tasks performed during World War II;" Albert E. Stauffer served in the US Navy as chief petty officer, electrician mate, 1936–1945; Ralph G. Stauffer was in the US Navy as chief petty officer, machinist mate, 1943–1945; Howard C. Stauffer served in the US Navy as 1st class petty officer, pharmacist mate, 1942–1946. (Courtesy of Wallace and MaryAnn Stauffer.)

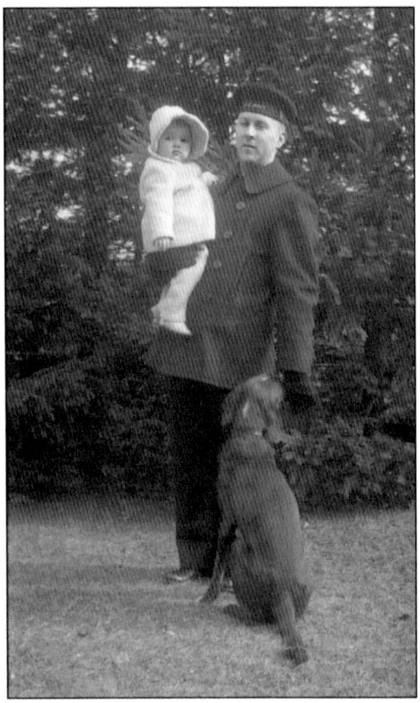

Thomas Unser of Kings Highway North served in the US Navy during World War II. Here, he was home on leave enjoying time with baby daughter Patricia and the family pet. Unser served the township first as secretary and then as supervisor for 26 years through 1985. Other township supervisors at or before Unser's time were James H. Heil, William H. Rupp, Horace S. Miller, Paul S. Schreiber, Walter H. Lichtenwalner, Harvey E. Schlicher, Wilbur S. Schultz, Albert D. Schell, and Paul D. Christman. (Courtesy of Sidney Unser.)

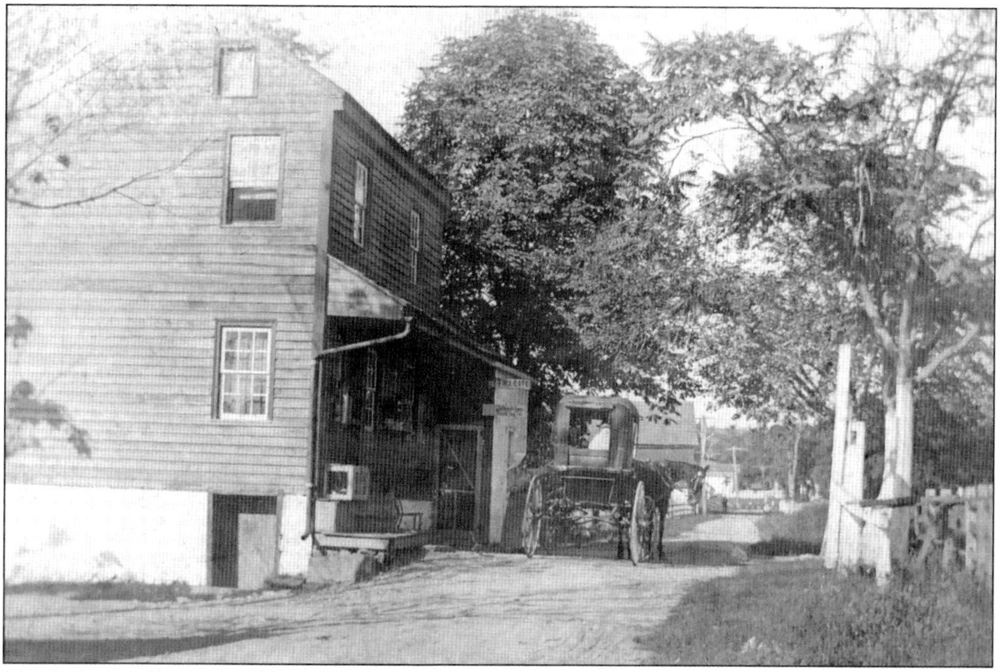

Until 1919, tollgates, such as this one at Treichlersville (Hereford), were all along four miles of the Lehigh/Berks County Turnpike from Shimerville to Hereford, now Route 29/100. Charles Y. Yoder's horse and buggy stopped to pay the 9¢ toll. A post barred the road until the toll had been paid, and keepers often had to bear abuse from travelers for the fee. In 1908, a single-seat automobile cost 10¢ and a double seat cost 20¢ to pass. (Courtesy of Ruth Yoder-Taylor.)

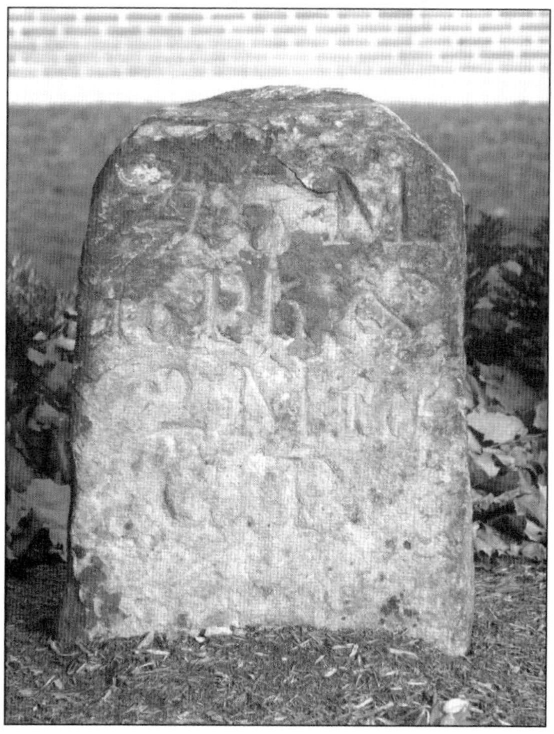

In the 1700s, the government placed stone mile markers, as pictured, one mile apart along the Kings Highway to inform early travelers of the distance from that point to Philadelphia. The markers were generally 24 inches high, 18 inches wide, and six inches thick. Most of these stones have disappeared. However, two existing markers have been preserved for the township through the foresight and generosity of Esther Martin and Dorothy Nicholas. Look for these mile markers, not gravestones, in front of the township municipal building in the landscaping done by Steven Lapp as an Eagle Scout project. (Courtesy of Sidney Unser.)

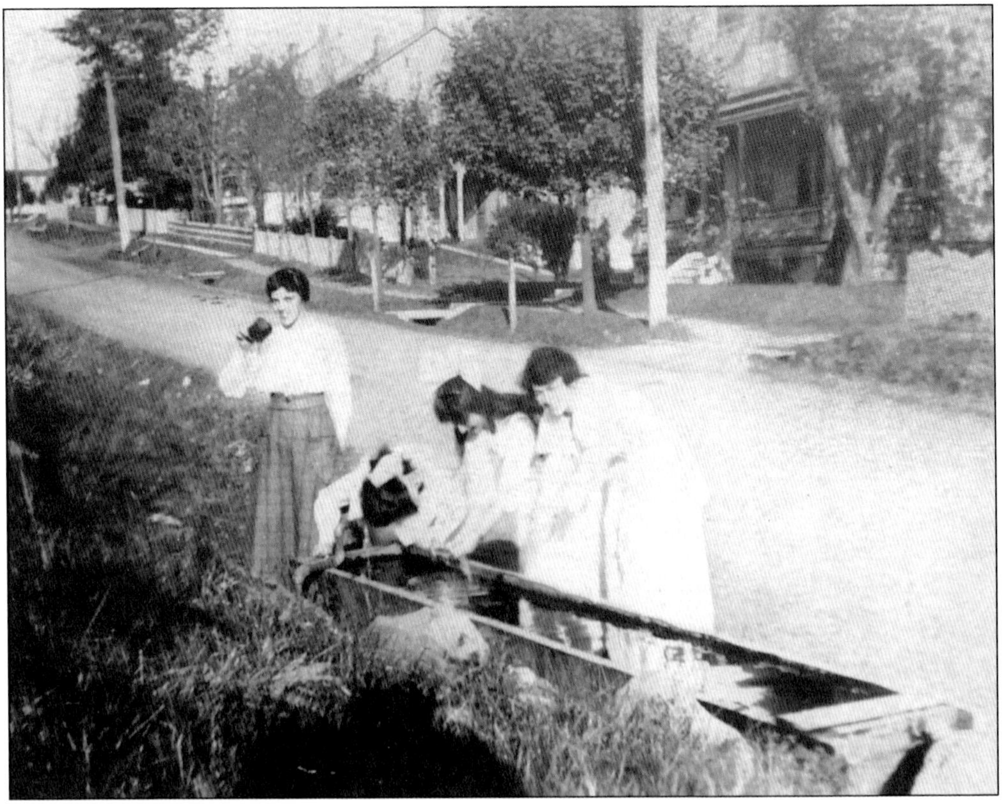

Before the memorial was built on Fountain Road in Old Zionsville, there was a trough to catch overflow water from the spring, which provided water for travelers and their horses. Seen here about 1916 enjoying a refreshing drink with friends from the spring is Ella (Miller) Schreiber, on the left with a cup. (UMHS.)

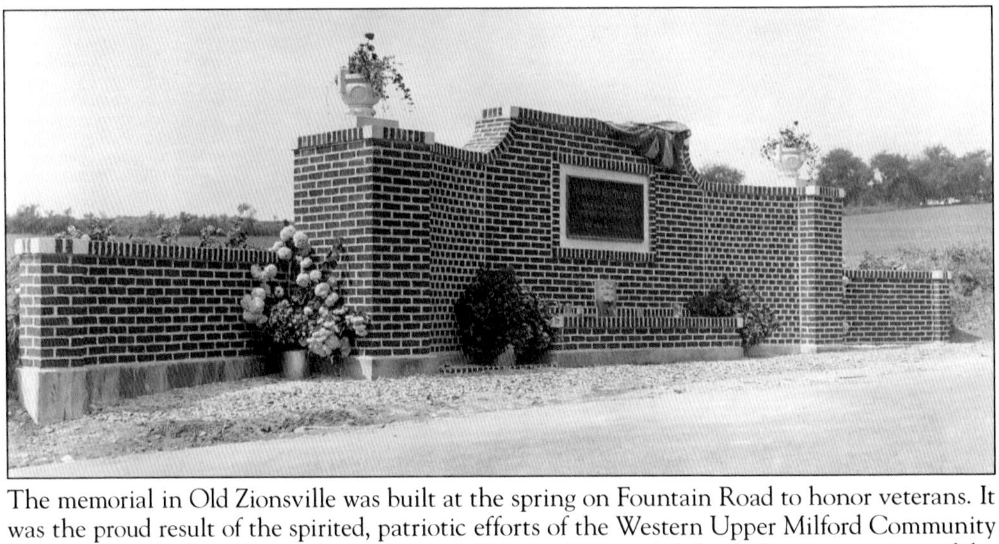

The memorial in Old Zionsville was built at the spring on Fountain Road to honor veterans. It was the proud result of the spirited, patriotic efforts of the Western Upper Milford Community Association, which no longer exists. About 2,000 people attended the dedication program of the memorial on May 21, 1922. Later, the water from the fountain was declared unfit for drinking, and the fountain was closed in 1980. (UMHS.)

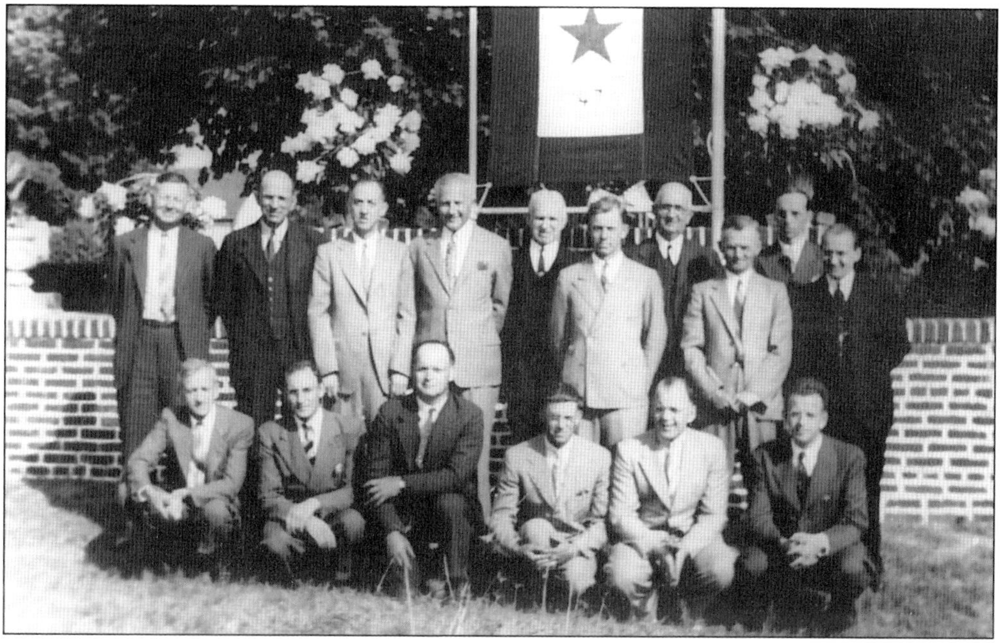

World War II air raid wardens and community leaders gathered at the Memorial Fountain in Old Zionsville about 1943. Pictured are, from left to right, (kneeling) Harry Miller, Earle Fegely, Paul Berger, Albert Hiestand, Wilmer Kline, and Warren Treichler; (standing) Readen Schantz, Clarence Mohr, Dallas Carl, Henry Snyder, Rev. James Blatt, Leonard Serfass, Rev. David Kauffman, Howard Stauffer, Dallas Gackenbach, Rev. Gordon, and W.J. Oplinger. (Courtesy of Shirley Walbert.)

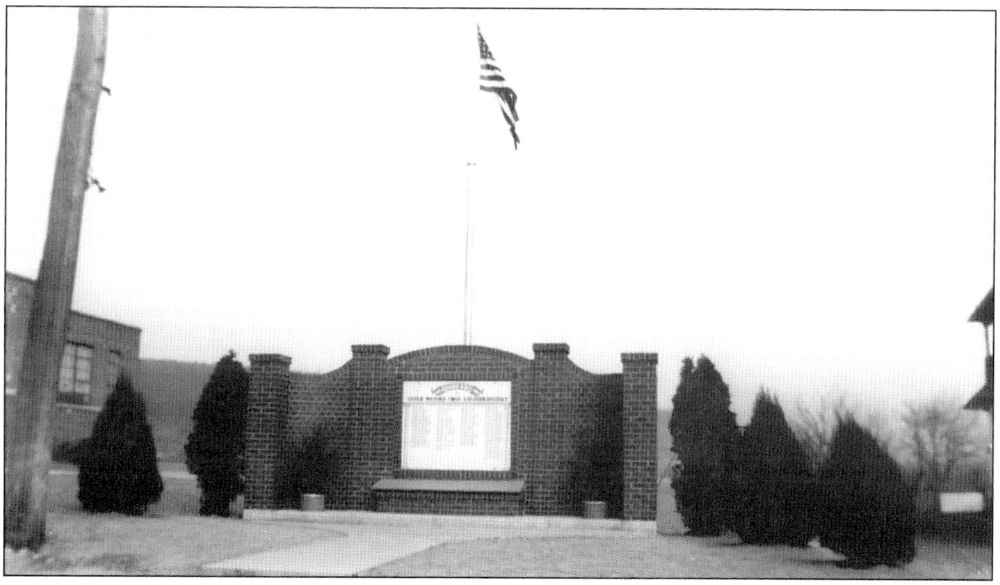

The monument to honor Vera Cruz area veterans stands next to the old Vera Cruz School. It was dedicated December 12, 1943, and listed the names of 103 men and two women. Additional names of residents who served in the military were added, but the list became too long over time. Therefore, the names were removed sometime before 1951 and generalized wording recognizing veterans was put in its place, as seen on the scaled-down present-day monument. (UMHS.)

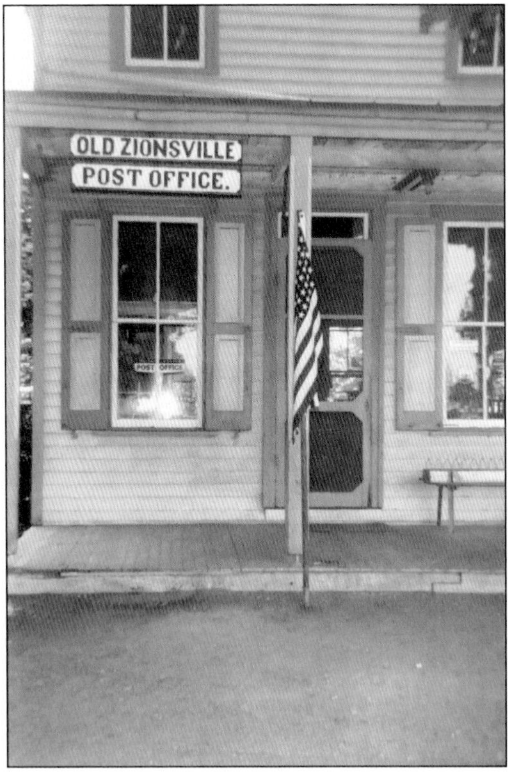

The post office on Kings Highway in Old Zionsville was provided a small room to the left of the front door in the M.J. Miller and Son Hardware Store from 1898 to 1971. Before that, the office had been in the local store, as was the custom in the early 1900s. In October 1971, the post office was relocated to its current location in the Municipal Building on Church View Road, Old Zionsville. (Courtesy of Henry Beitler.)

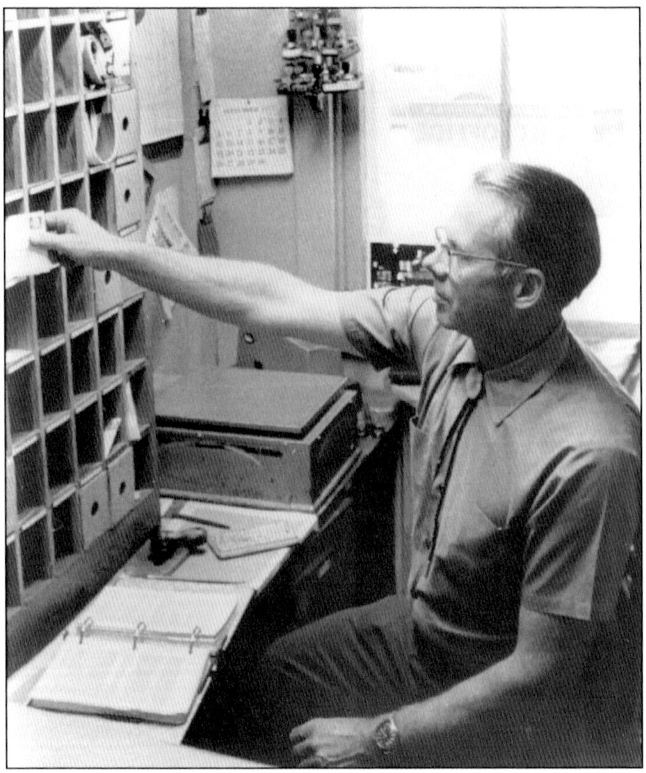

Postmaster Henry Beitler is shown putting the last letter in a resident's box at the Old Zionsville Post Office in the M.J. Miller and Son Hardware Store before the post office was moved to the Municipal Building. Beitler was postmaster in Old Zionsville from 1960 to 1987. Born and raised in the township, Beitler was a decorated Scoutmaster for 50 years. He continues as a church and community leader into his 90s. (UMHS.)

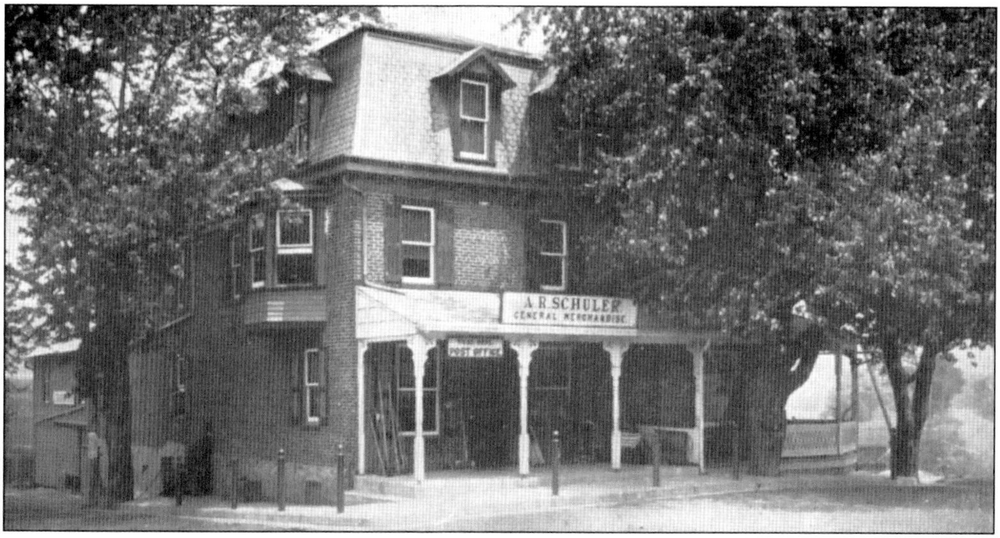

When the post office in Vera Cruz was established in 1861, it was located in the store building at the northeast corner of the crossroads. Alexander Weaver was the storekeeper at the time, and Charles Bernhard was the postmaster. The building has largely been a general store through these many years with many proprietors. Among some of the owners were Schuler, Reese, Heist, Roth, Remaley, Knauss, Utsch, and Kline. Today, it houses a pizza business. (UMHS.)

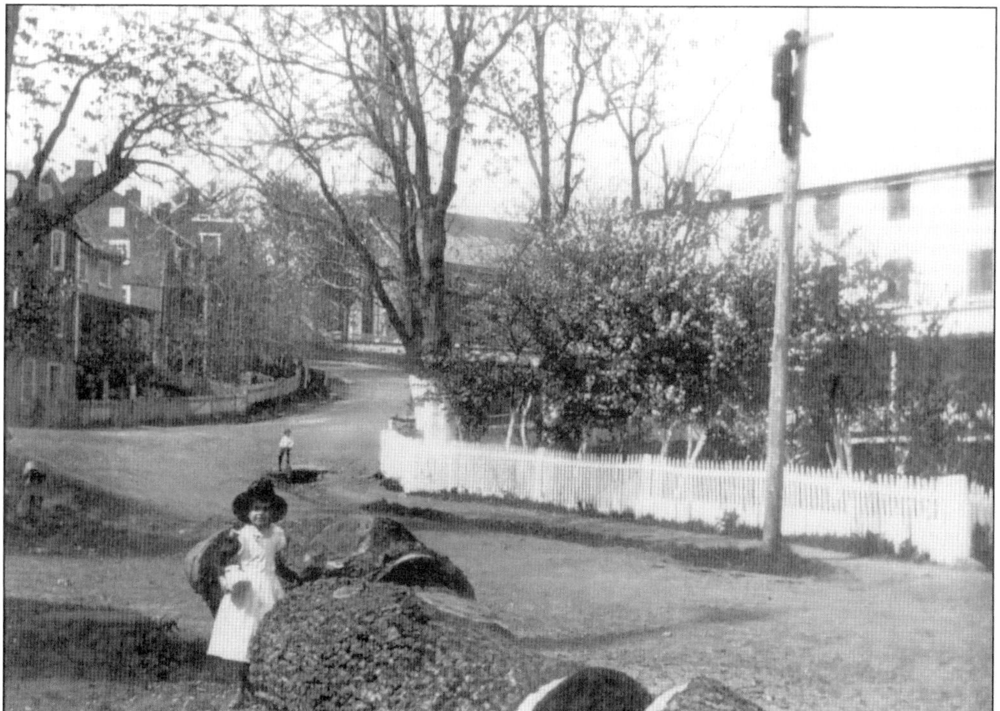

This portion of Old Zionsville, pictured around 1870s, is on Kings Highway near the old hardware store/post office building. Rupp's (Carl's) Store is on the right, and the UCC Church is on the left. Remember the telegraph? The focus of the photograph is the person on the utility pole installing a telegraph line. The child is Edna May Weaver at eight. (Courtesy of Richard Malburg.)

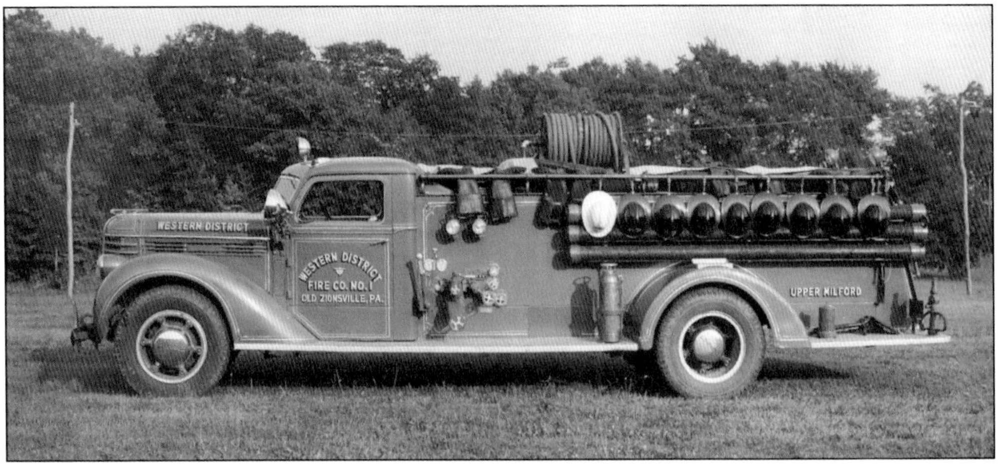

This Diamond T truck was originally a coal truck converted into a fire truck for the Western District Fire Company No. 1. It was housed in a garage owned by Irwin Sell, located next to where the current station was built on Route 29/100 in 1952. The first meeting of the all-volunteer company when it separated from the Vera Cruz Company was held in the Reformed Church on March 26, 1942. At that time, 37 members joined, but by April, 68 new members had joined, and by May 25, the company had been granted a charter. (Courtesy of Western District Fire Company.)

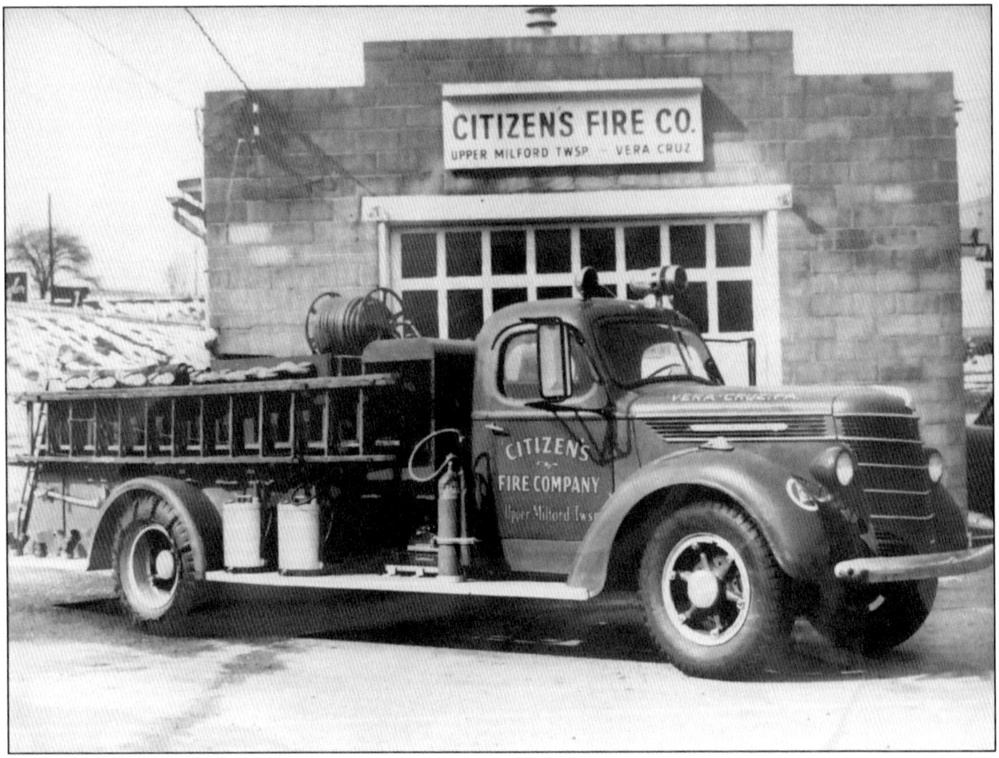

The Vera Cruz Fire Company's first fire truck was a truck chassis mounted with a military surplus pump. In 1957, a two-way radio was added to the truck, and in 1962, the surplus pump from the truck was transferred to a new GMC truck chassis. In 1983, the fire company got its first brand-new, factory-made truck, a Hahn pumper, for $109,000; it was an additional $20,000 for equipment. (Courtesy of Vera Cruz Fire Company.)

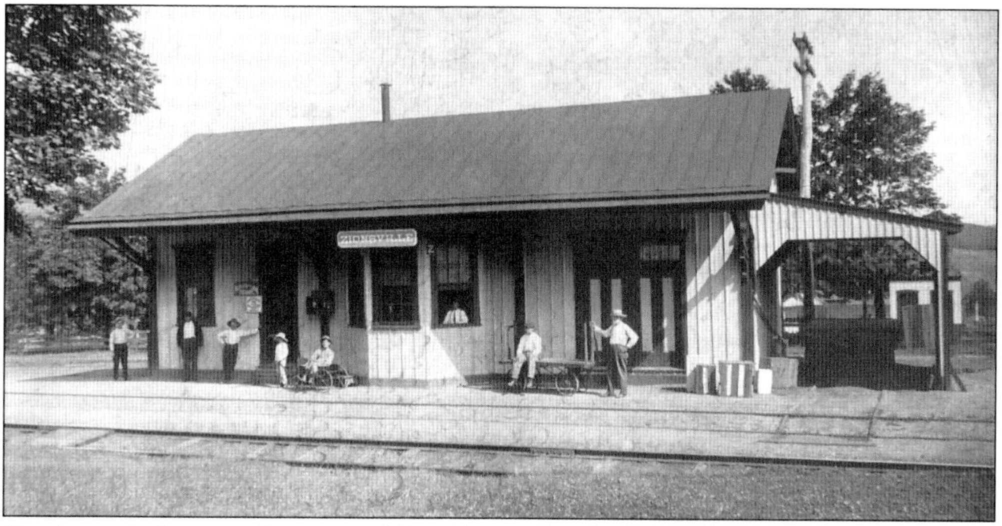

On the tracks between Emmaus and East Greenville, the Zionsville Railroad Station was the busiest stop. It was a large combination depot servicing both freight and passengers to the area. When the Perkiomen Railroad built this station in 1876, a hotel, a store, and houses soon followed, and the village of Zionsville was born. Four trains ran each way on weekdays and two trains each way on Sundays. (UMHS.)

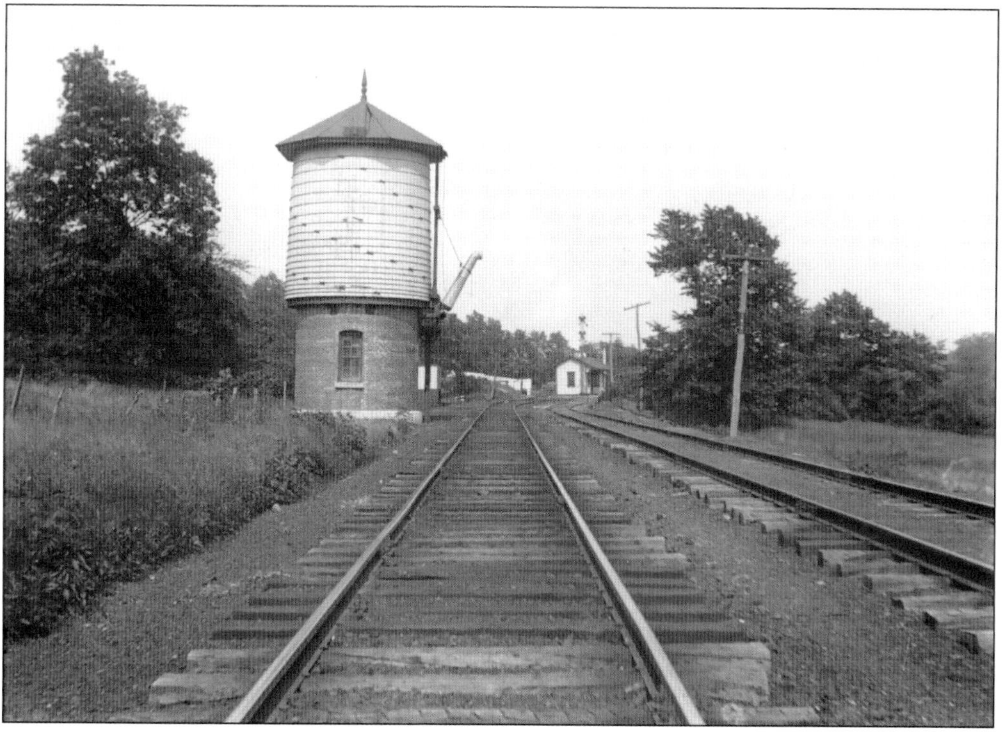

This metal-and-brick water tower stood a short distance down the tracks from the Vera Cruz Railroad Station in the days of steam locomotives. In the photograph, the tower stands as a great sentinel beside the tracks waiting for a locomotive to enter the siding, screech to a halt, take on water, and noisily steam away. With the coming of diesels, its usefulness was gone, and only remnants of the water tower's base remain. (Courtesy of Joseph Benner.)

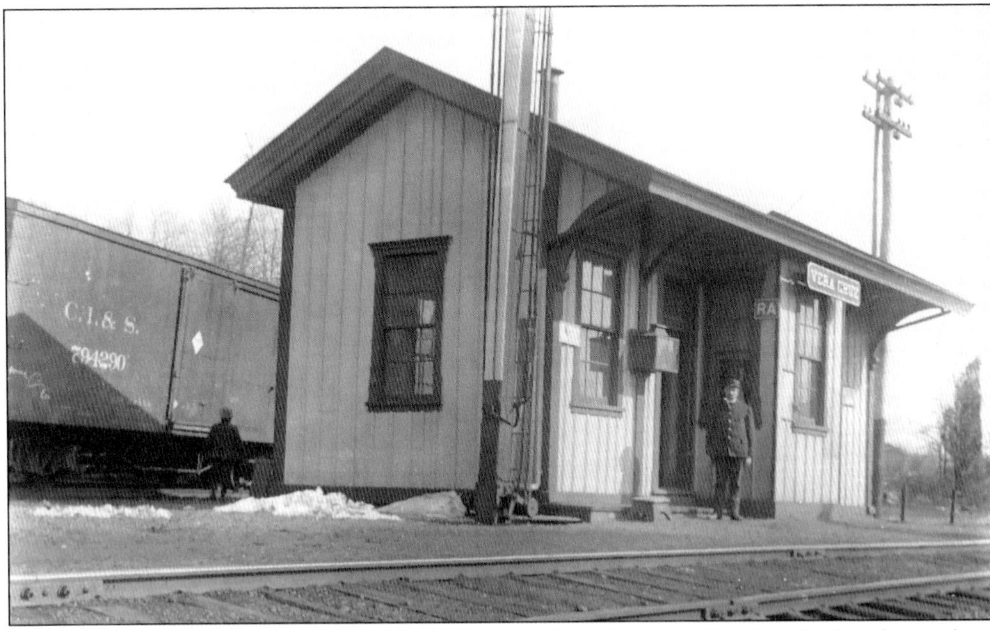

The Vera Cruz Railroad Station on the Perkiomen Branch of the Reading Railroad was about one mile east of the village. Henry Souders was station agent there for more than 30 years, and his son Howard was with the railroad for 51 years. The last station agent was Oscar P. Kuhns, who served 18 years in Vera Cruz and worked for the company 41 years. The station closed July 1, 1932. (UMHS.)

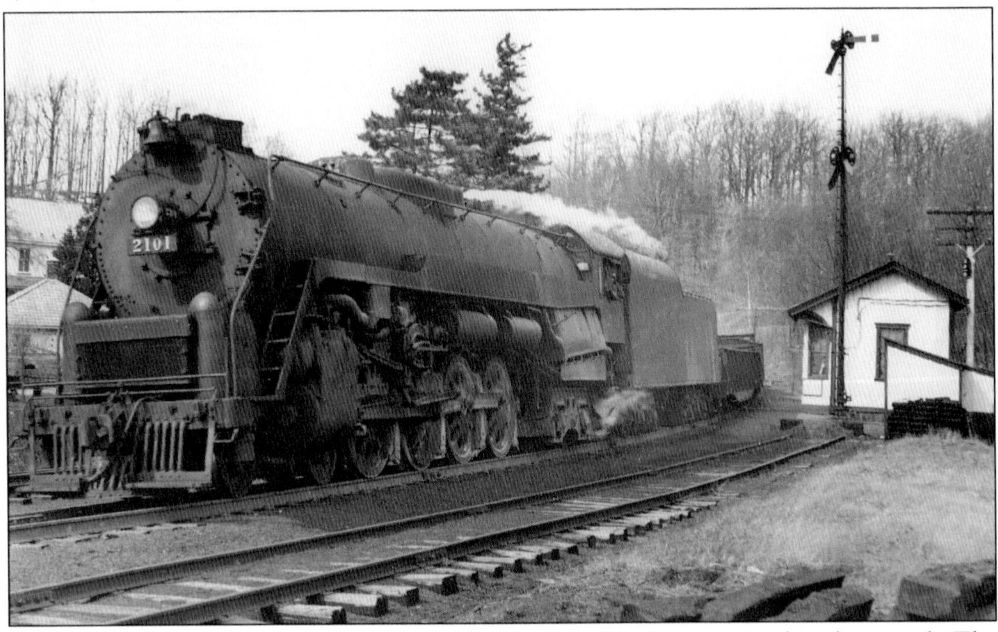

A mighty 2101 engine is steaming past the Vera Cruz Railroad Station in this photograph. The coal-fired 2101 was built in Reading in 1945. According to Joseph Benner, who fired and operated these types of locomotives early in his 38-year career, "It was the best of all locomotives. A youngster could have fired it!" Later, Benner operated diesels and was one of only six enginemen qualified to instruct incoming rookies. (UMHS.)

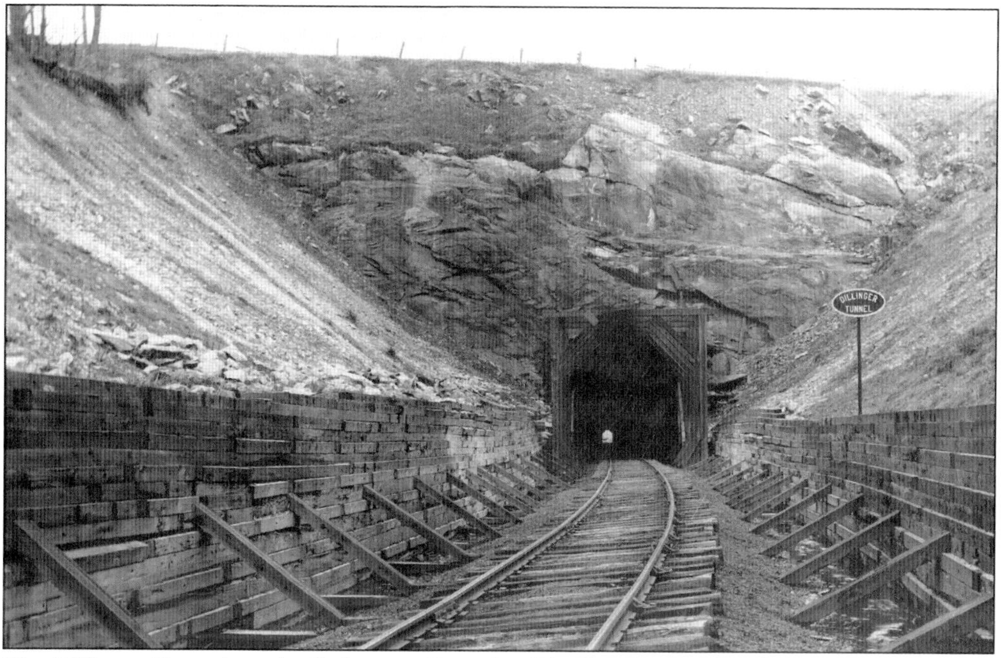

The Dillinger Tunnel on the Perkiomen Branch of the Reading Railroad in Vera Cruz is about one-third mile long and cut through a ridge in South Mountain. It was started in 1874 and completed in 1875 by contractor Judge Barney Reily and his son Thomas. They employed mostly Irish laborers who lived in six shanties housing 75 men each. Work was done by hand drills and powder, donkey engines and hoists, and 20 horses with dump carts. One man lost his life during construction. A rock above the tunnel entrance bears a white figure that legend has it is the ghostly image of that lost man. (UMHS.)

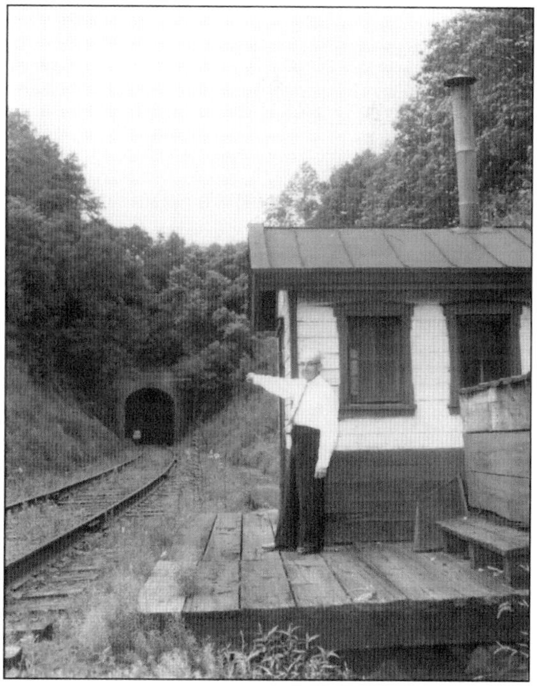

Robert Shelly is standing at the small Dillinger Station in Vera Cruz where he worked as watchman for many years. Shelly is pointing at the Dillinger Tunnel. When the watchman knew a train was approaching, it was his job to walk the tunnel first and check the structure for fallen rocks or any problems that would hinder the passage of the train. (Courtesy of Joseph Seem.)

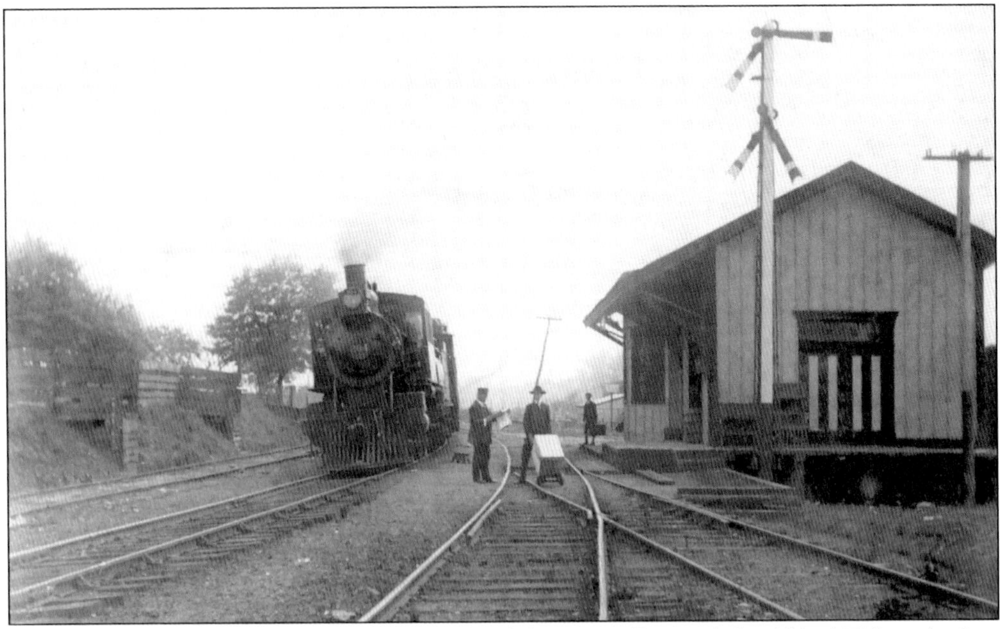

The railroad depot at Hosensack stood north of the post office and the Alfred Ehlert chicken farm and north of the Earl Lahr home. The many tracks indicate it was a busy stop for freight as well as passengers, such as the youth on the platform with suitcase in hand waiting to board the train. The nearby Hancock Company ice business, formerly in the area of the Meckling farms, had its own track to the depot for shipments of ice. (UMHS.)

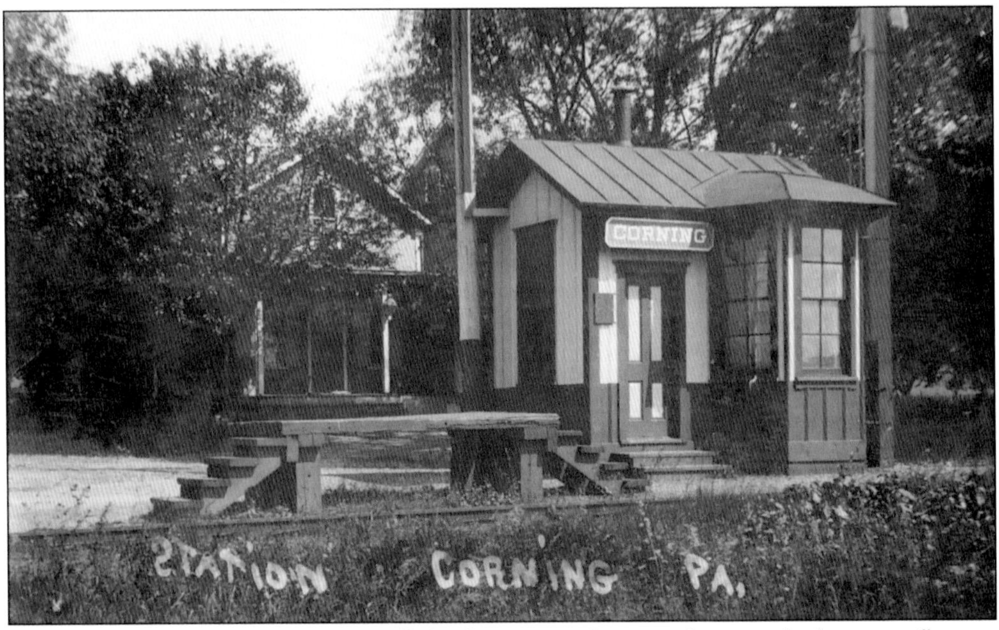

The Corning Railroad Station was called a flag station, because the agent had to put a flag out on a pole, the semaphore, whenever the train was supposed to stop to pick up passengers or mail. Small though it was, the station was an important service for the Corning area, such as delivering the Philadelphia newspapers. The building in the background was the store and post office. Today, that structure has been converted into homes. (Courtesy of Donald Schlicher.)

Seven

Rural Life and Leisure

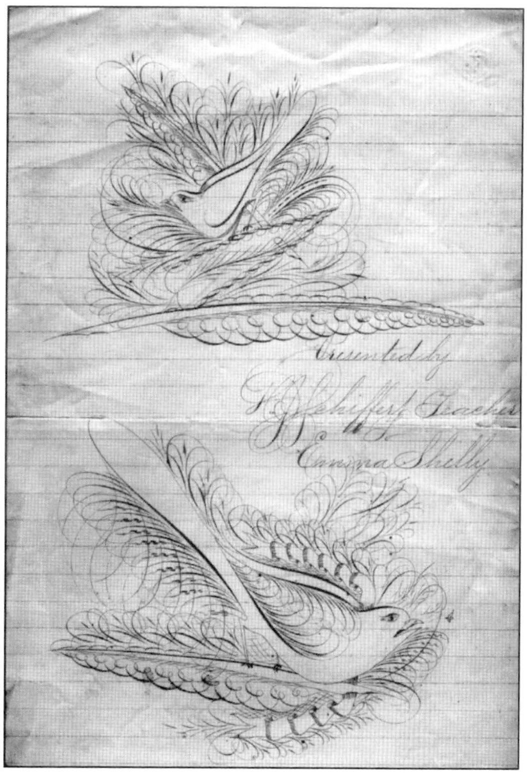

The decorative design and graceful script on this certificate is an example of the Pennsylvania German folk art known as fraktur. Many early teachers had a talent for such artistic works and gave them to students as rewards or small gifts. Teacher Solomom Shiffert presented this one to Emma Shelly from the Ortt School at Dillinger Station. (Courtesy of Barbara Harris.)

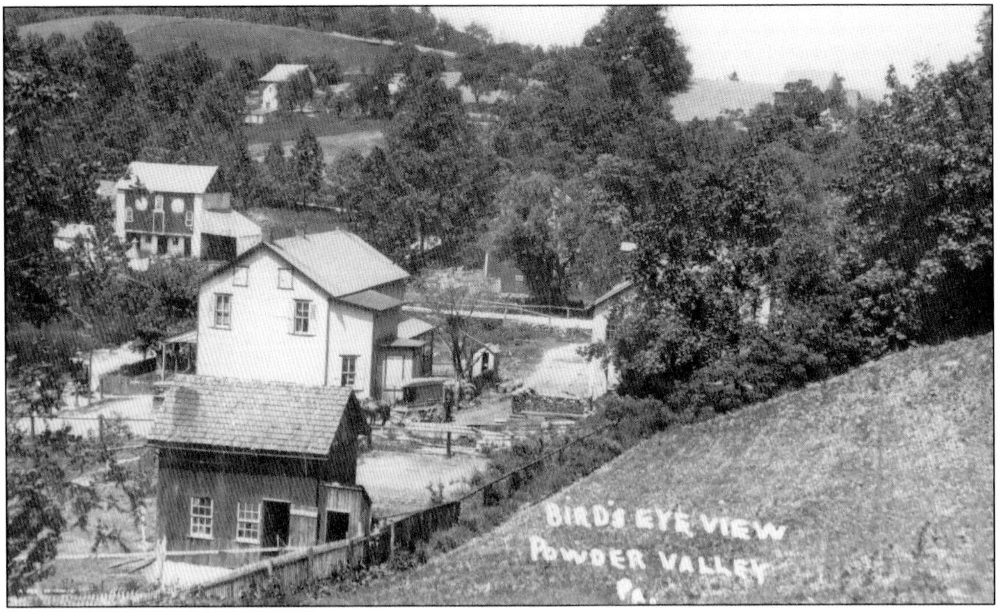

Captioned "a bird's eye view," Powder Valley nestles among the trees and hillsides in this photograph. The Powder Valley Store occupies the foreground of the picture, and the mill behind the store is still standing. Notice the horse and wagon waiting behind the building. The barn with hex signs is where Charles Stahl's Pottery originated. (Courtesy of Beulah Miller.)

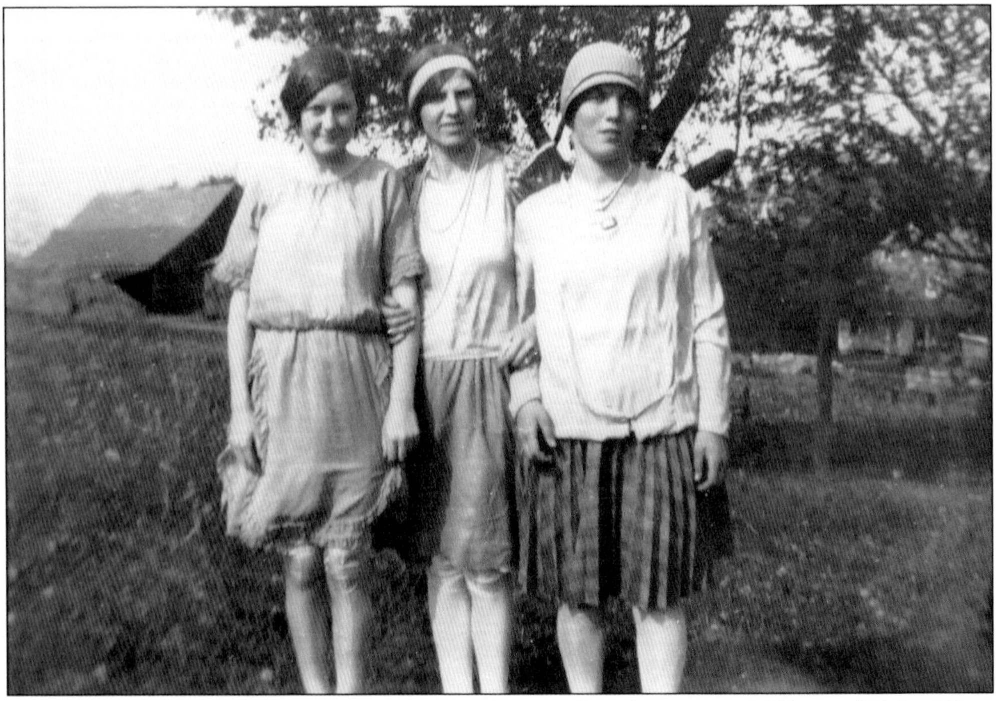

From left to right, Powder Valley residents Estelle Houseknecht, Marian Miller, and Helen Kline are stylish ladies of the late 1920s. The trio's skirt lengths fell modestly at the knee, hairstyles were conservative, and the cloche hat was the fashion of the time. Miller was a teacher in local schools. (Courtesy of Beulah Miller.)

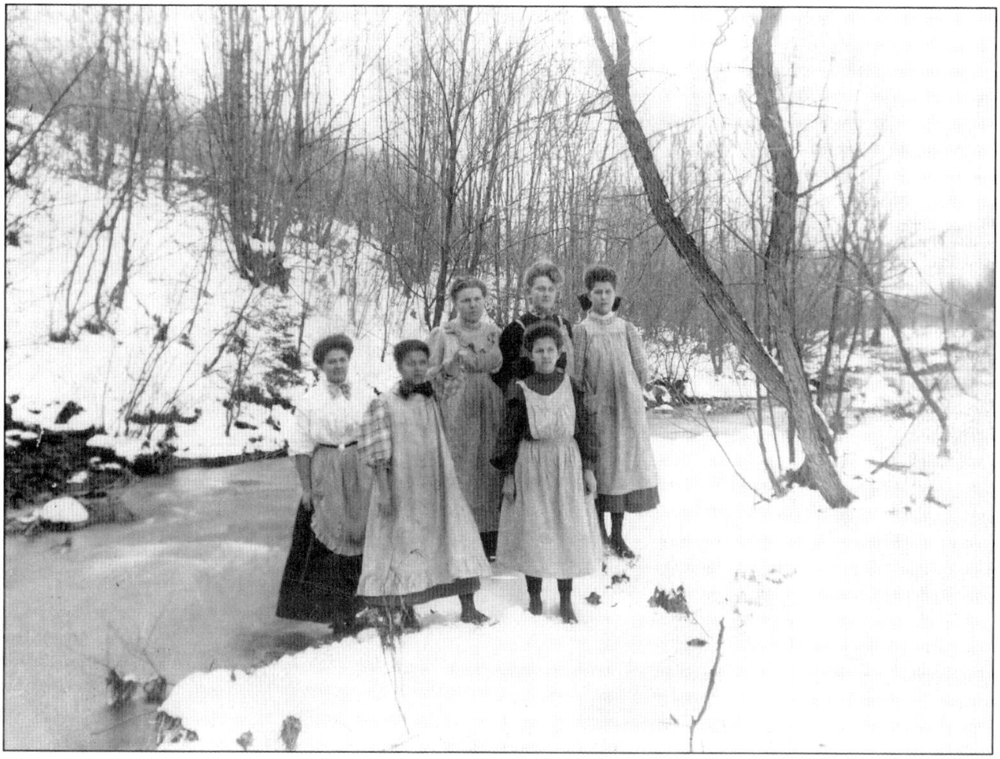

These young women worked at the cigar factory across the road from Indian Creek in Powder Valley. They gathered to take a refreshing break from their jobs making cigars. Pictured are, from left to right, Belva Miller, Esther Miller, Clara Krauss, Elsie Buhman, Daisy Miller, and Sally Hallman. (Courtesy of Beulah Miller.)

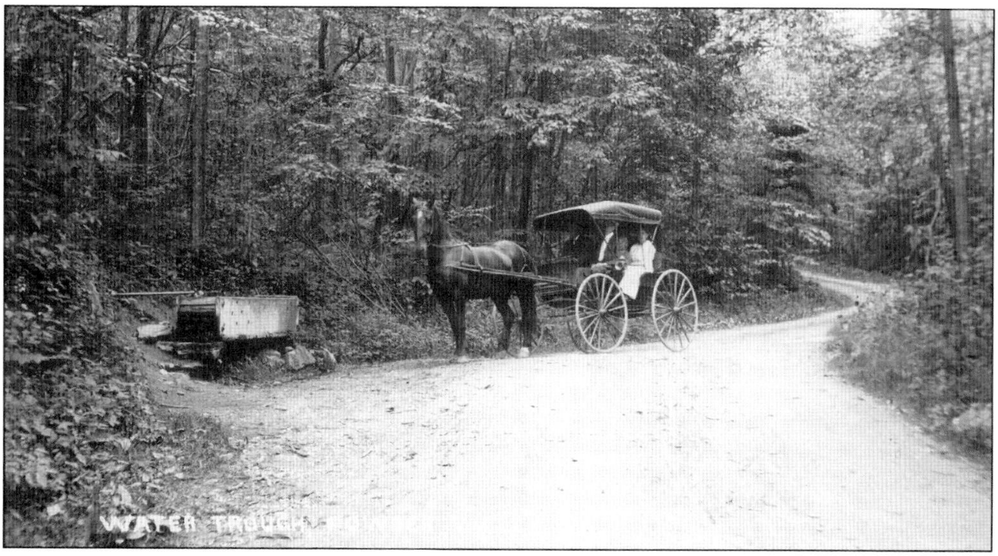

There was a water trough for horses on Powder Valley Road between Yeakel's Mill and the tobacco factory. People out for a Sunday ride are seen stopping their buggy to let their horse drink. The pipe from that spring, one of many springs in the area, is still there on the left side of the road but is no longer in use. (UMHS.)

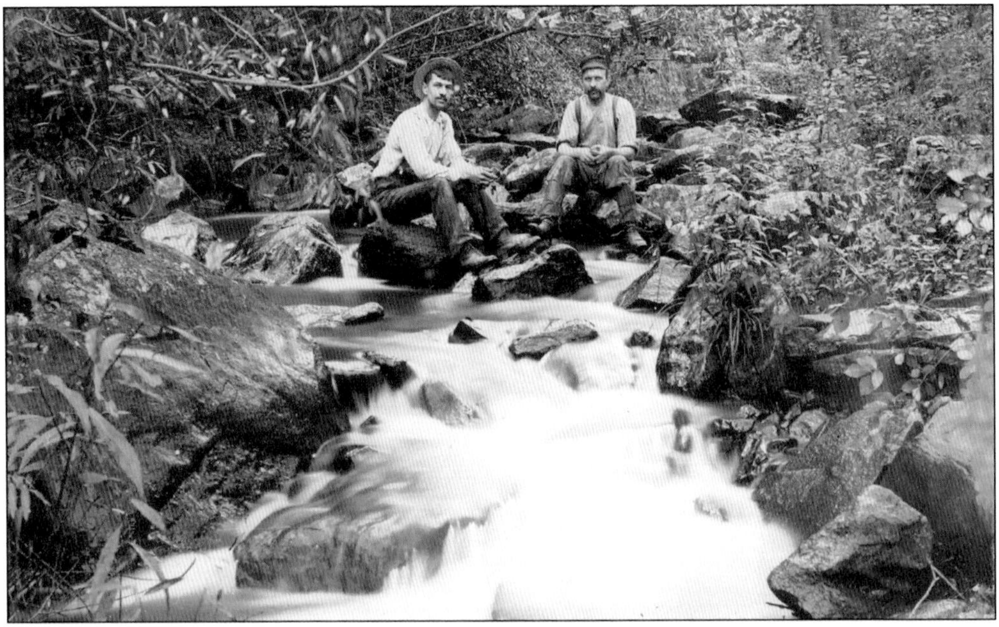

The waters of Indian Creek were an integral part of early life in Powder Valley. In this 1891–1892 photograph, two friends, Amandus Miller, left, and Asa Miller, right, are shown relaxing at a favorite spot along the creek. With the dredging and lowering of the creek after the 1935 flood, scenes like this with large rocks and rushing waters were eliminated. (Courtesy of Barbara Heist.)

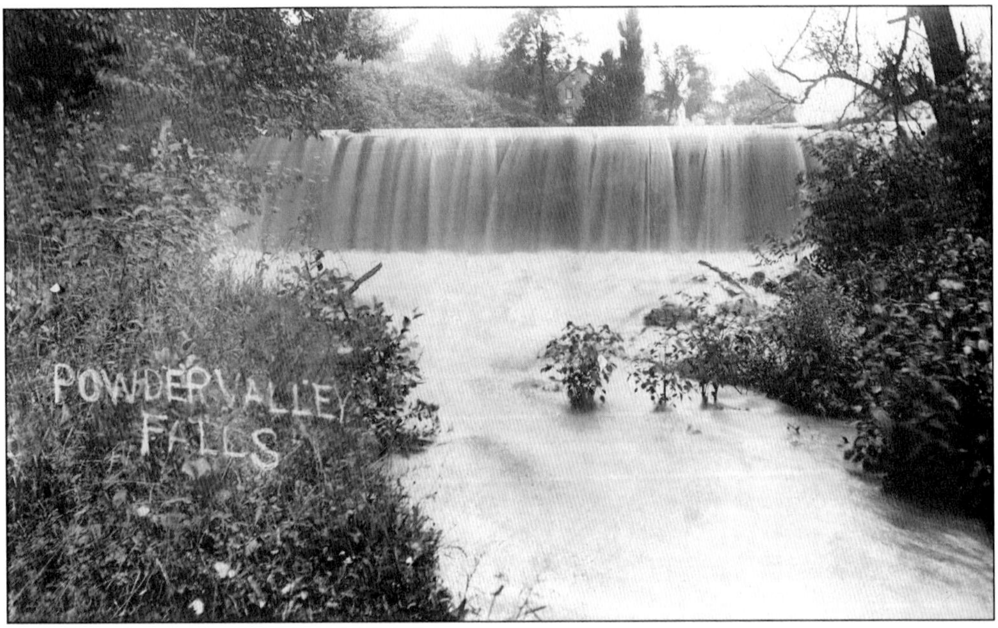

These beautiful falls were at the small dam on Powder Valley Road, with Miller's Lake above them and Indian Creek below. The lake and the falls provided countless pleasures for the leisure time of area residents and also provided waterpower for the many mills along the creek. An icehouse was located across from the dam until 1922. The scene changed drastically on July 9, 1935, when a mighty flood swept along the creek and destroyed these falls as well as all of the dams along the waterway. (Courtesy of Beulah Miller.)

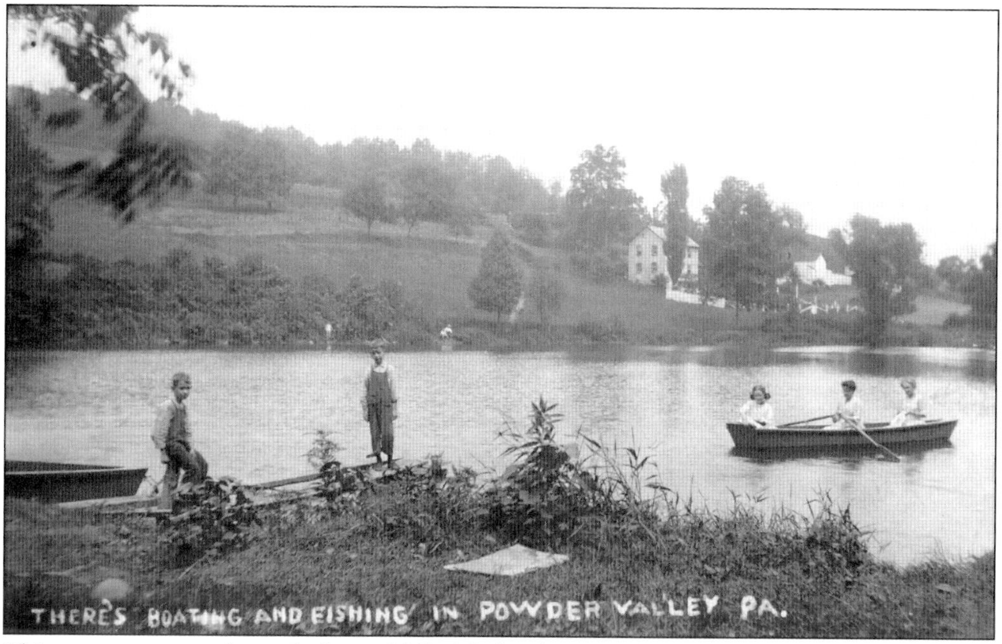

This scene captures a leisurely day on Miller's Lake along Powder Valley Road before the big flood of 1935. It was a peaceful oasis for relaxing activities, such as boating and fishing for big lake trout. Isabella Glass is shown rowing a boat with Mary Schell and her daughter. James Miller is the boy standing on the left. (Courtesy of Richard Zacharda.)

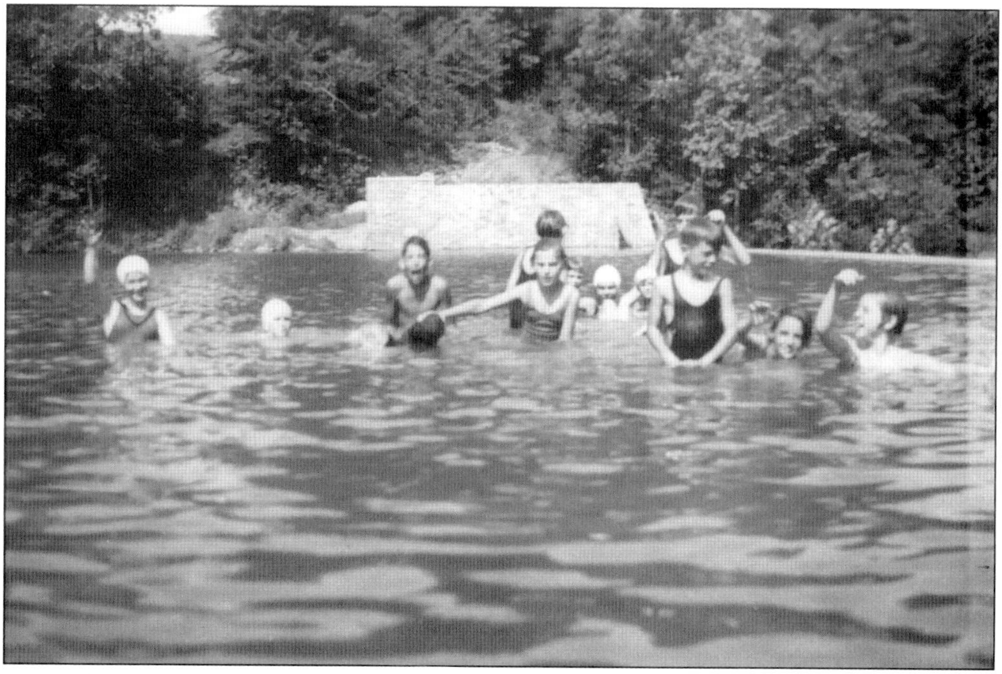

A popular pastime on a warm summer day in Powder Valley was to go swimming in the lake behind Stahl's Dam. It was a ready spot for people from the entire area to cool off in the 1940s, albeit somewhat dangerous, since there were no lifeguards to oversee the activities. (Courtesy of Beulah Miller.)

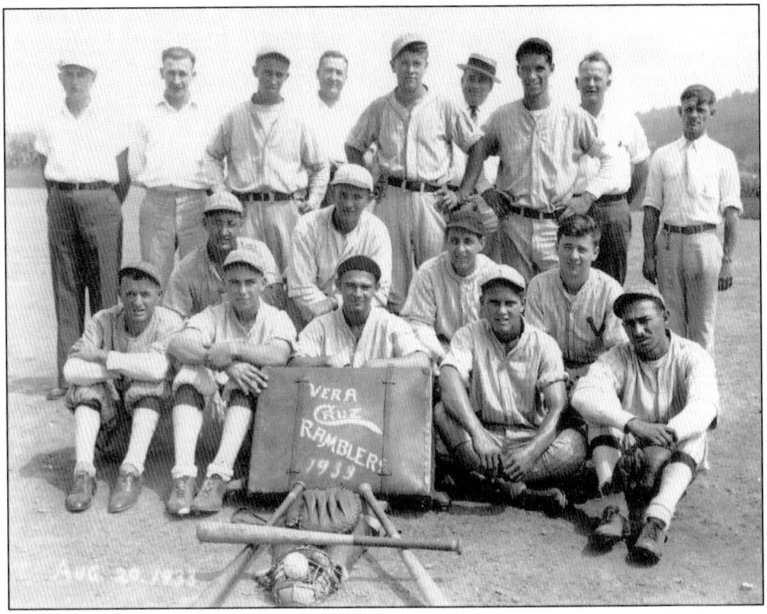

The Vera Cruz Ramblers baseball team was organized in 1933, with Worman Weaver as manager and Wharton Schuler as business manager. They played independent ball and later were part of various baseball leagues. In 1950, Raymond Buchecker organized a new Ramblers team, which played in the Valley B League. (UMHS.)

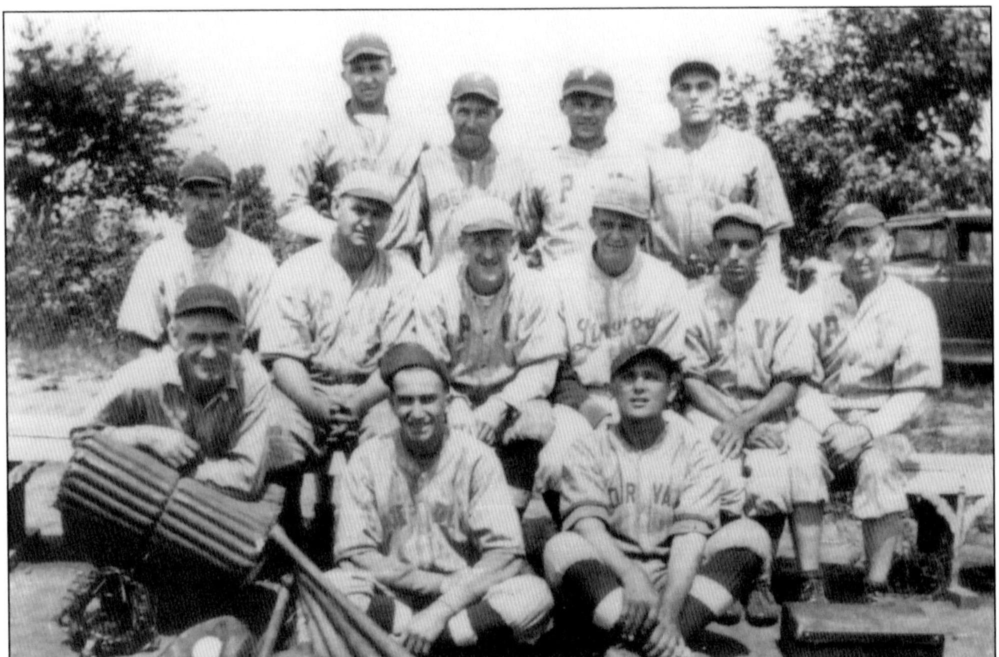

This 1932 Powder Valley baseball team compiled a 23-17 record. Manager Carl Cassler, of the Old Zionsville wooden shoe sole factory, was the best pitcher and also the manager. Due to limited open areas in wooded Powder Valley, the team played mostly on lots in and around Old Zionsville. Pictured are, from left to right, (first row) Aaron Carl, Leroy Schoenly, and Carl Cassler; (second row) Harold Bartholomew, Harry Riedy, William Boehm, Paul Brunner, Jacob Bartholomew, and Howard Schultz; (third row) ? Finkbone, Earl Houseknecht, Lester Heidler, and Elmer Heilman. (UMHS.)

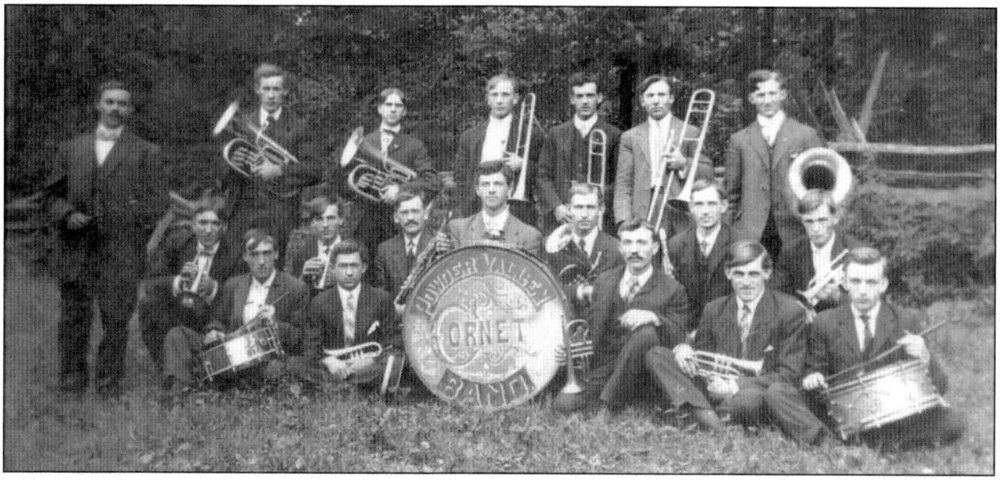

Around the turn of the 20th century, Powder Valley had its own band. Members practiced in the tobacco factory building and at the boardinghouse. Band concerts were usually part of the special Fourth of July festivities held at the store. Enos Krauss was the first director, and members' surnames included Bartholomew, Carl, Doney, Kemmerer, Miller, Treichler, Raudenbush, Rothenberger, Schultz, Stahl, and Sterner, which reflected the strong German heritage in the township. (Courtesy of Beulah Miller.)

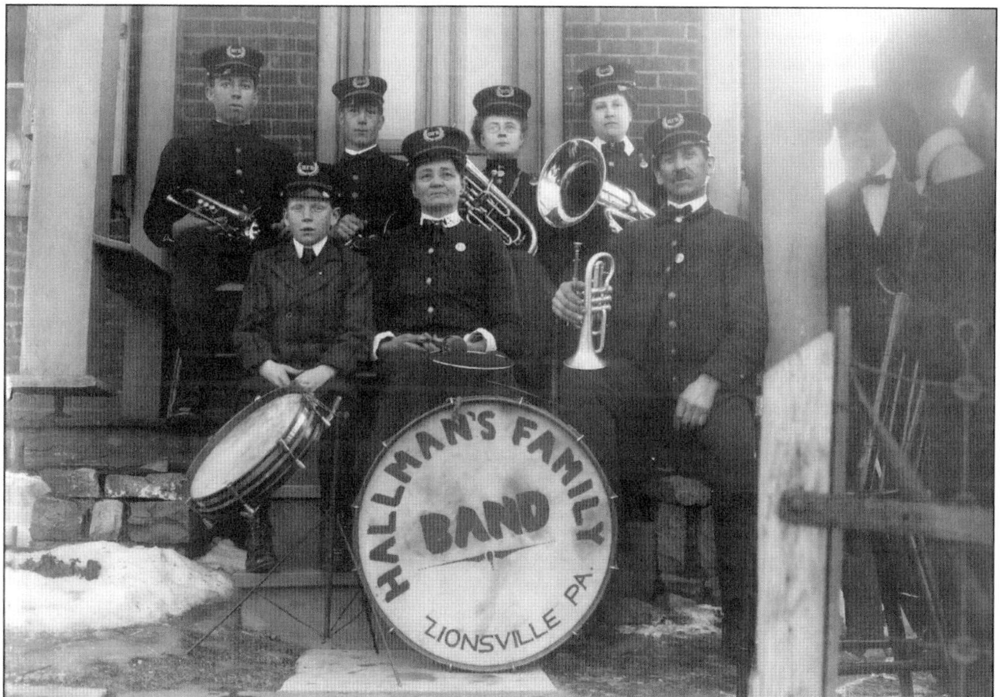

Wilson M. Hallman of Zionsville taught his entire family, wife included, to play musical instruments and organized the Hallman Family Band. The band was a popular source of entertainment at parks and church picnics from 1901 to 1914. Shown are, from left to right, (first row) Miles on the snare drum, mother Amanda on the bass drum, and father Wilson on the cornet; (second row) Lloyd on the cornet, Norman on the baritone horn, Elsa on the alto horn, and Erma on the bass horn. (Courtesy of Schwenkfelder Library and Heritage Center.)

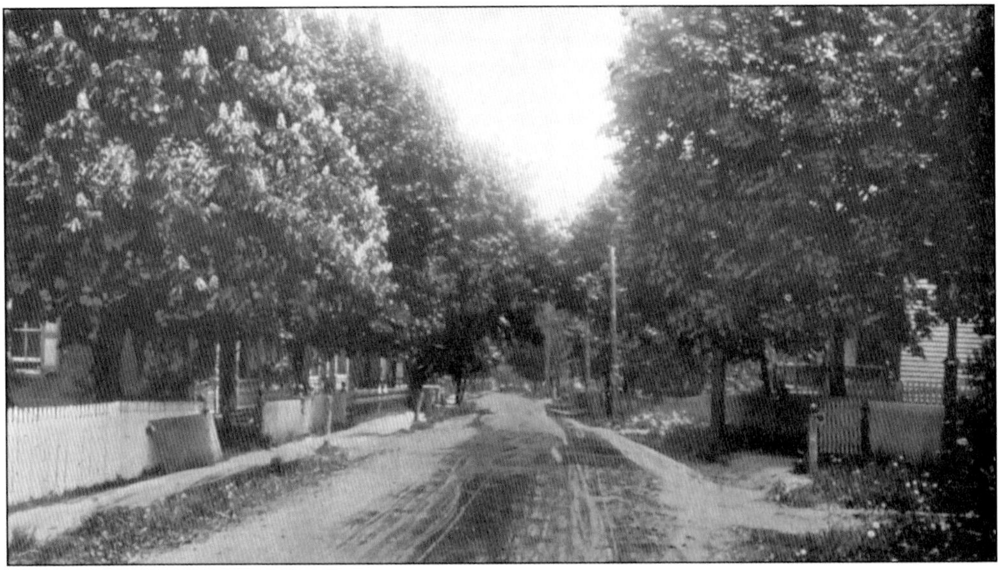

This is Main Road West, but looking east, in Vera Cruz. The Alexander Weaver Store in the top corner is where the Spanish name Vera Cruz allegedly originated for this decidedly Pennsylvania Dutch area. The village was as yet unnamed. Store regulars were discussing a newspaper article, at hand, about the 1851 uprising in Vera Cruz, Mexico, against the Spanish. Hearing a loud fight erupting in the street, the men rushed outside to have a better look. One of the brawlers had his finger bitten off in the skirmish! Weaver, ever the wag, declared, "Now we know what to call our town—Vera Cruz!" And, Vera Cruz it remains. (UMHS.)

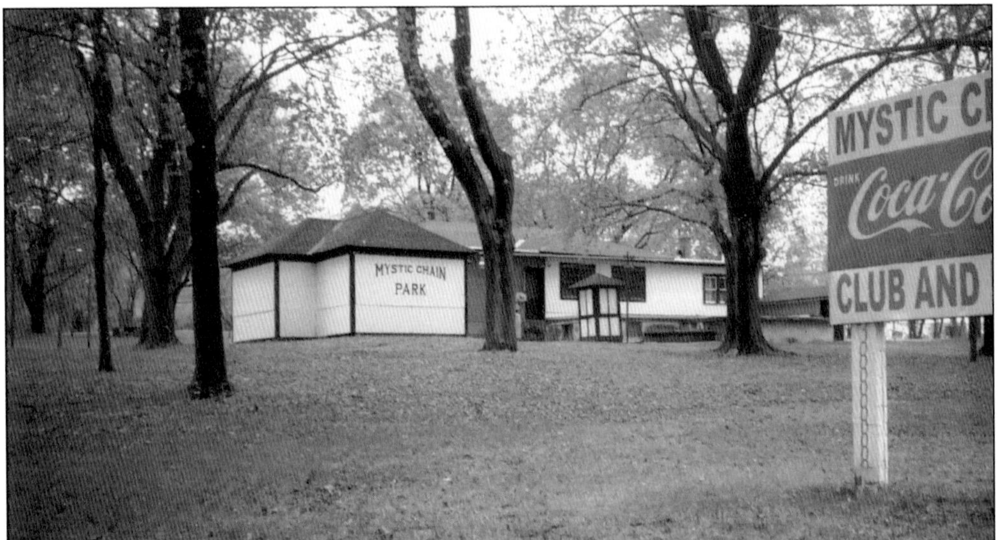

The oldest organization in Vera Cruz, Mystic Chain Lodge was instituted in 1900 in Creamery Hall. It later moved to Mystic Chain Park when two acres of land were purchased from Allen and S.K. Fetterman, with another acre being added later. The property was first called Milford Castle Playground but was incorporated as Mystic Chain Hall and Park Association in 1926. It has been the home for reunions, picnics, Saturday night dances, Friday evening auctions, wedding receptions, and more. The Vera Cruz Community Association holds its annual homecoming in the park every August. (Courtesy of Joseph Benner.)

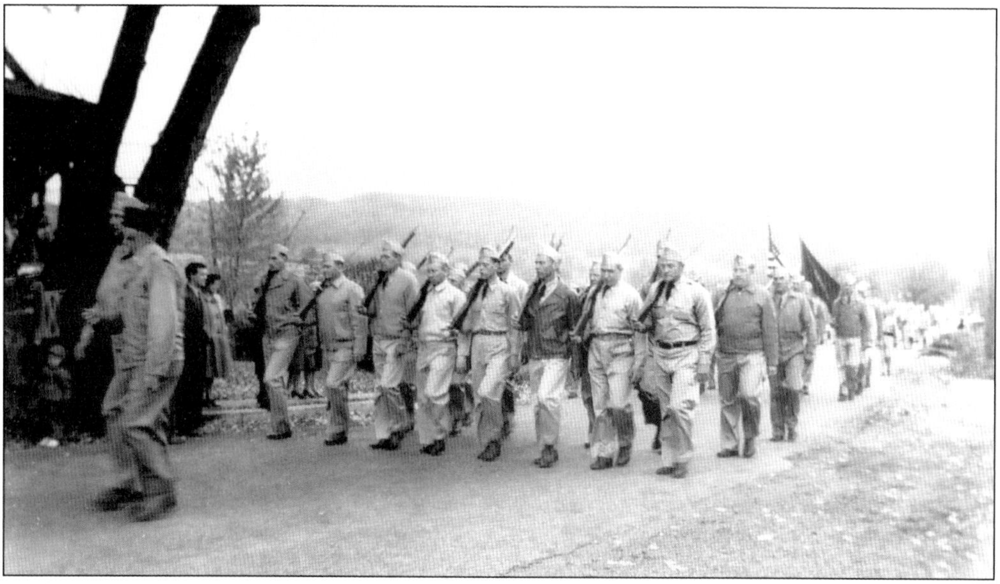

At the end of World War II, jubilant citizens celebrated with victory parades like the one in Vera Cruz in the fall of 1945. Seen above are the soldiers who marched proudly through the village streets along with the Emmaus High School Band, the Emmaus Drum and Bugle Corps, and the Pennsylvania State Guard Band. At right, eighth-grade student Cyrus Mohr had the honor to lead his classmates and teachers from the Vera Cruz School as he carried the American flag. In his adult years, Mohr spent over 50 years volunteering with the Vera Cruz Fire Company. (Both, courtesy of Ernest and Kathy Stoudt.)

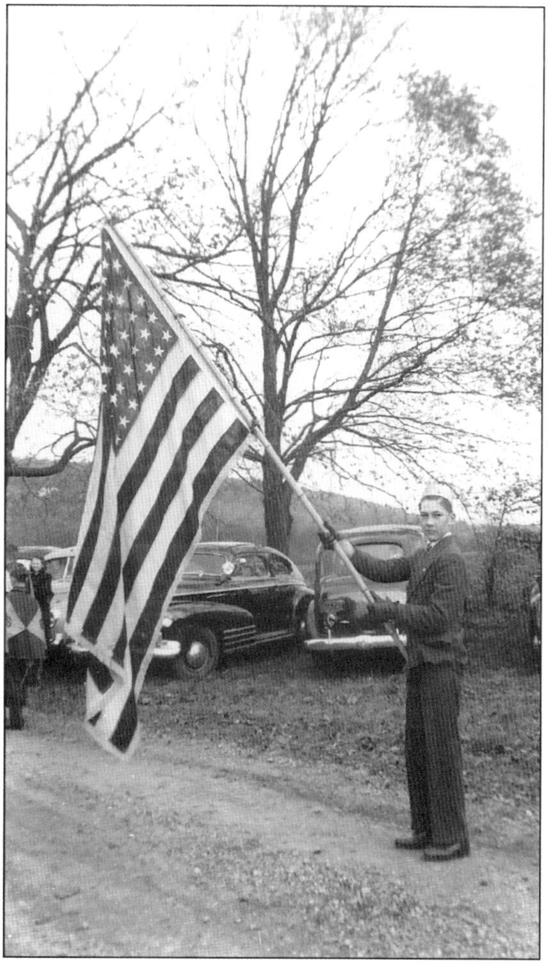

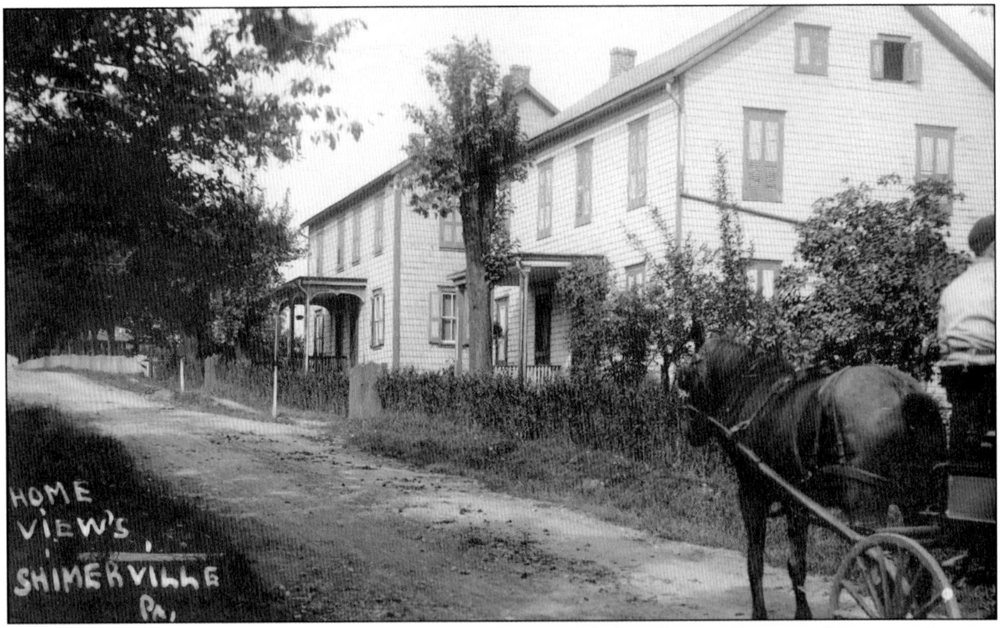

In the early 1900s, this person in the wagon on Shimerville Road passed many of the same houses as today's travelers do. The houses on the right remain. The buggy was heading to the intersection in Shimerville where the modern-day traffic light controls vehicles. (UMHS.)

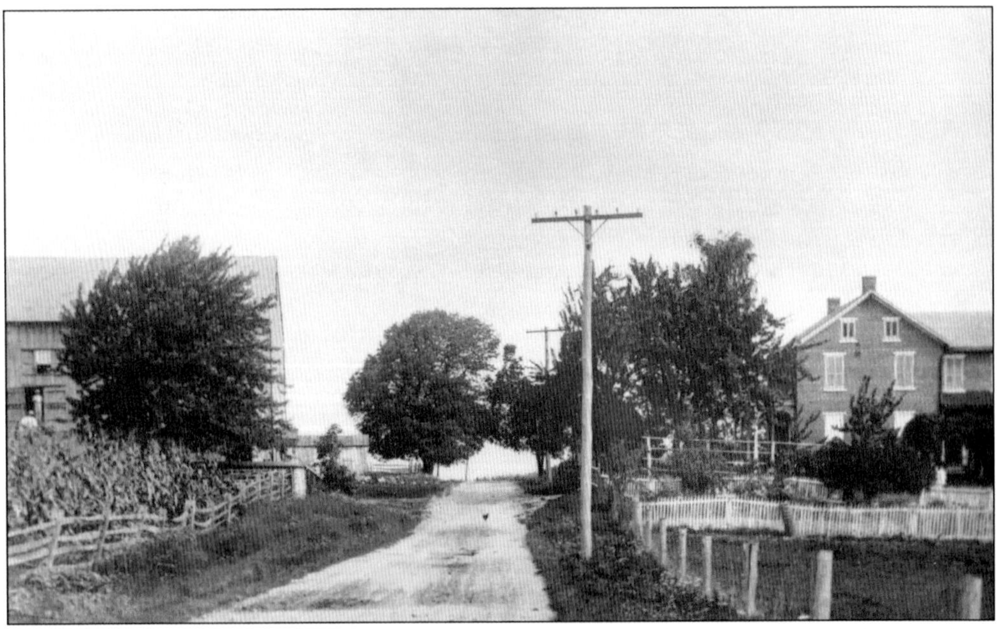

This portion of Kings Highway, Route 100/29, was still dirt road as it approached the top of the Shimerville Hill and led into Macungie. The other part of the road leading into Emmaus had not yet been constructed. The buildings on the left side of the road are no longer standing, but the house on the right remains. (UMHS.)

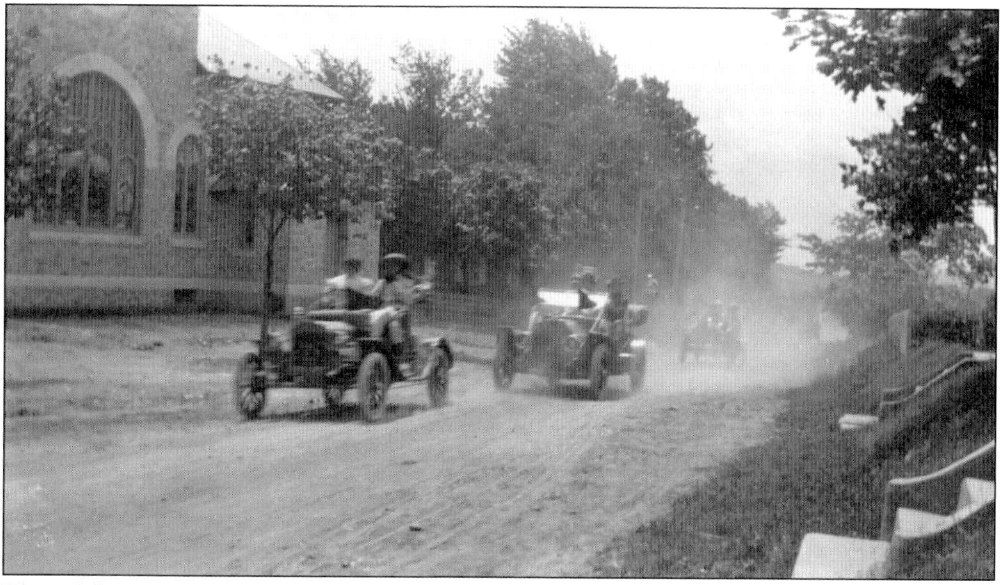

These folks were attending the dedication of the new granite Reformed Church (now the United Church of Christ) on Fountain Road in Old Zionsville in 1910. About 5,000 people attended the daylong dedication ceremonies in very hot weather. A special train was run from Allentown to handle all the visitors for the grand event. Notice that Fountain Road was still a dusty dirt road. (Courtesy of Barbara Harris.)

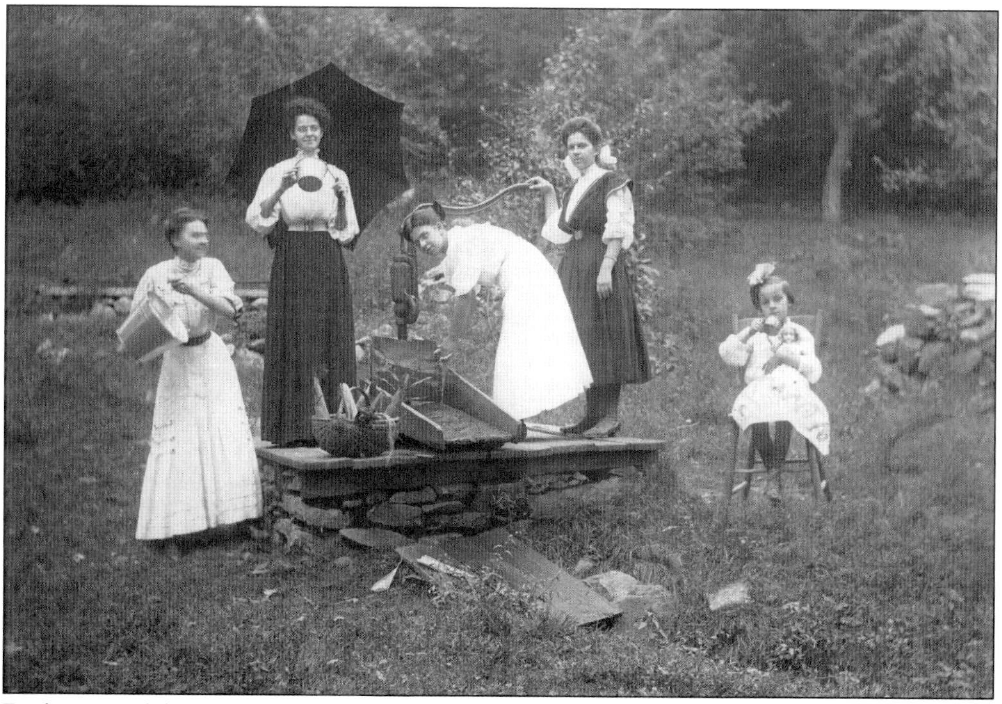

Finding a cool drink in years past often meant working the pump in the yard, as the daughters of Milton Miller are doing in this picture. The pump was across Sell Road from the Miller home in Powder Valley. From left to right are Jenny, Mary, Belva, Esther, and Verna Miller. Was someone about to be splashed with water from the bucket? (Courtesy of Beulah Miller.)

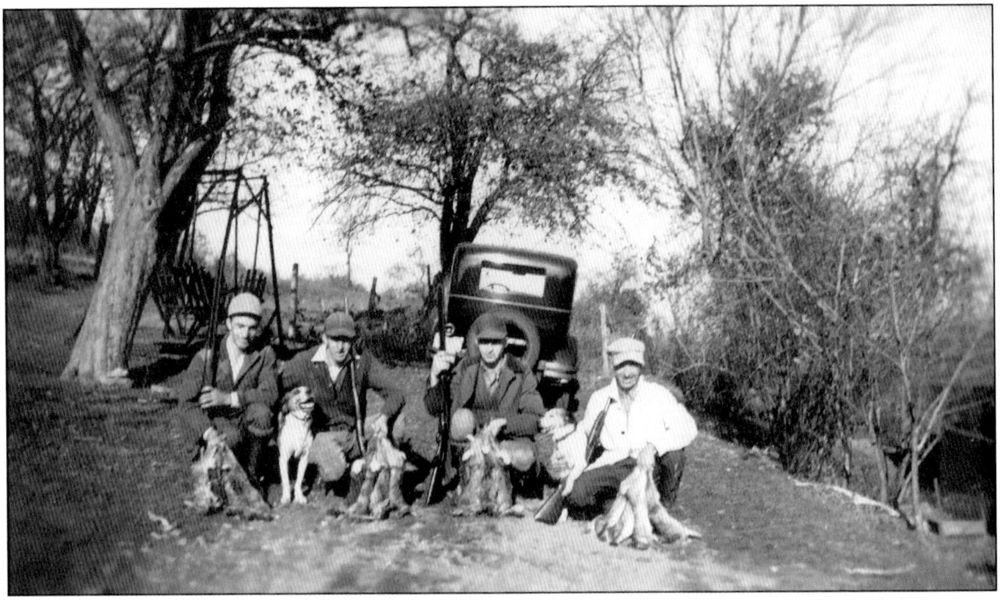

The Bartholomew family, who lived on Woodlawn Drive in Powder Valley, included these boys seen displaying their catches after hunting rabbits. With their trusty dogs, the boys made a good haul, perhaps some for the family's evening meal. Notice the c. 1928 automobile in the background. (Courtesy of Beulah Miller.)

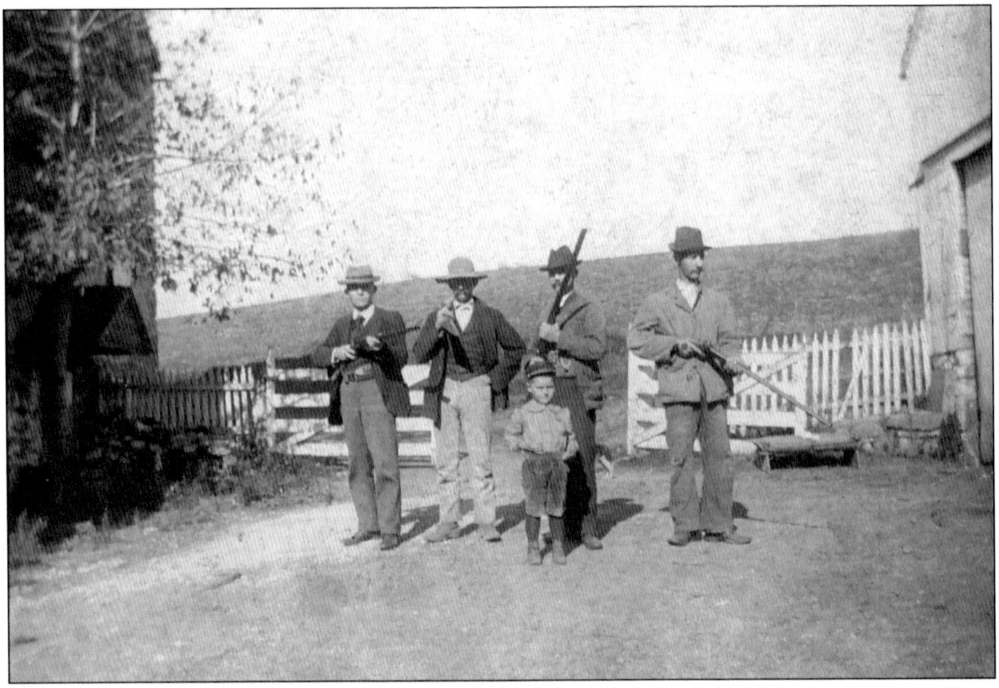

A group of men have gathered at the Hosensack farm of Harry Schreiber about 1900. Harry Schreiber is on the far right, and his son Raymond is in front of the men. Are they preparing to do some hunting? There is a large clear field behind them of seemingly prime hunting territory. Does one go hunting wearing those hats and a tie? Perhaps the men are merely posturing for the cameraman like their counterparts out west. (Courtesy of Barbara Harris.)

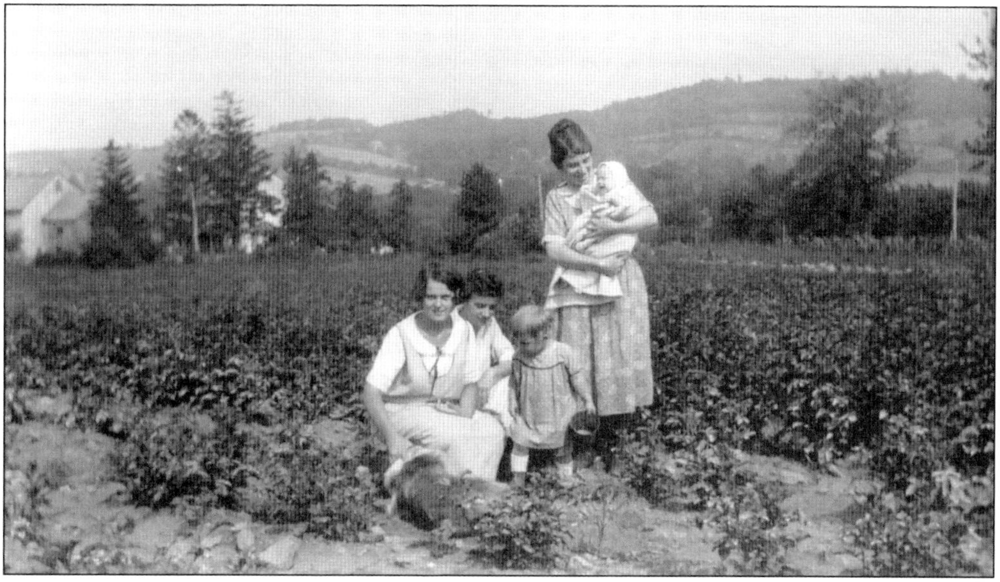

Ella Miller Schreiber, wife of Paul Schreiber, is out in the field behind the family farm on Vera Cruz Road in Zionsville in the early 1900s with two of her three daughters. Annabelle has a bucket ready to be filled, but baby Carolyn is not too happy in her mother's arms. Cousin Grace Edwards is kneeling in front. The other woman is unidentified. (Courtesy of Barbara Harris.)

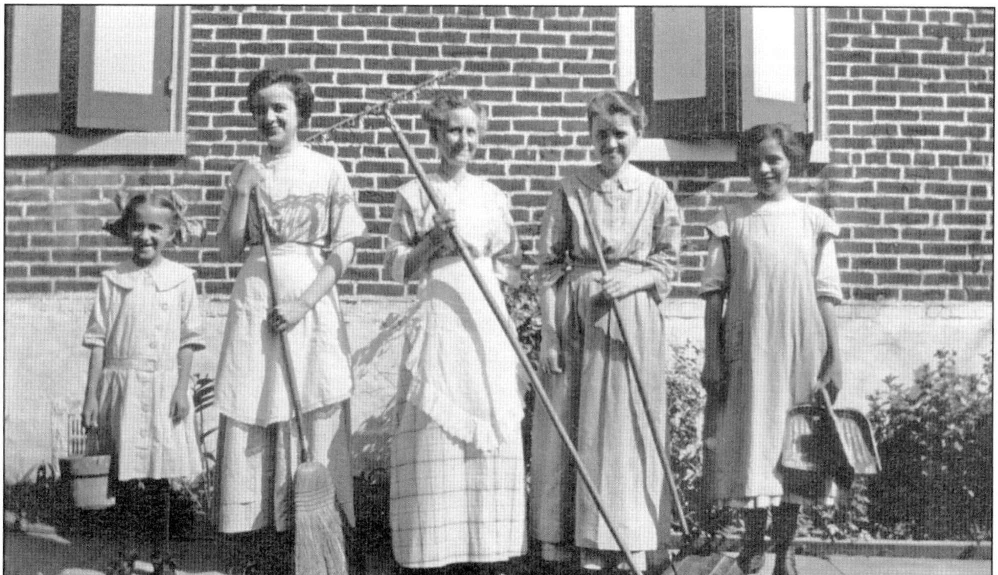

These women and girls from the Miller/Schreiber kin seem very happy about doing clean-up chores outside the house in Zionsville. Pictured are, from left to right, Marie Miller, Lulu Miller, Emma Shelly Miller, Mazie Miller, and Ella Miller Schreiber. The young Lulu Miller pictured here became the storied teacher of 45 years in township schools. (Courtesy of Barbara Harris.)

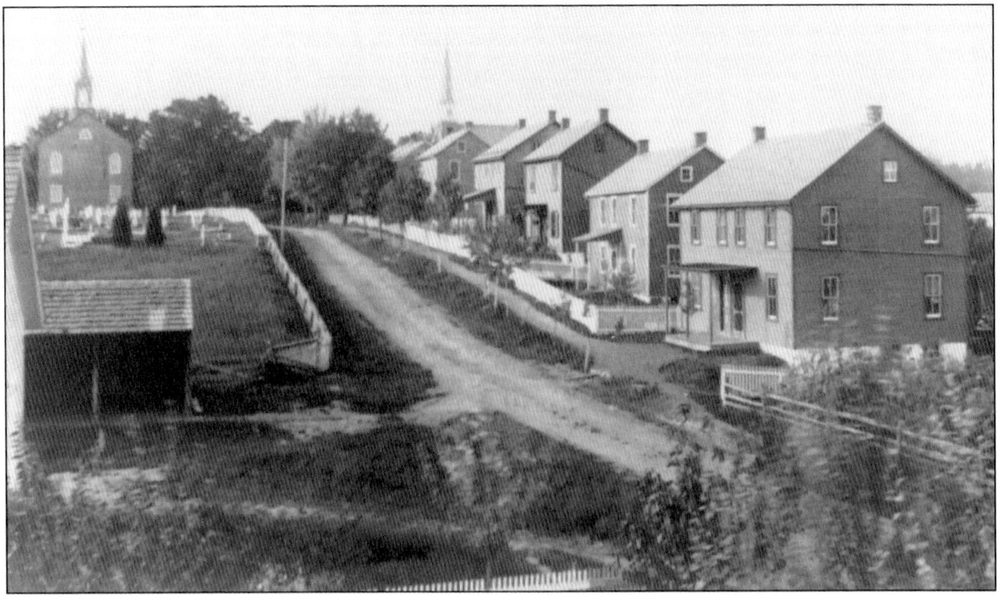

The lower end of the village of Old Zionsville is pictured. The lane on the lower left goes into the schoolhouse. Today, the school is a home, and the road continues into Lenape Park. At this time, the UCC Church building in the upper-left corner was brick, and Kings Highway is still a dirt road. Most of the houses that line the road had already been built, but the church cemetery had lots of space remaining in the early 1900s. (UMHS.)

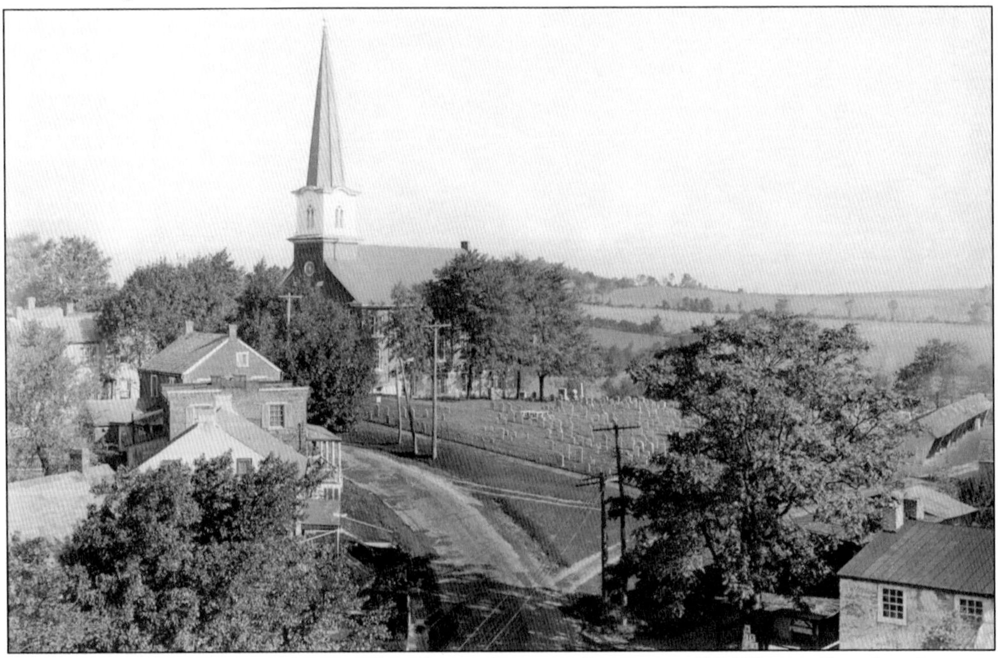

The steeple of the Zion's Lutheran Church stands out in this view of Old Zionsville taken from an elevated position in the village. One house on the left side of the highway was a bakery in early village life. In the lower-right corner is the upper edge of the Rupp/Carl General Store building, now gone. To the far rear of the store is a row of horse sheds that were used by members attending services at the Lutheran Church. (UMHS.)

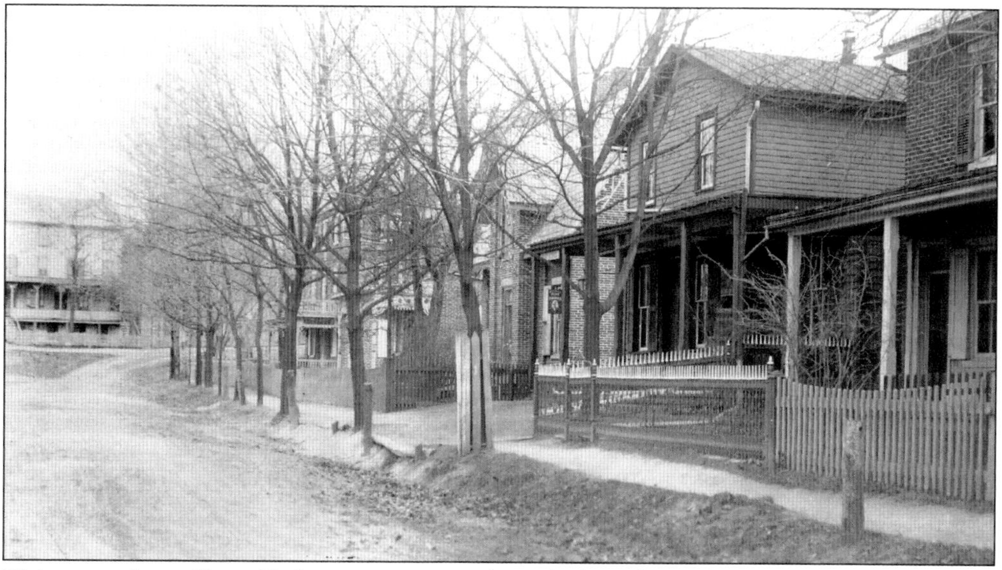

This scene shows Kings Highway as it passes through the village of Old Zionsville. The Miller Hardware Store is the large building on the right. The road follows to the curve where it bears to the right and up the small grade to the Lutheran Church. To the left, it becomes Fountain Road and the part of Old Zionsville pictured in the photograph below. Until 1926, the Patriotic Order Sons of America Camp No. 244 and the International Order of Odd Fellows Lodge No. 1077 met in the building directly ahead at the foot of the curve. (UMHS.)

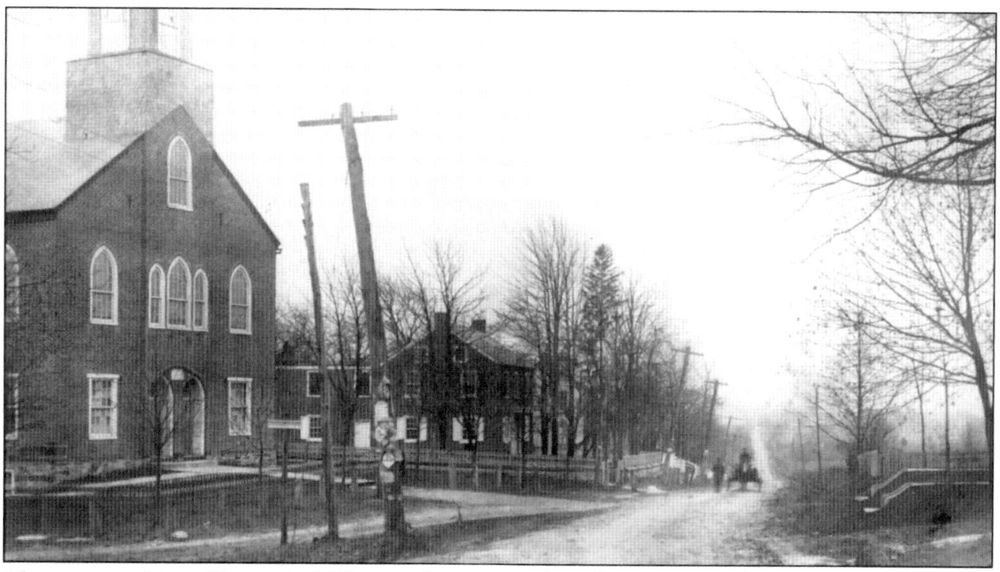

The center of the village of Old Zionsville is seen when Fountain Road was a dirt road and the third brick church of the Old Zionsville UCC congregation was still in existence. People with a horse and buggy are making their way along the road, passing the decorative metal fences fronting so many houses of early-1900s villages. (Courtesy of Jean Iobst.)

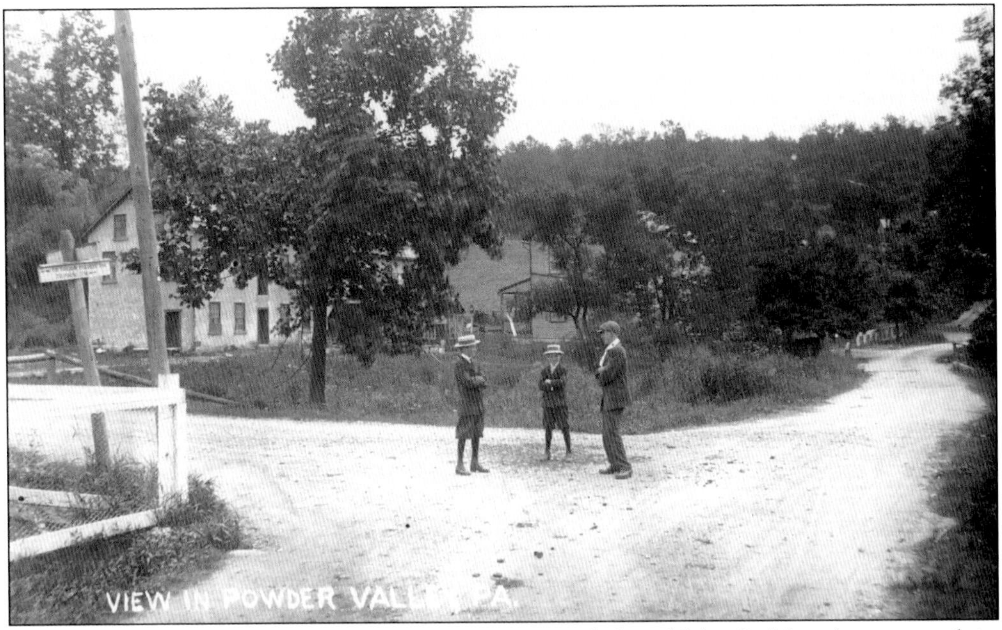

The Miller boys Elton and Newton are seen meeting with friend John Stahl at the crossroads in Powder Valley about 1912. Decked out in their Sunday best, they are standing at the intersection of Woodlawn Drive and Powder Valley Road in the center of the village. The sign indicates Palm is one mile to the right, and Treichlersville (Hereford) is to the left. (Courtesy of Beulah Miller.)

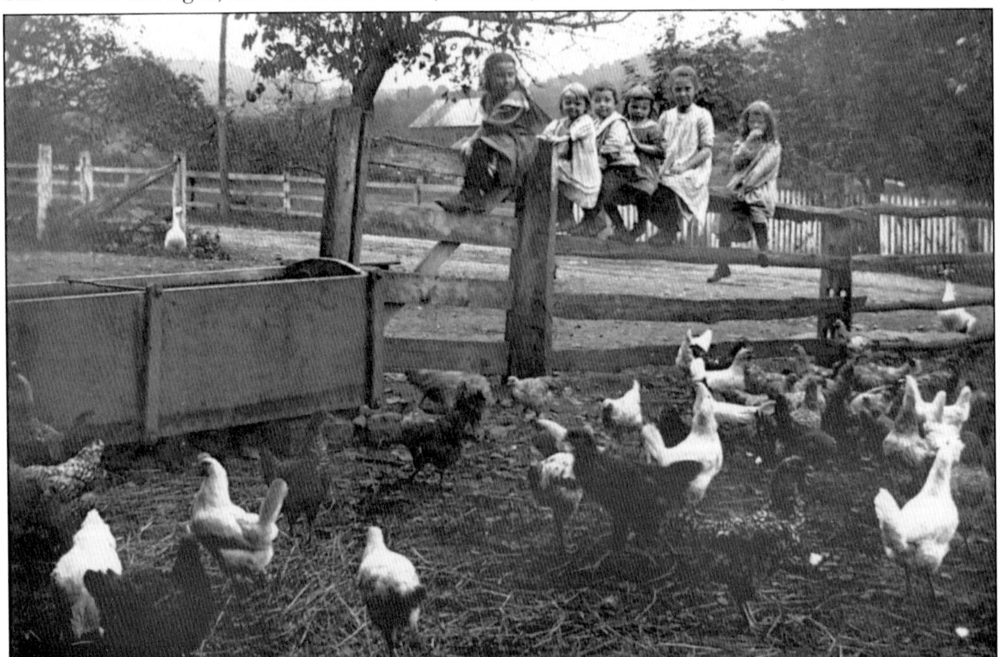

A young Roman Yoder is perched on the top rail of the Yoder barnyard fence in the early 1900s with girl playmates, all unidentified. Playing with friends may have included chasing the chickens at his farm home in Zionsville, Route 100, at the base of the Pennebacker Hill. (Courtesy of Ruth Yoder-Taylor.)

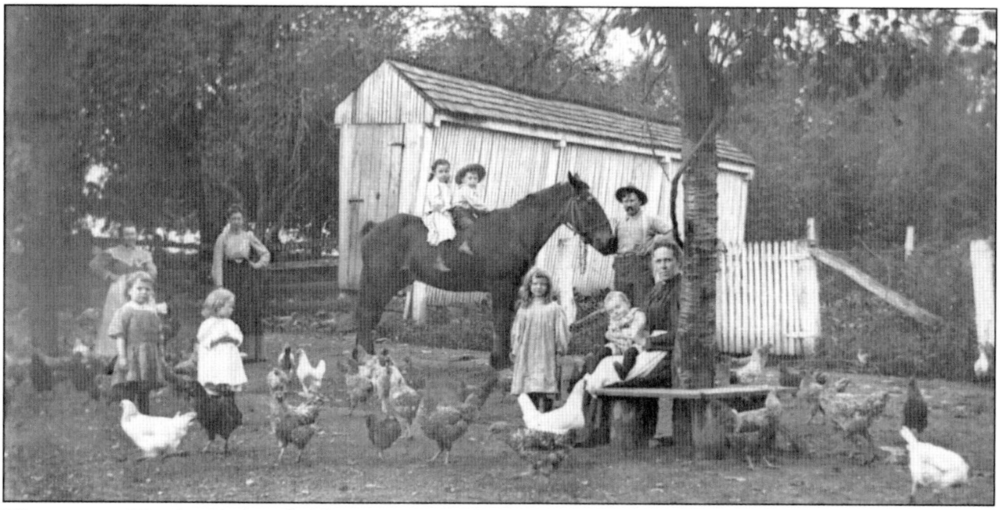

The young Charles Yoder children Verna and Roman are sitting on their family's big pet at the Yoder farm in Zionsville as their father steadies the horse. The children grew up living with horses and chickens all about their farm and therefore were comfortable around the animals at an early age. The other people are unidentified. Free-range chickens were the order of the times. (Courtesy of Ruth Yoder-Taylor.)

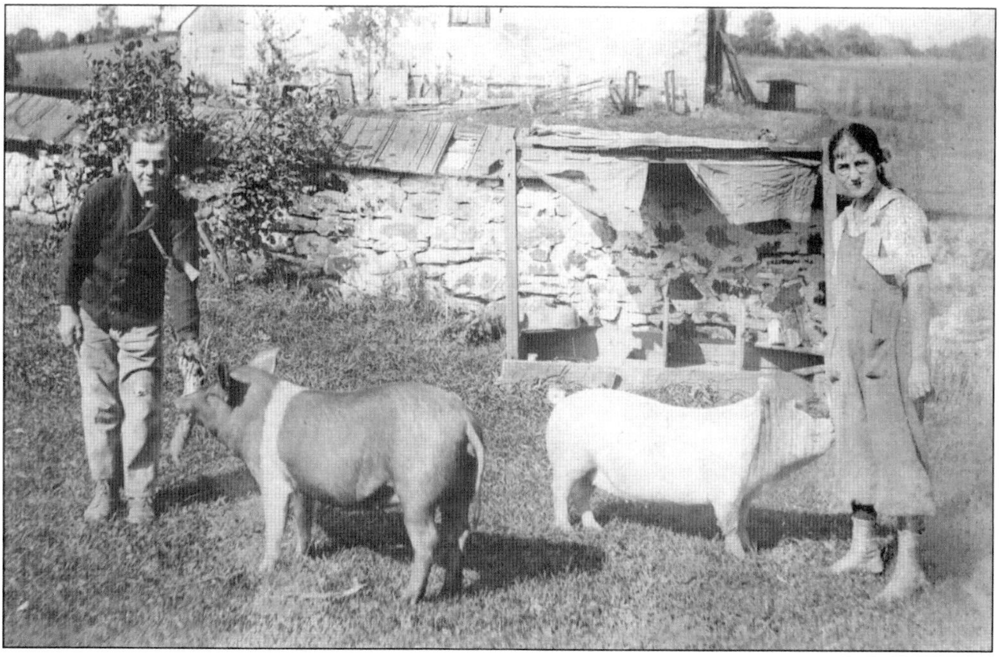

When Verna and Paul Clauser lived on their dairy farm on Church View Road in the 1920s, they raised pigs. Twelve-year-old Paul Clauser and his sister Verna are posing with their prize pigs, Lady Jane and Tessie. The children also had a calf they named Burke, as often farm animals became more than just a commodity. (Courtesy of Carolyn Lagler.)

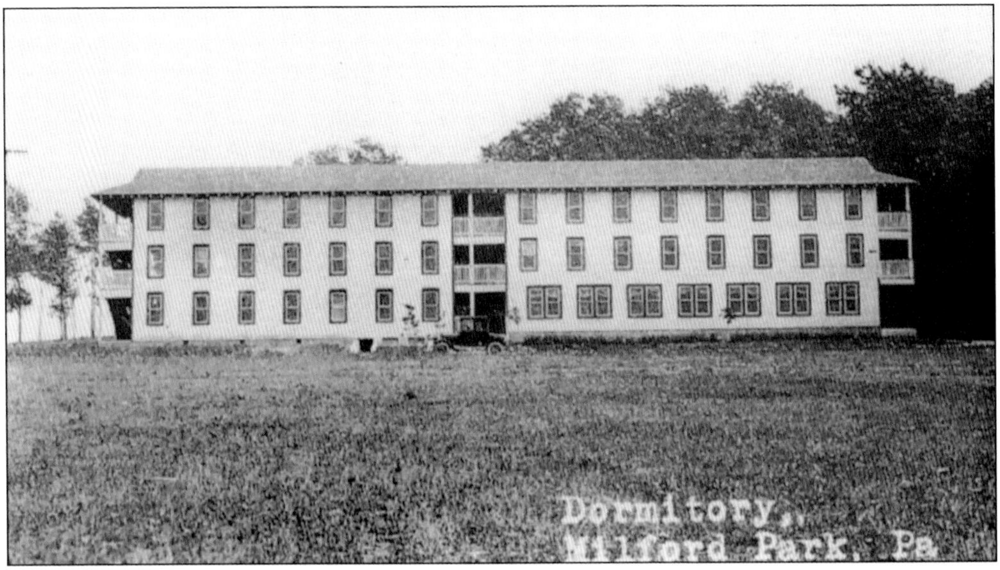

From 1913 to 1926, the Milford Circuit Camp Meeting was held in Schultz's Grove near Corning Station. In 1926, the Milford Park Camp Meeting Association was formed, and the land on Route 29/100 in Zionsville was purchased from Jacob Snyder. The first meeting was held in August 1927. Milford Park is a nondenominational Bible camp open to everyone for church and children's camps and Gospel concerts. (Courtesy of Jerald Lagler.)

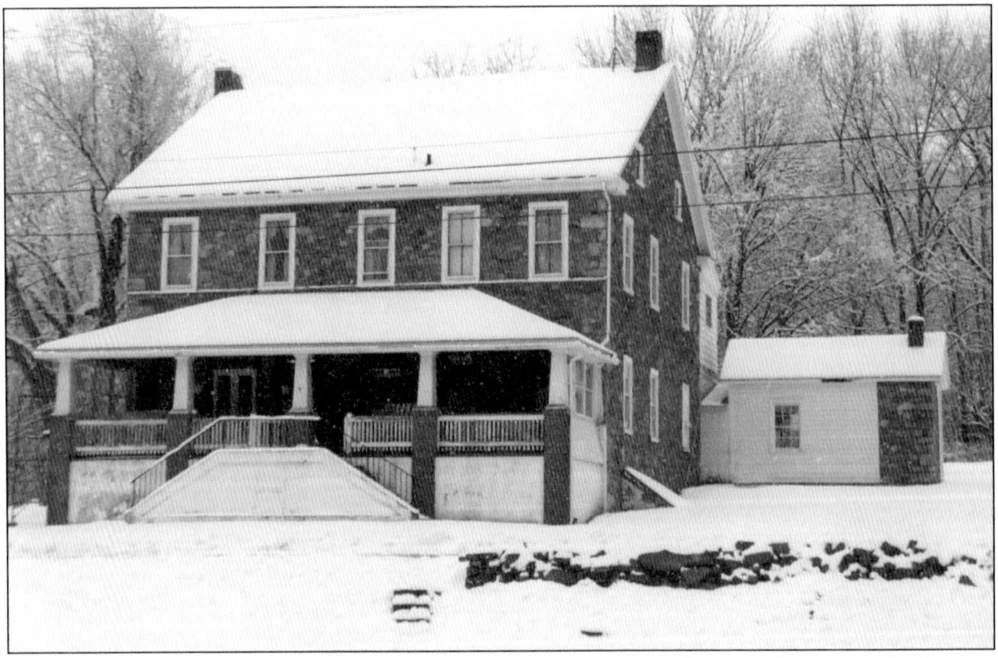

This 1871 stone building served as a general store, a post office, and a hotel for the hamlet known as Sigmund. In the 1920s, ? Henninger bought it for his home. His large "H" is still visible at the front porch and on the side chimney. Victory Valley Camp and Children's Ministry bought the place in 1956 and added cabins for their Christian camping programs. The building is now used as headquarters for the 73-acre camp and housing for the director and his staff. The small side building was added as a bathroom facility for campers. (Courtesy of Victory Valley.)

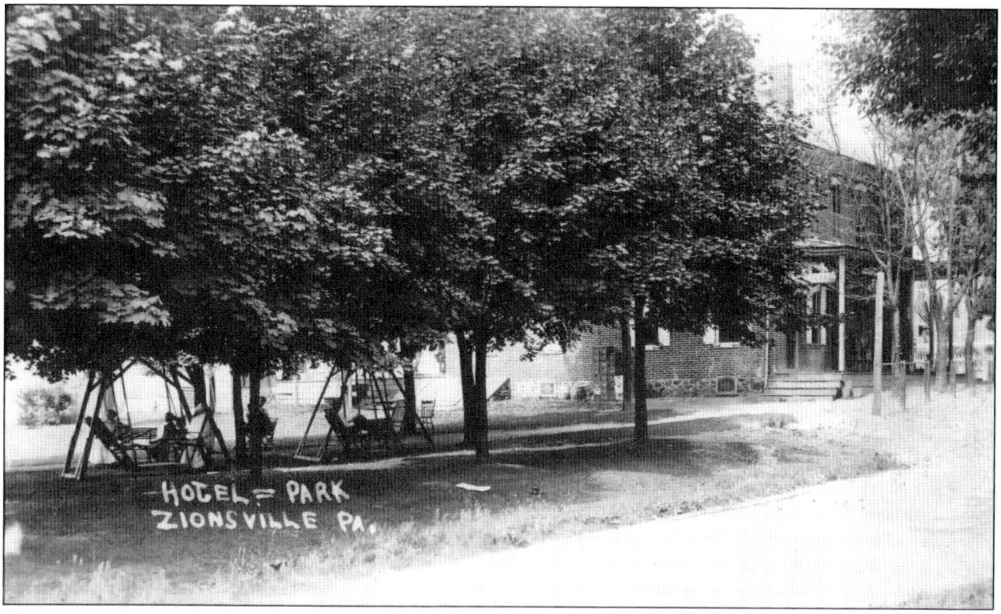

Guests staying at the hotel in Zionsville had access to this small shady park next to the building. In these simpler days of yore, the small pleasure of relaxing in the shade on a double swing could bring contentment in ways many folks today would find boring and unsatisfying. (UMHS.)

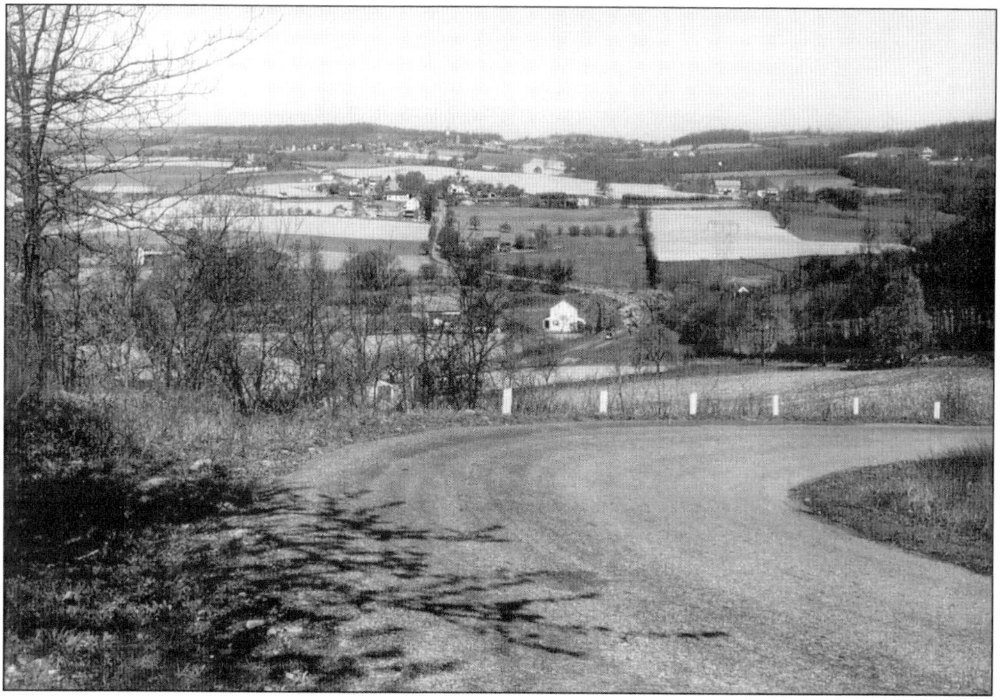

A panoramic view of the Zionsville area, taken from a sharp curve in the road leading to Dillingersville, embodies the rural character of Upper Milford Township. Historically, villages have been spread out between these farm fields, hills, and valleys. In recent years, development has reduced the open spaces, but not enough to take away the rich rural heritage recalled through this photograph and the images in this book. (UMHS.)